CIVIL AIRCRAFT
TODAY

GENERAL EDITOR:
PAUL E. EDEN

Published in 2006 by Silverdale Books
an imprint of Bookmart Ltd
Registered Number 2372865
Trading as Bookmart Ltd
Blaby Road
Wigston
Leicester LE18 4SE

ISBN 1-84509-324-0

Produced by
Amber Books Ltd
Bradley's Close
74–77 White Lion Street
London N1 9PF
www.amberbooks.co.uk

Project Editor: James Bennett
Design: Colin Hawes

Previously published in a different format as part of the reference set *World Aircraft Information Files*

All images courtesy of Aerospace/Art-Tech except
Airbus: 38b, 39tl, 39b
AFP/Getty Images: 38t
Corbis: 6
SIPA Press/Rex Features: 39tr

Printed in United Arab Emirates

Contents

Introduction 6

Airbus 10

Airtech/CASA 40

Antonov 42

ATR 50

BAe Systems 54

Boeing 62

Bombardier 116

De Havilland Canada 120

Douglas 126

EMBRAER 134

Fokker 138

Ilyushin 142

Lockheed 148

McDonnell Douglas 154

Raytheon 168

Saab 170

SATIC 174

Swearingen 176

Tupolev 178

Index 188

Introduction

Today, air travel to destinations around the world is seen not only as a vital tool in the ever growing globalisation of the world's economies, but as a fundamental benefit to millions of tourist and leisure travellers, using the extraordinary flexibility in price and unprecedented choice of destinations to visit parts of the world that were inconceivable even a generation before.

A major revolution in civilian air transport occurred in the late 1950s, when the first generation of reliable long-range jet airliners, typified by the Boeing 707 and Douglas DC-8, began to roll at an unprecedented rate from the factory floor. Once a preserve of the rich and powerful, intercontinental air travel soon came within reach of business travellers and enlightened tourists. Powered by noisy and environmentally unfriendly turbojets, the first generation of jet airliners has all but disappeared from the Western airlines. However, a dwindling number, many of them converted as freighters, still provide sterling service in Africa, where environmental concerns and economy of performance are outweighed by low acquisition costs.

At the end of the 1960s commercial aviation underwent a double transformation that has helped shape the way we travel today. The advent of quieter, more reliable, more powerful and fuel-efficient turbofan engines allowed Boeing to develop

Boeing made the most of twin-engined economics and advanced technology with its long-haul 777. The type competes head to head with the Airbus A330/A340 family and in its stretched versions has the passenger capacity of a 747. The latest -200LR development will challenge the A340-500 as the world's longest-ranged airliner.

the 747 'Jumbo Jet'. Having reigned as 'King of the Skies' for the last 35 years, the 747's size and unique shape still capture the public's imagination. Other widebody airliners such as the Lockheed TriStar and Douglas DC-10 followed, and continue to serve around the world today.

The second, less glamorous transformation occurred with the advent of the Boeing 737 and Douglas DC-9. Replacing piston and turboprop types on regional routes, these 100- to 130-seat aircraft

Many industry pundits consider the A380 to be as big a step forward in commercial aviation as the Boeing 247 and Douglas DC-3 of the pre-war era and Boeing's 707 and 747 of the jet era. The giant Airbus should first be delivered in 2006.

In the post-Cold War era CSA Czech Airlines retired its fleet of ageing and uneconomical Soviet-built airliners in favour of Western-manufactured types, including the Boeing 737-400.

finally allowed rapid and efficient transport for holidaymakers and business travellers alike. Selling in huge numbers, these aircraft have steadily evolved, introducing more efficient

With the 747, Boeing revolutionised the long-haul airliner market. Large numbers of 747-200 aircraft, as here in Cathay Pacific colours, and a smaller number of 747-100 machines survived into the 21st century, but the majority was either retired or converted for use as freighters in the aftermath of the 9/11 terrorist attacks in the US. The 747-200 survived in Cathay's fleet only in freighter form by 2005.

engines and computer technology in the cockpit, increasing safety and comfort for passengers and operating profits for the airlines. In the 1980s Airbus launched its A320

competitor to Boeing's 'babyjet' and the DC-9 family, incorporating a host of new technologies including an all-glass cockpit, fly-by-wire flight controls and the use of lighter and stronger composite materials in parts of the airframe. It is the latest versions of the 737 and A320 families that dominate the recently conceived and rapidly

growing low-cost carrier market that has reduced air fares to a level that allow every day travel at a cost undreamt of just a decade earlier.

In the communist world Tupolev similarly transformed air travel in the 1970s with the introduction of the Tu-134 and Tu-154. Although unable to compete economically with modern Western

Built by Brazil's EMBRAER, the ERJ 145 is typical of the new breed of regional jets that have managed to offer their operators the economics of turboprop aircraft, while offering their passengers the option of jet-powered flight; statistics prove that many passengers feel uncomfortable on an aircraft with propellers. The ERJ 145 and its derivatives have proved phenomenally successful.

designs, these served in considerable numbers into 2005, when the enforcement of new regulations affected many of the regional airlines flying them in ex-Soviet and communist states.

Boeing and Airbus currently dominate the large jet airliner market, and each manufacturer has introduced technologically advanced airliners as they battle for supremacy. Boeing's twin-engined 777 uses the most powerful turbofan powerplants in the world offering airlines economical performance, over ranges in excess of 17,000 km (10,500 miles). Airbus, following on from its successful A330 and A340 long-range airliner series, is revelling in the successful first flight of the A380. This giant of the air is capable of carrying

The DC-8 from Douglas was the main rival to Boeing's 707. Although it never sold as well, the Douglas machine has proved more apt for re-engining and conversion to cargo configurations. This Pratt & Whitney JT3D-powered Super 60 flew with Arkansas Air Transport International, at Little Rock-Adams Field.

more than 550 passengers in a standard configuration and employs the latest in computer-aided design and composite material construction techniques. Boeing has hit back with the launch of its 787 Dreamliner – a smaller but highly efficient aircraft

aimed at expanding the world's route network by introducing new point-to-point services and escaping the crowded hub airports into which the A380 must operate.

As the latest airliners are introduced, older designs are finding useful employ-

ment following conversion as freighters. Operating alongside the colossal purpose-built An-124 and An-225 outsize cargo carriers from Antonov, many other converted and largely unsung types carry vital goods and mail across the globe.

Airbus A300

The European challenge

Today, Airbus Industrie and Boeing fight as equals for almost every jet airliner contract. This remarkable situation has developed in the three decades since the A300 made its first flight.

In the early 1960s, when the concept of a new European wide-bodied aircraft was first mooted, there were many who expressed serious doubts about the venture, especially those across the Atlantic. Yet today Airbus Industrie is on course to achieving parity with the mighty Boeing Airplane Company. The decision to develop a pan-European aircraft by Britain, France and Germany to challenge the domination of US manufacturers – a leap of faith both politically and economically – has proved right.

The emerging mass travel era, made possible by powerful new jet engines and plummeting air fares, directed attention to high-capacity short-range aircraft, and most manufacturers on both sides of the Atlantic began to develop a variety of interesting wide-bodied concepts.

After discarding many imaginative and fanciful design concepts, which included jet flaps, canards, tandem wings, and horizontal and vertical double-deck layouts, the Airbus partners eventually settled on a fairly conventional 200-250 seat aircraft designed by a Hawker/Breguet/Nord team.

Designated the HBN 100, it proposed a circular fuselage and two Rolls-Royce high by-pass ratio turbofan engines mounted under the low wing. When Britain pulled out on 10 April 1969 and, with Rolls-Royce concentrating on the RB.211 turbofan for the Lockheed TriStar, Airbus decided to go with the 50,000-lb (222.5-kN) thrust General Electric CF6-50, under development for the DC-10. The aircraft, then referred to as the A250, was renamed as the A300B, alluding to the maximum seating capacity.

Design definition

By the beginning of 1969, the overall definition was complete. The length of the aircraft had been fixed at 167 ft 2 in (50.95 m), with an 18-ft 6-in (5.64-m) fuselage diameter. The cabin would accommodate 250 passengers in comfortable eight-abreast seating, with standard freight containers in the lower cargo hold. Economic considerations dictated a cruising speed of Mach 0.84 and a typical range of 1,367 miles (2200 km).

The Hawker Siddeley-designed high-speed 28° swept wing was notable for the application of the rear-loading principle. This technique was designed to increase lift over the rear portion of the aerofoil before the onset of flow separation and buffet.

Plans were being drawn up to build four development aircraft, designated A300B1, around the General Electric CF6-50 turbofan, although the smaller Rolls-Royce RB.211 engine remained an option, primarily to win orders from British customers. Across the Channel, Air France was pressing for the inclusion of 24 more passengers, and this was

F-WUAB, the first A300B1 prototype, flew initially on 28 October 1972. The excellence of the design was soon revealed, but for a while it seemed as though the Airbus would never sell in numbers. Eventually, European co-operation, on an unprecedented scale, drove the programme on to success.

achieved by inserting two extra fuselage frames ahead and three aft of the wings, providing space for three more rows of eight seats each. It was decided that the last two development aircraft were to be built to this A300B2 configuration.

The long-expected first order for the Airbus was finally signed on 9 November 1971, with Air

Building an Airbus

Hawker Siddeley worked on the A300 wing design for almost nine years. The wings of all subsequent Airbus aircraft have been designed and produced in Britain, latterly at British Aerospace's Filton and Chester works. Main components are also constructed in France and Germany, with various sub-contractors responsible for more minor systems, and components spread throughout Europe. Final assembly of the A300, as with all Airbus types except the A319/A321, is carried out at Airbus's Toulouse headquarters.

A triple-slotted trailing-edge flap arrangement had become accepted as the normal system for large airliners. In its quest for reliability and maintainability, Airbus ruled out this traditional flap installation in favour of tabbed Fowler flaps, which offered greater mechanical simplicity.

out ceremony at Toulouse on 28 September 1972. Exactly one month later, on 28 October, A300B1 F-WUAB took off on its maiden flight, returning one hour and 23 minutes later.

Service debut

In 1973, the prototype, joined by the second A300B1, fitted in an ambitious demonstration programme, including an extensive world tour, to stimulate interest in Europe's new airliner. The final certification flight was made on 31 January 1974, with French and German certification granted on 15 March 1974, two months ahead of schedule. Launch customer Air France took delivery of its first A300B2 on 10 May 1974 and introduced the type into service on its Paris-London route 13 days later.

France contracting to buy just six A300B2s and taking options on 10 more. That same month, Airbus Industrie decided to offer an increased-range model, the A300B4, to widen its market appeal, and it was this which became the standard model. The B4 differed in having an additional centre wing tank, and a changed fuel-management system which increased the range to more than 2,300 miles (3700 km). Iberia was the first to place a contract for the A300B4 in January 1972. Lufthansa signed a contract for three A300B2s on 7 May 1973.

The Airbus work was shared among the partners roughly in proportion to their financial holdings. From the aircraft's inception, it had been planned that each partner would contribute complete sub-assemblies in a 'ready-to-fly' condition, with all cables, pipe runs and equipment installed and checked. The result was that just 4 per cent of the man-hours were spent on the final assembly line. The completed A300B was introduced to the public at a roll-

First customers

Air France and Lufthansa were obvious first customers for the all-European airliner. With the UK government having withdrawn at an early stage, leaving Hawker Siddeley to make Britain's contribution privately, it was unlikely that an order would hail from British Airways. Boeing was already the dominant manufacturer represented in BA's fleet, while Lufthansa had to be persuaded to break its 'all-Boeing' policy. Air France flew its first A300B2 service on 23 May 1974, Lufthansa its first on 1 April 1976.

A300 variants
Family planning

Above: The extended-range A300-600R first flew on 9 December 1987 and features the tailplane trim tank developed for the A310. This example is seen prior to delivery to Thai Airways and is one of 10 - 600Rs currently operated by the airline.

Left: With two extra rows of seats, the A300-600 can carry more passengers than the standard A300B4 (361 in all-tourist class). Saudi Arabian Airlines currently operates 11 examples.

As sales of the A300 boomed, Airbus introduced the A300C4 convertible freighter. Hapag-Lloyd of Germany was the first customer and introduced the type into service in 1980.

The short/medium-range A300 was the first wide-bodied twin-engined aircraft to enter airline service. It evolved through the design stage to meet different and changing airline requirements, and later benefited from the application of new technologies as they became available.

Only the first two aircraft were built to the original A300B1 configuration before a demand for more seats produced the A300B2, which became the first model to go into service. South African Airways specified Krüger flaps on its A300B2s to improve hot-and-high airfield performance, as the A300B2K.

Increased range was provided in the A300B4 through the addition of a new centre wing fuel tank. The A300B4 made its first flight on 26 December 1974 and received its type certificate on 26 March 1975, entering service with Germanair in May. To bring some semblance of order to the growing number of variants and permutations of weights and engine combinations, Airbus devised a new designation system, which took effect from 1978. Standard A300B2 and B4 models were given the -100 suffix, while aircraft with higher gross weights took on the -200 suffix. A special heavier model for Scandinavian Airlines System (SAS), the first to introduce the Pratt & Whitney JT9D turbofan, was designated A300B2-300. The two engine types also had their own groupings, so that aircraft numbered from -100 to 119 and -200 to -219 had CF6-50 engines, and those numbered from -120/220 to 139/239 were powered by the JT9D-59A.

As a means of extending the market appeal of

Built originally as an A300B2-320, which was a specially-developed heavier version for SAS with Pratt & Whitney JT9D turbofans, LN-RCA was converted to an A300B4-120 in 1983. At this time the aircraft was leased to Scanair, SAS's charter and inclusive tour subsidiary, and operated on summer flights to the Mediterranean. The aircraft operated with Scanair until bought by Conair of Denmark in 1987.

Right: The needs of South African Airways prompted the development of the A300B2K, which featured Krüger flaps to improve hot-and-high take-off performance. SAA introduced the variant into service in 1976.

Left: Delivered in 1980 A300B4-203 SX-BEE typifies the durability of the A300, having racked up almost 20 years' service with Olympic.

the aircraft, Airbus also offered convertible and all-freighter versions of the B4, both fitted with a 23-ft 2-in x 8-ft 4-in (7.07 x 2.54-m) upwards-opening cargo door on the port side and capable of carrying a 40-tonne payload a distance of 1,150 miles (1850 km). Only three and two respectively were later built on the production line, although there were some subsequent conversions. Hapag-Lloyd took delivery of the first convertible A300C4-200 in January 1980, while Korean Air Lines followed in August 1986 with the A300F4-200 all-cargo variant

New variant

In parallel with the development of the advanced shortened A310, Airbus produced what it called the 'world's largest twin-aisle

aircraft'. Designated the A300B4-600, generally simplified to A300-600, this model was launched on 16 December 1980 with an order from Saudia. It incorporated many new design features, headed by a new two-crew cockpit with digital avionics and flight management systems and a unique electronic centralised aircraft monitor (ECAM) providing extensive aircraft systems information. Other key improvements were a substantially modified wing, electrical signalling for flaps, slats and spoilers, wingtip fences for drag reduction, carbon brakes, and a saving of 1.5 tonnes in weight through the use of composite materials. The new aircraft provided typical two-class seating for 266 passengers in a slightly longer fuselage, or up to 361 in an all-tourist layout. The

A300-600 made its first flight on 8 July 1983 and received its type approval on 9 March 1984.

Next to fly, on 12 April 1984, was the convertible A300C4-600. Equipped with a large forward port-side cargo door and capable of being operated in all-passenger or all-freight modes with a maximum structural payload of 46.8 tonnes, the first 'C' variant was delivered to the Kuwait Airways on 30 May 1984. The A300-600 replaced previous models after the last deliveries of the A300B4 were made in early 1985, but the process of product improvement was far from complete.

Extended range

On 2 March 1987, American Airlines launched the extended-range A300B4-600ER, but soon shortened to A300-600R. The -600R differed in its installation of a 1,620-US gallon (6,150-litre) fuel tank in the horizontal stabiliser, with a computerised fuel transfer system for active centre-of-gravity control, and the required equipment fit for 180-minute ETOPS (extended range twin-engine operations) approval. The A300-600R first flew on 9 December 1987 and entered service with American Airlines the following May.

Apart from a handful of orders, cargo versions of the A300 had attracted little interest from airlines until the giant US package operator Federal Express signed a huge order for the all-cargo A300-600F. This definitive freighter version can accommodate a single or double row of standard pallets, plus four pallets and 10 LD3 containers, or 22 LD3s, on the lower deck. Main structural changes from the passenger aircraft include the addition of a large maindeck cargo door on the port side (as fitted to the convertible 'C' models), a reinforced main deck floor, and the deletion of cabin windows. The A300-600F took to the skies on 2 December 1993, with the first delivery to Federal Express taking place on 27 April 1994.

The introduction of the vastly improved A300-600/-600R models created a buoyant market for freighter conversion programmes, carried out on older passenger service models. Both ChryslerBenz Aerospace Airbus (Dasa) and British Aerospace Aviation Services developed conversion kits, which include the same large port-side cargo door, reinforcement of the main deck floor and other features from the production freighter.

Above: With the widest fuselage in its class the A300-600F is an ideal aircraft for cargo-carriers such as Federal Express. The aircraft features a large maindeck cargo door and a reinforced floor.

Right: Delivered in April 1998 to ACS Cargo of Costa Rica, this Airbus A300B4 was the fourth freighter conversion completed by BAe Aviation Services at Filton, UK.

A300 operators

Despite entering service in the early 1970s the A300 is still popular with major and smaller airlines around the world. Many operators are utilising the A300's widebody fuselage and operating the type as a freighter, whereas the increased capacity and range of the A300-600 has proved popular for passenger operations in the Far East.

China Airlines

After cancelling an earlier order, China Airlines signed a new deal in July 1980 for five A300B4-220s with Pratt & Whitney engines. A further option was later also taken up. The first A300 service was flown on 1 August 1982 on a Taipei-Manila-Taipei round trip. Between September 1989 and December 1992, China Airlines bought six new A300B4-622Rs, and has added a further eight since December 1996. Two were lost in tragic accidents in 1994 and 1998. Twelve remain in service today.

American Airlines

American Airlines became the launch customer for the extended-range A300-600R on 2 March 1987, with an order for 25 aircraft plus options, which brought the eventual fleet to 35. The first of the General Electric CF6-80C2A5-powered aircraft went into service with American in May 1988 and the airline took delivery of the 35th and last Airbus in February 1993. The A300 is still used extensively into the Caribbean from American's New York and Miami gateways, as well as on a few transatlantic routes.

China Eastern Airlines

The Civil Aviation Administration of China (CAAC) placed the first order with Airbus for its Shanghai branch, which became China Eastern Airlines after reorganisation of China's civil aviation structure. The new airline took delivery of 10 A300B4-605Rs between November 1989 and July 1995, and put the big Airbus onto its domestic trunk routes and regional services. Shenyang-based China Northern Airlines and Xian-based China Northwest Airlines also later acquired Airbuses, operating eight A300B4-622Rs and five A300B4-605Rs from October 1992.

EgyptAir

The Egyptian flag-carrier has become a prolific operator of Airbus types since leasing a pair of A300s in spring 1977. It placed its own order on 29 April 1979 for three A300B4-203s, plus four options, later taken up, with an eighth also ordered. Deliveries were spread over three years, with the first arriving in Cairo in September 1980. Ten years later EgyptAir started taking delivery of nine advanced A300-622Rs (seven in service today), which have replaced the earlier model, except for two converted for cargo carriage.

FedEx

The world's largest express freight transportation company placed an order for 25 A300-600F freighters on 3 July 1991. Subsequent take-up of options brought orders to 36 aircraft. The first was delivered to FedEx at its Memphis 'superhub' in April 1994, with deliveries completed in October 1999. Another six second-hand converted aircraft were added between 2000-2002. FedEx operates its 42-strong fleet out of domestic hubs, as well as international locations in Europe and the Far East.

Iberia

The Spanish flag-carrier was the second Airbus customer when it signed an order for four A300B4-103s, plus one option, on 14 January 1972, becoming the launch customer for the extended-range B4 model. Nearly seven years elapsed before Iberia came back to Airbus, buying four Pratt & Whitney-powered A300B4-120s on 28 December 1978. Tw A300B4-203s were bought on 28 April 1989, and eight aircraft remained in service until 2002.

Indian Airlines

Indian Airlines became the sixth customer for the Airbus twin, signing for three A300B2-1C machines, plus three options, on 24 April 1975. On 1 December 1976, the airline put the Airbus onto its main trunk routes linking Bombay, Delhi, Calcutta, Madras and Bangalore. Conversions of options brought the fleet to eight, with the final delivery on 7 August 1980. Two new A300B4-203s and two ex-Lufthansa A300B2-1Cs were bought in 1982. Indian Airlines' 3-strong fleet (two were lost in accidents and five sold) is scheduled primarily on major domestic routes.

Japan Air System

Japan's third-largest airline placed a contract on 21 May 1979 for six A300B2K-3Cs, adapted with Krüger flaps for improved performance. That same year, Toa Domestic Airlines (TDA) – later renamed Japan Air System – increased its commitment to nine. The airline later acquired eight second-hand A300B4-203s (including an A300C4-203 not taken up by Libyan Arab Airlines). Orders and options for 17 larger A300-622Rs, since increased to 23, were placed on 30 March 1989. Deliveries were completed in May 1998, and the current A300 fleet totals 35 aircraft.

Korean Air

South Korea's national airline signed a contract for six A300B4-103s on 5 September 1974. Others were added in subsequent years, including one more A300B4-103, one convertible A300C4-203, and a launch order on 11 October 1985 for two A300F4-203 all-freighters. The airline then went over to Pratt & Whitney-powered models, first acquiring some A300-620 and -622 models, before placing a massive launch order on 11 March 1988 for 16 A300-622Rs with deliveries being completed in May 1994.

Kuwait Airways

Kuwait Airways converted three A310 options to the A300C4-620 convertible, for which Kuwait Airways became the launch customer. However, on 2 August 1990 all three were seized by Iraq and flown to Baghdad, where two were destroyed by Allied bombing at the height of the Gulf War on 15 February 1991. The other was returned to Kuwait in September 1990 and joined in 1993/94 by five General Electric-powered A300B4-605R models. The six aircraft have been used to link Kuwait to destinations in Europe, the Middle East and the Indian sub-continent

Lufthansa

Lufthansa signed a contract for three A300B2s, plus four options, on 7 May 1973. The first A300B2-1C entered service on the Frankfurt-London and Frankfurt-Paris routes on 1 April 1976. Three more A300B2-1Cs and five A300B4-2Cs followed, but all had left the fleet by 1988, at which time, Lufthansa was taking delivery of 11 new A300-603s. Four extended range A300-605R aircraft have since joined the fleet.

Olympic Airways

Olympic took delivery of six A300B4-103s for its high-density European services between 1979 and 1981. Two A300B2-1Cs were also leased in 1985/86, while two improved A300-605Rs were acquired in June 1992 and October 1993, as part of a fleet expansion and modernisation programme.

Saudi Arabian Airlines

On 12 December 1980, Saudia signed for 11 of the larger, advanced A300B4-620, powered by the JT9D-7R4H1, but leased two A300B2-103s from Korean Air for one year from November 1980 to provide much-needed capacity. All 11 aircraft were delivered during 1984. The aircraft are used mainly on regional services and the high-density domestic trunk routes.

Thai Airways International

Thai International signed up for two A300B4-2Cs on 15 April 1977. The conversion of options and regular subsequent orders brought the fleet to eight A300B4-2C and four A300B4-203 models by the time of the final delivery in March 1985. The Airbus fleet was built up on a regular basis, with further deliveries of a total of six A300B4-601s, two A300B4-605s and eight A300B4-622Rs by October 1993. Five more A300B4-622Rs delivered at the end of 1998, bringing its total to 33 ordered new from Airbus.

South African Airways

SAA was an early customer, and the first on the African continent, when it placed an order for four A300B2Ks on 4 September 1975. The A300B2K introduced the Krüger flaps of the A300B4 to provide enhanced hot-and-high performance. The Airbus fleet, all powered by the CF6-50C turbofan engine, was enlarged by adding two A300B4-200s, one A300C4-200 convertible, and an ex-Singapore Airlines A300B4-200. Phase-out began in 2000 and all had been sold by May 2001.

Airbus A310
Shortening the A300

Developed initially as the Airbus A300B10, one of the many proposed versions of the original A300, the A310 was launched in 1978 after interest was shown in the project by Lufthansa and Swissair.

The A310 first flew in April 1982 and, by September that year, the order book stood at 102 due to the aircraft's excellent performance and fuel economy which had become evident in test flights.

Left: As with all early-generation Airbus aircraft, the final assembly of the A310 took place at Aérospatiale's factory in Toulouse-Blagnac, southern France.

Recognised at the time as one of the most fuel-efficient, medium-haul transports in the world, despite keen competition from Boeing's 767, Airbus Industries' A310 was originally planned as a huge airliner, with a fuselage diameter of 20.9 ft (6.4 m). Airlines thought this too big and it was subsequently cut back to a diameter of 18.50 ft (5.64 m). The number of seats (typical mixed-class) was reduced from 300 to around 250.

Originally called the A300B10, it eventually matured into the A310. Lufthansa and Swissair, were the main backers for the new smaller aircraft.

In late 1977 the brilliant aerodynamics team of British Aerospace at Hatfield – which a decade earlier had designed the wing of the larger A300B – began scheming a totally new wing for the proposed 'all-new' A300B10. But BAe was not a member of the consortium, so other new wing designs were started by German partners MBB, VFW-Fokker, and French partner, Aérospatiale.

Has anything changed?

The public first saw the A310 in the form of a model at the Hanover airshow in April 1978. It looked very much like the A300B, but the wing was smaller and the fuselage was 12 frames shorter.

The engines were expected to be lower-thrust versions of those used on the A300B. The only real argument still concerned the wing, but a solution was in sight when, in January 1979, British Aerospace returned to Airbus as a full partner. BAe accordingly handled the main responsibility for the wing.

The final wing configuration however, differed significantly from that of the A300B. Seen from the front it looked very thin, apart from the portion inboard of the engines – where the wing grew thicker rapidly – and its undersurface curving sharply down towards the very bottom of the fuselage. Fowler flaps were fitted outboard, while

Along with Lufthansa, Swissair was the launch customer for the A310, the aircraft illustrated here being the first pre-production example painted in Swiss colours. With deliveries commencing in 1985, six A310s served with the airline, operating on high-density, short-/medium-haul services, until the last example was withdrawn in 1999.

Left: Operating with the Dutch airline, KLM, and supplementing its Boeing 737s were six A310-200s. The aircraft served on KLM's short-haul routes throughout Europe. They were later sold to Fed Ex in summer 1996, and converted to an all-freight configuration.

Below: British Caledonian was absorbed by British Airways in 1988. The remaining A310s were sold by BA a short time later.

inboard the flaps were of the double-slotted variety.

The A310 fuselage had a redesigned rear end, with the rear pressure bulkhead nearer the tail. So while the fuselage was reduced in length, by 13 frames, compared to that of the A300B the cabin is only 11 frames shorter. Other changes included a smaller horizontal tail and revised engine pylons, that were able to accept either General Electric or Pratt & Whitney engines without modification. Regarded as the main pioneering breakthrough, however, was the adoption of Airbus Industrie's FFCC (forward-facing crew cockpit), with multifunction cathode-ray tube displays and digital avionics.

Workshare changes

In organising the A310 manufacturing programme, there were a few changes compared to that of the A300B. Aérospatiale constructed the nose, including the cockpit, the lower centre section, including the wing box under the floor, the engine pylons and airbrakes. This taking place, along with the assembly of the aircraft and

flight testing, at Toulouse-Blagnac. MBB constructed almost all of the entire fuselage, as well as the vertical tail, flaps, spoilers and final assembly of the wings. When completed they were subsequently dispatched to Toulouse. British Aerospace at Chester made the wing inter-spar boxes, which are by far the strongest and heaviest parts of the whole aircraft. CASA's plants in Spain constructed the horizontal tail, forward passenger doors and landing-gear doors. In the Netherlands, Fokker made the all-speed ailerons between the

flaps, wingtips, main-leg doors and flap-track fairings. A specially formed Belgian consortium, Belairbus, supplied the full-span slats and forward wing/body fairings.

Production begins

Aérospatiale did not set up any separate assembly line for the A310, but slotted the smaller aircraft in among the A300Bs and A300-600s. There was no prototype, though the first four differed from production aircraft in various ways. The first two had an emergency crew escape route

through the nose-gear bay and another had provision for explosive bolts on one of the main cargo doors, to comply with FAA regulations.

Airbus had planned a short-haul A310-100, but this was never built and the first aircraft were A310-200s, which became the basic passenger version, with an internal fuel capacity of 12,098 Imp gal (55000 litres).

The first flight took place on 3 April 1982 and from the very beginning it was clear that the new Airbus was a winner. The stage had been set for Airbus's incredible future successes.

Lufthansa demonstrated its fleet renewal policy with the purchase of nine A310s in 1982, receiving the -200 model (illustrated). This was later replaced by the -300 variant.

Airbus A310
Further development

Proving its critics wrong with a series of publicity-staged long-distance flights, Airbus Industrie's A310 was ordered by a host of airlines to fulfil the niche for a twin-engined, long-distance airliner. Although now overshadowed in production by later Airbus models the A310 remains in service around the world.

Having completed its first flight, the A310's performance directly contributed to the design of the new wing, which was absolutely 'clean' in having no flaws (such as gaps in the slats at the inboard end or above the engine pylon), an outstanding aerofoil profile with a flat-top section, and an average thickness/chord ratio of almost 12 per cent. Perhaps the greatest surprise was the buffet boundary (the combination of speed and altitude at which aerodynamic buffet will be encountered even in level flight) which exceeded expectation by almost 10 per cent, which meant either that the A310 could cruise 2952 ft (900 m) higher for any given weight, or else carry 10.8 tons more payload at a typical cruise altitude.

Confounding the critics

The no. 2 aircraft (F-WZLI)) flew on 13 May 1982, and soon made a route-proving trip to the Far East. Up to this time, an army of rivals, led by America's Boeing

Above: Two A310-300s, delivered in 1991, were operated by the former Czechoslovakia's national airline, CSA. Following partition of the country, the aircraft continued to serve with the airline, although in a slightly revised colour scheme.

Before Pan Am's demise, the airline was one of the major US airlines to embrace Airbus products – ordering significant batches of A300s and A310s. At one stage its A310 fleet stood at 19, made up of seven -200s and 12 -300s. Several served on Pan Am's European network.

The first prototype of the A310-300 wore this striking colour scheme during its publicity sales tour. The aircraft was displayed at both the Farnborough and Paris airshows.

Company, had poured scorn on the European A310, pointing out how poor its high-altitude performance would be, being penalised by so small a wing. On this trip, the aircraft silenced such critics forever. It carried a full load, equivalent to 218 passengers and baggage, a distance of 2,994 miles (4818 km) from Toulouse to Kuwait. It then fought against headwinds of 53 mph (85 km/h) all the way to Singapore – a distance of 4,607 miles (7415 km), once more with a full load. But it was the sector from Kuala Lumpur to Bangkok that surprised the critics. Again with a full payload, F-WZLI took off and climbed straight up to a height of 42,979 ft (13100 m). Throughout the 16,155-mile (26000-km) trip, the Mach 0.8 cruise returned an average fuel burn of 2.7 Imp gal/ nautical mile (6.67 litres/km) – 6.5 per cent below the prediction of the Airbus engineers.

Powerplant choices

The first two aircraft were powered by Pratt & Whitney JT9D-7R4D1 engines, each rated at 48,000 lb (213.5 kN). An alternative launch engine was the JT9D-7R4E1, or the lighter General Electric CF6-80C2A2,

Below: FedEx currently operates the largest fleet of A310s. All their A310-200F aircraft have undergone conversion to a freighter configuration, which involved introducing a large cargo door on the front port side of the fuselage.

Above: Air India still operates a fleet of 20 A310-300s (12 of which are leased) on its medium and long haul routes. This example is seen wearing a trials colour scheme, that was ultimately not adopted by the airline fleet.

both rated at 50,000 lb (222.4 kN). In 1980, widespread interest in the aircraft from the Middle East appeared to offer an opening to Rolls-Royce which, by this time, was beginning to realise that it had been mistaken in not becoming involved in the development of the A310.

In the course of production of the A310-200, various improvements were introduced, the most visible being the addition of winglets. Airbus Industrie called these 'wingtip fences', and they are larger than those of the A300-600, and of a quite different shape. The first example to receive these additional winglets was a Thai Airways aircraft, delivered on 7 May 1986. They subsequently were retrofitted to a few A310-200s in service. Another version,

first delivered to Martinair of the Netherlands in November 1984, was the A310-200C convertible. This had an upper-deck cargo door with a width of 11.7 ft (3.58 m), and a convertible interior which can accept 16 cargo pallets or any combination of cargo and passengers. Martinair's two examples were later sold to FedEx. In response to a request, Airbus developed the -200F, a dedicated all-cargo version, with a weight-limited payload of 38.7 tons.

Cargo conversions of the aircraft have firmly established the A310 within the United States. FedEx operates the aircraft on freight routes around the world, the aircraft having proved themselves to be extremely versatile and economical to operate.

In 1982, Airbus announced a third version, the A310-300, aimed at even longer routes. The programme was announced during the handover of Swissair's first A310, and that same airline again became the launch customer. Visually, the A310-300 is almost identical to the -200, although it does carry the distinctive winglets as standard. Again, there was a choice of powerplants; the first Swissair A310-300 example took to the air on 8 July 1985, powered initially by JT9D-7R4E1 engines, although Pratt & Whitney PW4000-series engines were intended for the final aircraft. The first -300 powered by CF6-80C2 engines flew on 6 September 1985.

Perhaps the most important development for the new longer-range version was the tailplane trim tank. Most conventional aircraft have a natural tendency to go into a dive. It is prevented by the tailplane or elevators continuously being angled to push the tail down. This fights against the lift of the wing and increases drag. In the A310-300, the tailplane is full of fuel, and this exerts the required download with no drag.

Optional 1,853 Imp-gallon (7,200-litre) tanks can be carried in the hold but, without these, the A310-300 still has remarkable range – 5,157 miles (8300 km) with a full payload. This ability has allowed many airlines to quality the A310 for ETOPS overwater routes.

Military service

Although aimed purely at the commercial market, the A310 has adopted a limited military role within some armed forces. The first military delivery was in September 1991, comprising one aircraft for the Royal Thai air force for governmental transportation tasks. In the following year, the German Luftwaffe took delivery of three A310s originally operated by the East German airline Interflug. Similarly, the Canadian Forces adopted five A310s as replacements for its five elderly Boeing 707s (CC-137s) used by No. 437 Sqn, designating the type CC-150 Polaris. At present, the only other European military operators are Belgium and France's Armée de l'Air, operating three A310s, replacing DC-8s operated by ET 3/60.

Thailand was the first to put the A310 into military service, one being employed on VIP transport duties. France, Germany and Canada later followed.

Operational history

The A310 still serves with a number of operators around the world. Some examples, however, are operated by smaller carriers, and are in the hands of their second, or even third, owner. This cross-section of A310 operators serves to demonstrate the success of this highly popular airliner.

Uzbekistan Airways

In 1992 the government of the newly-formed Uzbekistan assumed air sovereignty over its national territory. At the same time, the aircraft of the former Tashkent directorate of Aeroflot became the property of Uzbekistan, with Uzbekistan Airways being founded as the national airline. Particular attention was paid to new routes from western Europe to the Far East. In order to be able to meet the needs of travellers from Western countries, Uzbekistan leased two A310-300s, the first arriving in July 1993, for services to London and Middle East cities. One further A310-300 joined the airline in 1998 and all three remain in service.

Air Jamaica

Established by the Jamaican government, together with Air Canada, in October 1968, the airline operated a limited network of routes to destinations within the United States and Canada. A major expansion to the airline in May 1994 brought with it a new colour scheme (illustrated) and new aircraft, six A310-300s. These aircraft allowed the airline to reopen the London service in 1996.

Pakistan International

Founded in 1951, PIA operated a limited global network until a major restructuring in late 1972. After acquiring six A310-300s in the early 1990s PIA added a further six examples in 2004 and the fleet is utilised on long-distance routes to cities such as Moscow, London and Tokyo. The new additions coincided with the retirement of PIA's Airbus A300B4 fleet after two decades of service.

Aerolineas Argentinas

Created from the merger of four smaller airlines in May 1949, Argentina's national airline, Aerolineas Argentinas, acquired three A310-324s from US operator Delta Airlines in July 1994 to replace its Boeing 707s. Utilised on routes to the USA, the aircraft have now been withdrawn from use with the airline.

Royal Jordanian

King Hussein declared the establishment of Jordan's first national airline, Alia, on 8 December 1963. Having lost several aircraft during various wars within the Middle East, the airline emerged in 1984 as the first Arab national carrier to commence schedules to the USA. With the introduction of the A310 in 1986, a new colour scheme was introduced and a new name, Royal Jordanian. The current A310 fleet comprises five A310-300s and two -300 freighter conversions.

Kuwait Airways

Kuwait Airways Corporation came into existence in 1953 as a national airline set up by local businessmen. It was named Kuwait National Airways. The present name was adopted in 1958 when the British airline BOAC took over management of the airline. The airline became wholly-government owned in June 1963, and it underwent a rapid expansion in the following years with Boeing aircraft. After the Iraqi occupation of Kuwait in summer 1991, flights were discontinued and some aircraft destroyed. Following the conclusion of the war the airline ordered a host of new Airbus aircraft, including four A310-300s.

Air Afrique

The airline was established on 28 March 1961 with the objective of creating a comprehensive internal service within the former French colonies. In the 1960s and 1970s, the airline operated leased DC-8s before acquiring its first widebody aircraft, a DC-10, in 1973. Boeing 747s were used from October 1980 to March 1984, but this aircraft turned out not to be flexible enough for Air Afrique's purposes. Airbus A310-300s were increasingly used; these proved ideal for opening new routes to South Africa. Unfortunately, the airline ceased operating in 2002 and the four A310s were repossessed due to financial difficulties.

Sudan Airways

Founded in February 1946 for domestic operations, the airline expanded in the 1950s and 1970s, operating aircraft that included the Boeing 707, which was used for flights to Europe. During 1993, the airline acquired a fleet of Airbus aircraft, including at one time five A310s. Beginning operations in 1990 the last A310 was withdrawn from Sudan Airways service in 2004.

Emirates

The independent state airline of Dubai was formed in 1985 with the support of the Sheikh of the United Emirates, and operations commenced on 25 October 1985. From 1987, flights to London, Frankfurt and Istanbul were established using the newly-delivered A310-300s; further examples followed in 1988 and 1990, to comprise a total of 10 such aircraft. The A310s were replaced from 1999 by larger A330s in a fleet modernisation programme.

Turkish Airlines

Founded in 1933, Turkish Airlines concentrated on the development of domestic rather than international routes; only in the late 1960s were services to European cities developed. Airbus A310s were brought into service from 1984, serving on regional routes only. From 1985, further examples were acquired to expand Turkish Airlines' services to overseas destinations. At present, the A310 fleet comprises seven A310-200/-300s.

Airbus A320
The first FBW airliner

After successes with the A300 and A310, Airbus turned to the A320, hoping that it would emulate the successes of its relatives. A delay in development allowed the A320 to become the most advanced airliner in the world on its introduction into service.

Airbus Industrie has, from the start, been identified in the minds of the public and of its customers with fat wide-body, or twin-aisle, aircraft. But for commercial success a manufacturer (of almost anything) needs to be able to offer a broad spectrum of products. From as early as 1970 the Airbus management studied possible single-aisle (SA) aircraft, much smaller than the A300B and A310 and more in the class of the 737 or DC-9.

Dassault was building the Mercure (and losing all its investment, with a production run of 10). BAC wanted to build the One-Eleven 700 or 800, as well as wide-body 3-11s. BAC was also a partner in the rival Europlane consortium. Hawker Siddeley wanted to build a QTOL (quiet take-off and landing) aircraft in partnership with Dornier and VFW-Fokker. Later came a whole spate of national or international projects, including the European JET family and the Dutch Fokker F29. But in 1979 British Aerospace became a member of Airbus Industrie, and the JET family became the Airbus SA-1 and SA-2, single-aisle projects with different body lengths to seat from 130 to 180.

In 1980 it looked as if such aircraft could be designed for propfan propulsion, offering reduced fuel consumption, without any significant loss in cruising speed. Airbus carried out

Above: When it entered service, the A320 completely outclassed the market in terms of high technology, both in its aerodynamics and onboard equipment. The A320 set a standard that is only being challenged today by other manufacturers.

The A320 is a true multinational project, with sections built by Aérospatiale, BAe, CASA and Deutsche Airbus (MBB and VFW). The various components are then assembled in Toulouse.

*Above: Very soon after **BA** and Air France received their aircraft, Air Inter began replacing Super Caravelles and Mercures with the A320. These three airlines are the only ones to have bought the A320-100, at a gross weight of 68 tonnes, total production of this model being 21. It was quickly replaced on the assembly line by the A320-200.*

Left: The first A320 was ceremonially rolled out at Toulouse on 14 February 1987 and flew on 22 February. Certification was achieved on 26 February 1988, and scheduled services began with Air France and British Airways in April 1988.

The first customer to put the IAE V2500-engined variant into service was Cyprus Airways, which started receiving a fleet of eight A320s in April 1989.

a prolonged study of propfans, in partnership with Hamilton Standard and Pratt & Whitney. The outcome was a decision to stick to advanced turbofans. The resulting A320 was announced in February 1981 and given the go-ahead at the Paris air show four months later. The go-ahead was more in spirit than in practice, however. For one thing, no decision had been made between a number of candidate engines in the thrust range 20,006-27,000 lb (90-122 kN), some of which existed only on paper. But far more serious was the fact that, running true to form, the British government had failed to reach any agreement with British Aerospace regarding support and launch costs. Not until 1 March 1984 could BAe at last announce an agreement, in which the early part of the programme was to be assisted by a loan of £250 million, repayable by BAe, to help the company with massive tooling costs in building the wings.

Design refinement

The 'three lost years' were not wasted, because throughout this period both the design of the A320 and its exceedingly advanced systems were refined and improved. The main externally obvious development was to make all aircraft the same length and, though this was fixed at only 123 ft 3 in (37.70 m), not much longer than the 'short' Dash-100, the internal cabin length was almost the same as that of the previous 'long' -200. The wing passed through several evolutionary stages with six

different spans, finally settling at 111 ft 3 in (33.91 m). It was long and slender, with an aspect ratio of over nine, making for an aerodynamic efficiency significantly greater than that of the wings of the 737 or MD-80. Another advantage over those older-technology rivals was that the fuselage diameter was greater: the internal cabin width is 12 ft 1 in (3.70 m), compared with 10 ft 8 in (3.25 m) for the 737 and 757, and 10 ft 1 in (3.07 m) for the MD-80 series.

To look at an A320, it hardly seems revolutionary. An aerodynamicist might comment on the almost perfect external form, and on the unique way in which the wings have only two sections of slotted flaps on each side, running aft and down on

tracks to form an unbroken lifting surface from root to aileron. Whenever an A320 flies through turbulence, accelerometers in the fuselage sense vertical accelerations and, via the universal electrical FBW (fly-by-wire) signalling, power the ailerons and spoilers to damp out and virtually eliminate disturbance.

In the end, CFM International came up with an engine specially tailored to the new airliner, and Airbus went ahead with this. The CFM56-5-A1 has active clearance control and full authority digital control, with a take-off thrust of 25,000 lb (112.5 kN).

When the A320 was launched, this was the only engine available. Subsequently, IAE (International Aero Engines, a

powerful five-nation consortium including Rolls-Royce and Pratt & Whitney) offered a newer and even more advanced engine, the V2500. It was soon clear that the V2500 was a superb engine, clearly the toughest and also the quietest in its class, and from 1989 it offered the very keenest of propulsion competition.

Range extension

Except for the 100 series, all aircraft have a large centre-section fuel tank, which increased fuel capacity from 3,429 Imp gal (15588 litres) for the -100 to 5,154 Imp gal (23430 litres), giving the aircraft a range with 150 passengers and baggage of around 3,000 nm (3,450 miles; 5550 km). And, except for the early Dash-100s, all A320s have winglets, or as Airbus calls them, 'wingtip fences', which further enhance aerodynamic efficiency and correspondingly save a significant amount of fuel.

State-of-the-art equipment

Probably the most visible aspect of the avionics is the flight deck. At first sight there seems to be no way to fly the aircraft, because the traditional control yoke is missing! In its place is a small SSC (sidestick controller), as in the F-16, which responds electronically to the force exerted upon it by the pilot (complex laws have been followed to enable two pilots to transfer control, and to allow one pilot to override another, should this ever become necessary). Absence of the yoke makes room for a pull-out table in front of each pilot, and also gives a perfect view of the instruments. But again there is a surprise, because there seem to be no instruments. Instead, there are just six multi-function colour displays, two facing each pilot and two on the centreline. These displays are bigger than any seen previously, at 7¼ in (18.4 cm) square. They comprise a PFD (primary flight display) and an ND (navigation display) for each pilot, while the two in the middle serve the ECAM (electronic centralised aircraft monitor). Each display can be made to tell the pilot

almost anything, driven by three management computers. When one counts all the displays and instruments, the total comes to 12, compared with 42 in the 737-300 and 43 in the MD-80, yet the A320 pilot can call up a far greater amount of information.

On the central console are the usual throttles (which are not connected to the engines but to the FADECs (full-authority digital engine controls)) and other controls. There are also new systems, such as a compact and totally integrated RMP (radio management panel) on each side of the engine controls, giving instant and faultless control of every radio and navaid in the aircraft, and two NICD1Js. The latter, the multi-function controller display units, are the human interfaces with another piece of equipment possessed by older aircraft, a CFDS (centralised fault display system). Previous BITE (built-in test equipment) developed haphazardly, but in the 320 the CFDS is a perfect system from nose to tail and from wingtip to wingtip. It records every error or fault, or even a fault about to happen.

Airbus A320/A321

Stretching the family

Moving from strength to strength, the A320 and higher-capacity A321 have now, together with the A319, created a family of mid-sized airliners that compete directly for orders with Boeing's 737 family.

From the third quarter of 1988, the standard A320 version became the Dash-200, with the manufacturer placing emphasis on this model's greater capability compared to the initial A320-100 series.

In early 1989, A320s started rolling off the Airbus production line with the new IAE V2500 engine. This powerplant was first flown on a Boeing 720 in Canada, and first powered an Airbus Industrie test A320 in July 1988. Visually, the V2500 engine pod is differentiated from the CFM56 by its smooth unbroken curve from the inlet to the single nozzle at the rear. The CFM56 pod, by contrast, has a large forward section which discharges fan air, followed by a slim aft fairing over the core.

First V2500 sales

The first customer for the V2500-powered A320 was Cyprus Airways, which began receiving a batch of eight of the type in 1989. These allowed the airline to replace its ageing BAC One-Elevens and Boeing 707s, to become an all-Airbus operator. Shortly afterwards, V2500-engined A320s were delivered to Indian Airlines, fulfilling an initial order for 19 of the type. Indian Airlines' A320s were the first examples to be fitted with new four-wheel bogie main landing gears. Originally, it had been intended that A320 customers would have been offered the option of a two-wheel main landing gear with enlarged tyres inflated to reduced pressure, giving a bigger footprint area, and thus enabling the A320 to operate from unimproved surfaces. However, it was found that a four-wheel main gear bogie would complete this task more effectively.

Future developments

From 1985 onwards, Airbus Industrie began to study a range of A320 developments, the first – which was launched in 1989 – being the A321-100. The A321 had begun life as the projected 'A320 Stretch' or 'Stretched A320', a longer-fuselage higher-capacity version of the A320. In June 1989 it

Above: The A320 was the first commercial aircraft to be equipped with fly-by-wire (FBW) control throughout the flight regime. Bahrain-based Gulf Air operates a fleet of 12 A320s.

Left: British Airways' A320s were ordered by British Caledonian. The airline currently operates a mixed fleet of A320-100 and -200 models, the latter now being the standard production variant.

A subsidiary of Cyprus Airways, Eurocypria Airlines operated a fleet of three Airbus A320s in the 1990s. The airline replaced its A320s with new-generation Boeing 737-800s in 2003.

formally became the A321, with accommodation for 185 passengers within a lengthened fuselage.

Fuselage stretch

Remaining a minimum-change version of the A320, the A321 incorporates a 273-in (6.93-m) fuselage stretch, with a reinforced centre fuselage and undercarriage, and redesigned trailing-edge flaps. The fuselage stretch comprises two plugs forward and aft of the wing. This length increase dictated the repositioning of the four emergency exits, which are now positioned to either side of the wing leading and trailing edges.

The first A321 prototype (F-WWIA) made its maiden flight with V2530 engines, on 11 March 1993. The second, CFM56-5B-powered, prototype first flew in May 1993. The A321-100 is offered with a choice of CFM International CFM56-5B or IAE V2530-A5 turbofans. It was initially planned to assemble the A321 alongside the A320 on Airbus Industrie's Toulouse production lines. However, the A321 became the first Airbus to be assembled in Germany, with the airframes being constructed at DASA's facility in Hamburg.

Launch customers for the A321 were Lufthansa, choosing the higher-powered V2530 for its 20 aircraft, and Alitalia, which ordered 40 examples. Lufthansa took delivery of the first production A321 on 27 January 1994, followed by Alitalia, whose first CFM56-5B-powered A321 arrived on 22 March.

Launched in April 1995, the A321-200, meanwhile, was developed as an extended-range version, incorporating greater fuel capacity and a maximum take-off weight increased from 182,980 lb (83000 kg) to 196,200 lb (88996 kg). The A321-200 was introduced in 1997, after making its four and a half hour maiden flight from Hamburg on 12 December 1996. The A321-200 has an increased range of 2,700 nm (3,107 miles; 5000 km), an increase of approximately 350 nautical miles (404 miles; 650 km) over the baseline A321-100.

Sales success

With the introduction of the A320/A321, Airbus Industrie has succeeded in conquering a share of the North American market, where the family (including the A319) has accumulated in excess of 1,600 orders. United Airlines became the largest A320 operator, and in April 1999 took delivery of the 1001st A320 family airliner. United Airlines ordered 50 A320s in July 1992, followed by options on a further 50, and received its first V2500-engined example in November 1993. Today, United has received a total of 153 A320 family examples with a further 42 on order.

Another North American Airbus operator, US Airways introduced the A320 on its Washington, D.C.-Reagan National to New York-La Guardia shuttle service in October 1999. Replacing the Boeing 727 on this heavily travelled East Coast route, the US Airways' A320s have inevitably proved themselves quieter, more fuel-efficient and more comfortable for passengers (each seat also provides a laptop computer port and there is a telephone in every row).

In March 1998 three South American airlines (Chilean flag carrier LanChile, Brazilian TAM and the Central American TACA group) signed a contract for the joint purchase of 179 Airbus aircraft, comprising A320s and A319s, the then largest-ever order for Airbus Industrie.

1998 saw the first Airbus operator within the former USSR, as Kyrgyzstan Airlines flew its first A320 service between Frankfurt and Bishkek on 3 July. Furthermore, on 24 September, Chengdu-based Sichuan Airlines received its first A321, marking the entry of the A321 into the Chinese market.

Impressive figures

It is more than 17 years now since the first A320 entered commercial operations, and to date the A320 family has carried well over a billion passengers. Some 2,500 examples of the A320 family have been delivered with another 1,000 on order. Some 240 customers have selected the A320 family, which comprises the 124-seat A319, 150-seat A320 and the 185-seat A321. From just 16 deliveries in the first year of production, Airbus Industrie now delivers in excess of 16 A320 family airliners every three weeks.

Left: Launch customer for the A321 was Lufthansa, introducing the type on its European routes in March 1994. Lufthansa chose the more powerful IAE V2530 turbofans for its 182-seat airliners.

Right: A stretched version of the A320, the Airbus A321 was launched in November 1989. The extra fuselage length offers 24 per cent more passenger seating and 40 per cent more hold area than its A320 brethren.

A319/A318

The A319 has been a tremendous sales success for Airbus. A total of 1053 had been ordered by June 2005. Many customers, such as TAM Brasil, were already A320 operators and commonality of maintenance made the A319 an obvious choice.

Having stretched the A320, Airbus then addressed the possibility of 'shrinking' the aircraft to produce a 124-seat version. The result was the A319, which not only kept the Airbus consortium intact, but became a best-seller and an essential element of the Airbus single-aisle family. Airbus followed this with the introduction of the 'baby' A318.

The roots of what became the A319 can be traced back to the original 130- to 140-seat SA1 designs of the early 1980s. By 1990 Airbus had revived these plans as the A320M-7 (minus seven rows of seats), or the A319. However, several of the Airbus group members already had plans for similar small airliners on their own drawing boards, such as British Aerospace's 146NRA and the Aérospatiale/DASA Regioliner projects. It took some time to get a unified Airbus design back on track, then disagreement broke out between France and Germany over where the final assembly site should be. A formal launch, once scheduled for March 1992, was delayed until a decision was reached to allocate A319 assembly to DASA, while the A320 stayed at Toulouse. This paved the way for the marketing launch of the A319 on 22 May 1992. Both Northwest Airlines and Air France were touted as major early customers, but in December 1992 Northwest cancelled most of its Airbus commitments and ceased to be a near-term prospect. In June 1993 Airbus finally announced the formal launch of the A319 with just six orders from ILFC. Only in January 1994 did Air France's long-awaited interest emerge when a letter of intent for nine aircraft and nine options

Above: The first two A319s were retained by Airbus and completed the 650-hour flight test programme which resulted in certification of the aircraft with both CFM56-5A/-5B and IAE V2500-A5 turbofans. The aircraft has subsequently been certified to operate with IAE V2524 engines.

Above: Air Canada was one of the first airlines to order the A319, receiving the first of 35 CFM International CFM56-5A5-powered A319-114s on 12 December 1996. The airline has progressively increased its fleet and currently operates 48 examples

Left: German airline Eurowings operated five A319-112s on both charter and scheduled flights to European destinations. To maximise profit the aircraft had a single-class layout accommodating up to 142 passengers – the largest number carried by any A319 operator.

After a troubled start the A318 has managed to garner 61 orders, although this number pales in comparison with other members of the A320 family. An early order of 15 was from Air France (as illustrated by this computer-generated image).

Below: The Airbus A320 made a significant impact on the US domestic market and many customers, such as United Airlines, have returned to Airbus to order the A319.

Below: Pictured is a representation of a TWA A318 powered by two PW6122 turbofans. TWA became the second US airline customer for the aircraft when it ordered 25 examples in December 1999.

was signed. Swissair next became the first airline to place a firm order, for three aircraft, and in June 1994 the Air France interest was elevated to the status of a firm order.

Short fuselage

Some 12 ft 4 in (3.77 m) shorter than the A320, the stubby A319 was the smallest Airbus available, until the A318 arrived. The A319 is aimed at sectors of approximately 2,000 nm (2,300 miles; 3700 km) with a load of 124 passengers. It is an integral member of the Airbus single-aisle family and shares many common features with the A320 and A321. The A319's wing is identical to that of the A320, although minor software changes have been made in the flight control system to account for different handling characteristics. The use of composite materials in the A319 is even more extensive than in the A320 and includes the wing leading edges, landing-gear doors, the fuselage belly fairing, spoilers, fin leading edge, elevators, rudder and tailplanes.

Maiden flight

On 23 March 1995 the first A319 entered final assembly at Hamburg; it was rolled out on 24 August and made its maiden flight on 25 August 1995. This first of two prototypes flew with CFM56-5B6/2 engines. The second A319 also took to the air powered by CFM56s, on 31 October 1995, and this allowed the first aircraft to be re-engined with IAE V2524-A5 engines. The first A319 to enter airline service was delivered to Swissair on 25 April 1996, followed by Air Inter, Air Canada and Lufthansa. Slow initial sales were compensated by subsequent substantial deals with customers like United Airlines and British Airways. In April 1999 an A319 delivered to Air France became the 1,000th single-aisle Airbus. The A319 has now outsold the A321 by a factor of nearly 2:1 and, in just four years, it has secured almost half as many orders as the A320.

Airbus 'Baby'

In April 1999 Airbus Industrie formally launched the A318, adding the latest and the smallest member of the single-aisle A320 family. After a relatively short development period, the A318 made a successful 3-hour 44 minute first flight from the company airfield at Finkenwerder near Hamburg, Germany, on 15 January 2002.

The A318 can carry 107 passengers in a standard two-class layout up to 2,300 miles (3700 km) in its baseline version.

Airbus Corporate Jetliner (ACJ)

In 1996, to compete with the Boeing Business Jet (BBJ), Airbus launched a derivative of the basic A319 airframe, the A319CJ (Corporate Jet). Available from 1999, the A319CJ is designed to accommodate between eight and 50 passengers in relative luxury, with a maximum range of 7,250 miles (11667 km) – representing non-stop flights from Frankfurt to Los Angeles, Los Angeles to Tokyo and Tokyo to Frankfurt. Most significantly, the A319CJ features minimal changes to the standard A319, so that it retains a high residual value to customers, as it is readily capable of conversion back to standard airline configuration. On 13 June 1999 an Airbus Corporate Jetliner (ACJ) flew non-stop from Toulouse to Buenos Aires, in a 14-hr 50-min flight covering an air-distance of 6,553 nm (7,543 miles; 12140 km), setting a new record for its class. On 16 August 1999 the ACJ received its basic certification from the European JAA prior to the first two aircraft being delivered for interior outfitting. The type certificate for the ACJ is not a new one, but is an amendment of the existing A319 type certificate required by the additional modifications implemented in the ACJ. These include the installation of up to six auxiliary fuel tanks which permit the maximum 7,250-mile (11667-km) range. The first A319CJ was delivered to a Kuwaiti corporation in 1999 and the type has also entered Italian air force service, where it replaced VIP-configured DC-9s. Further orders by private companies and VIP-specialist carriers has seen the ACJ firmly established within the VIP market.

Airbus A330
The A330/A340 concept

Family members: Airbus Industrie's A330 and A340 long-range, high-capacity airliners fly together with an A321, a member of the smaller A319/A320/A321 family.

Airbus Industrie was a latecomer to the commercial airliner market and initially struggled to win orders away from the well-established US giants, Boeing and McDonnell Douglas. Part of Airbus's strategy for success was to offer its customers distinct families of aircraft that could be tailored to meet a wide range of performance and capacity demands. Key to this strategy was establishing a place within the important long-range, high-capacity market with the A330 and A340.

In August 1994, Airbus received cross-crew qualification for pilots transitioning from the A320 to the A330/A340. This allows crew to fly all three types and represents a major cost-saving for airlines.

Airbus's first designs, the A300 and A310, were both high-capacity aircraft that ultimately evolved into long-range airliners. Their development gave Airbus valuable experience in designing and developing true long-range airliners. Airbus perfected the family concept with the A320, which has led to the A318, A319 and A321. Each of these types is essentially the same, but they offer different fuselage lengths (and thus seating capacities), with a range of engines to suit different markets and airline requirements. Furthermore,

there is commonality between engines, systems and, most importantly, cockpits, which allows airlines to maintain and operate the aircraft with the same personnel and flight crews. This is where the family concept starts to make serious economic sense. The concept of cross-qualification of crews, pioneered by Airbus (whereby a crew could step out of one type of aircraft and go and fly another without extensive re-qualifications) was

one of the most valuable 'family' benefits and became essential to A330 and A340 operations.

While the A300, A310 and A320 family were able to take on and beat the best the competition had to offer in their market, Airbus still had to develop an aircraft that could

compete with the long-haul 'kings' – chiefly the Boeing 747 and to a lesser extent, the McDonnell Douglas MD-11 (now the Boeing MD-11). Airbus also realised that there was a sizeable number of older, wide-bodied aircraft, such as the DC-10, L-1011 TriStar and 767-200, that

French carrier Air Inter was the first airline to begin A330-200 operations. European support for the A330/A340 programme was predictably strong, with Lufthansa and Air France taking the A340 into revenue-earning service.

In a dramatic demonstration of its long-range ability, an A340 departed the Paris Air Show on 17 June 1993 for a one-stop around the world flight. It returned a record-breaking 48 hours 22 minutes later.

would need replacing. Drawing on its 'family' experience, and in close consultation with the airlines, Airbus proposed two designs (with two and four engines) that would seat approximately 326 to 410 passengers. After several revisions these designs emerged in 1986 as the twin-engined A330 and four-engined A340.

Two-aircraft programme

The A330 and A340 are essentially the same aircraft, with a different number of engines and some important, but not obvious, structural changes. Each type is built around the same wing, uses the same advanced (two-pilot) cockpit and uses the same 18 ft 6-in (5.67-m) fuselage cross-section. Airbus treats the two types as one programme.

The A330 is a medium-range, twin-aisle aircraft, offered in two versions. The shorter-fuselage A330-200 can carry 256 passengers over 6,400 nm (7,347 miles/11824 km). The longer A330-300 (the first version developed) can carry 335 passengers over 4,650 nm (5,338 miles/8590 km). The A340

The A330-300 is the high-capacity, medium-range version of the A330. Airbus has faced strong competition from Boeing's 777 as the two manufacturers continue to struggle for dominance of this important market.

is the same basic aircraft, but with four engines and a much-increased fuel load to give it extra range. The A340 was rolled out first, appearing in October 1991. The first production aircraft was delivered to Lufthansa in February 1993. The A330 followed in November 1992 and entered service, with Air Inter, in January 1994.

Tough competition

Upon its introduction, the A330 became the largest twin-jet in service. Though the Boeing 777-200 has greater range, a larger cabin and more payload, the A330 had the advantage of being first and is better suited to operations on routes between 4,000 nm and 5,000 nm in length (4,592 to 5,740 miles/ 7390 to 9237 km). The A330 and A340 have been targeted towards so-called 'long thin routes' which demand long range but not very high capacity.

While the A340 cannot rival the 747-400's ultra-long range credentials, it has successfully challenged the total dominance of Boeing at this 'top end' of the market. The Boeing 777 was Seattle's response to the European challenge, but it was a long time coming. However, Boeing has now adopted the family concept with the highly-advanced 777 and can claim that what Airbus does with two

aircraft, it can do with one.

Airbus had its problems with the A330/340, and sales (particularly A330 sales) were sluggish to start. This trend was reversed after initial A330 engine faults were rectified. As of June 2005 total A330 orders stood at 524, with 348 delivered. A340 orders stood at 381, with 301 delivered. Airbus now faces a straight fight for orders with the Boeing 777. New versions of the Boeing 777, increasing range and capacity, have been mirrored in the development of the A340 with the introduction of the 'stretched' A340-600 (the longest airliner in the world) and the ultra long-range A340-500, capable of flying sectors in excess of 18 hours.

'Family' design offers benefits to the manufacturer as well as to the customer. The A330 (illustrated) and A340 exhibit a high degree of commonality of major components.

A330: Developing the twin

The A330 is the 'junior' member of the long-range, high-capacity Airbus family. It shares a common fuselage and wing design with the A340, but has only two engines for more economical operation over shorter routes.

By the early 1970s Airbus was looking at launching a larger family of airliners, based on the A300 design. Two concepts took shape, the A300B9 – which was bigger than the original A300 – and the smaller A300B10. The B10 design went on to become the Airbus A310, but the 330-seat A300B9 was joined by another new design, the B11, a 200-seat, four-engined aircraft which was based on the B10. However, driven by market demand, Airbus proceeded with the A310.

By 1980, it had the confidence and the financial security to return to the B9 and the B11. The two designs were redesignated TA9 and TA11 (TA for twin aisle) and partially revealed at the 1982 Farnborough Air Show. TA9 would have an A300-like fuselage stretched to 203 ft 6 in (62 m). Seating capacity would be approximately 326 to 410. Two variants were sketched out, the TA9-100 and the TA9-200. The -100 was optimised for 1,500-nm (1,722-mile/2771-km) routes, while the -200 would be aimed at sectors of 3,300 nm (3,788 miles/ 6096 km). The final

designs were smaller, but far surpassed this performance.

By the 1983 Paris Air Show, Airbus was treating the TA9 and the TA11 as a common design, using as many components from the A300/A310 as possible. By 1985, a variable-camber wing had been introduced and the size and shape of the two aircraft were becoming virtually identical – only the number of engines remained different. The variable-camber wing idea was abandoned as being too expensive to develop and employ, however, and then, in 1986, TA9 received its designation.

A330 christened

In January 1986, the TA9 was officially christened as the A330, while the TA11 became the A340. The two aircraft shared a common fuselage length of 194 ft 10 in (59.16 m), with a cockpit design based on that of the A320. The A330 would be powered by two General Electric CF6-80C2 or Pratt & Whitney PW4000 turbofans, allowing it to carry 308 passengers over 5,800 nm (6,658 miles/ 10715 km). Development of the

A340 proceeded first as competition in its intended market was more immediate (the McDonnell Douglas MD-11). As the A340 progressed, changes were made to the basic A330, lengthening its fuselage to allow 24 more seats to be accommodated, while cutting back its range slightly.

Just before the 1987 Paris Air

Show, the A330 and A340 received their official launch. The A330 had been sized to fit between the two planned versions of the A340 – the longer A340-300 and the shorter A340-200. During 1987/1988, the A340 underwent several changes which influenced the A330. The A330 was stretched again to match the fuselage length of the

Composites account for some 13 per cent of the structural weight of the A330/A340 wing, while the principal structures are of aluminium alloy. BAE Systems manufactures the wings in the UK.

Below: In August 1997, Airbus flew the first example of the shorter A330-200. With the CF6 and and PW4000 engines already test-flown, operations with Trents began in the summer of 1998.

Above: An A330 test airframe undergoes vibration testing. Simultaneous European and US certification for the A330 with CF6 engines was achieved in October 1993, and 120-minute ETOPS approval was granted in November 1994. Aer Lingus flew the first transatlantic ETOPS service with a CF6-powered aircraft in May 1994.

Pratt & Whitney delivered the first PW4168 turbofans for the A330 to Toulouse in the second half of 1993.

A340-300, and became the A330 300. The A330-200 then became equivalent in size to the A340-200. Up to that time, the -200 designation had been applied universally to the A330.

In 1987, British Aerospace completed design of the new wing. The wing is swept to 30° and has distinctive 9-ft (2.74-m) tall winglets. The wing is identical to that of the A340 and only small structural changes are needed to adapt it to carry the A340's extra engines. In 1987, the flight-deck configuration was also finalised. The A330 has a six-screen EFIS cockpit fitted with a sidestick controller. The only difference between it and that of the A340 is in the number of throttles.

The A330 was the first Airbus design to be offered with powerplants from all three major engine manufacturers, General Electric, Pratt & Whitney and Rolls-Royce.

A330-300

The A330-300 can seat up to 440 passengers, but a typical seating arrangement is 335 in a two-class layout. With 335 passengers and baggage, the A330-300 has a maximum take-off weight of 467,400 lb (212013 kg) and a typical range

of 4,500 nm (5,166 miles/8313 km).

The twelfth airframe from the A340/A330 production line became the first A330 – though it was actually the seventh to take to the air. The A330-300 prototype made its maiden flight on 14 October 1992. The CF6-powered A330 was certified jointly by the US FAA and the European JAA on 23 October 1993. The A330 entered revenue service with Air Inter on 17 January 1994. The PW4168-powered version was certified on 2 June 1994, but deliveries were delayed after problems were found with the engine's thrust-reversers. The first PW4168-powered aircraft entered service with Thai International on 19 December 1994. Rolls-Royce Trent-powered A330s were the last to enter service. This version was certified on 22 December 1994 and deliveries were made to the launch

customer, Cathay Pacific, on 27 February 1995.

On 30 June 1994, tragedy struck the programme when one of the test aircraft crashed during trial flights at Toulouse, killing all eight on board. The accident was blamed on pilot error and this led to a revision of the cockpit operating procedures. Further difficulties struck the A330 in 1996 when Cathay Pacific and Dragonair temporarily grounded their aircraft after three in-flight shut-downs of their Trent engines. Following the incidents, each aircraft continued to fly on its remaining engine and landed safely. The problem was traced to a fault in the gearbox – though it was not experienced by Garuda which also operates Trent-powered A330s.

A330-200

In 1995 Airbus announced a major development of the basic A330, the short-fuselage, increased-range A330-200. A 256-seat aircraft with a 6,400-nm (7,347-mile/ 11824-km) range, the A330-200 is fitted with an additional centre wing fuel tank, a revised tail fin and has a maximum take-off weight of 507,055-lb (230000 kg). Leasing company ILFC placed the first order, for 13, in March 1996. The -200 made its first flight on 13 August 1997, received its FAA/JAA and Transport Canada certification on 31 March 1998, and the first aircraft was handed over to Canada 3000 (via ILFC) on 30 April 1998.

Above: Sparks fly from the protected underside of an A330's rear fuselage during trials to determine the aircraft's minimum unstick speed. An intensive period of test-flying followed the 1992 first flight.

Right: On 25 April 1995, just two years after the A340 entered commercial service, the hundredth airframe was rolled off the A330/A340 line. The historic machine was an A330-300.

In its early days, the A330 struggled with a sluggish order book and bad publicity. It is a measure of the soundness of the basic design, and Airbus' high-powered sales technique, that the A330 became the best-selling aircraft in its class, beating off stiff competition from the Boeing 777 and all other comers.

LTU International Airways of Germany operates four A330-300s, all of them leased.

A330: In service

On 31 March 1987, Airbus announced that it had signed a letter of intent with Northwest Airlines for 20 A340s, with options on 10 A330s. This was a major order from an important US carrier, just the kind of deal needed by Airbus to launch its new twin-jet. The trail was soon to grow cold on the Northwest order, however. Instead, the real launch orders for the A330 were gained, also in March, from Air Inter (five aircraft and 15 options), and Thai International (eight aircraft). The next significant order came from Cathay Pacific, in 1989, which signed a contract for nine A330s (later increased to 11) for delivery from 1995 to 1998.

The first delivery of a CF6-powered A330 was made to Air Inter on 30 December 1993, the aircraft entering service on 17 January 1994. First deliveries of PW4168-engined aircraft to Malaysian Airline System (MAS) and Thai International, were delayed by delamination faults in the composite materials of the

engine thrust-reversers. MAS should have received its aircraft in August 1994 and Thai in September, but the timetable was further delayed by the tragic crash of one aircraft involved in PW4168 certification.

The first A330-321 for Thai International was introduced into service on 19 December 1994, on routes from Bangkok to Seoul and Taipei. Airbus paid compensation to Thai for the late delivery of its A330s. Initial A330 operations were then further affected by 'wing weeping' – leakage from the wing fuel tanks – which postponed delivery of Thai's third aircraft until the problem was corrected by British Aerospace. The first MAS A330-322 was delivered on 1 February 1995, but the airline then rescheduled the deliveries of the 10 aircraft it had on order.

The launch customer for the Trent/A330 combination was Cathay Pacific, which took delivery of its first A330-342 on 27 February 1995. Cathay

discovered that it could operate profitable night-time pure freighter operations with its A330s (and A340s), using the lower cargo hold only. Operating charters for express package delivery firms, the Airbus could carry loads of 1-25 tons, but still be profitable. Cathay Pacific also

Above: The A330 has been particularly successful in the Asian market where almost every major airline has placed orders for aircraft from the family.

Right: Cathay Pacific currently operates 23 A330-300s. All of Cathay's A330s are powered by Rolls-Royce Trent 700 engines.

Left: An Airbus A330 powered by Pratt & Whitney PW4168s made a successful first flight (of 3 hours 28 minutes) from Toulouse on 14 October 1993. This flight was part of a 500-hour programme which was aimed at certifying the PW4168 engine in the A330.

Below: Air Inter received its first A330 in December 1993 and so became the first airline to operate the type.

became the first airline to have pilots triple-rated on the A320, A330 and A340.

During the early 1990s, A330 orders dropped off and Airbus entered an alarming period when orders for the A330 and A340 came in at no more than a trickle. One important new operator of the type was Aer Lingus which took delivery of its first aircraft, via International Lease Finance Company (ILFC), in May 1994. Aer Lingus was the first airline to operate the A330 on ETOPS (Extended-range Twin-engined OPerationS) routes across the North Atlantic. It was instrumental in gaining full 180-minute ETOPS qualification for the (CF6-80E1-powered) A330-300, which was awarded on 6 February 1995. Like Cathay, Aer Lingus too discovered that its A330s made good freighters and, by mid-1995, the four aircraft initially in service were soon carrying half of the airline's yearly cargo business (approximately 15,000 tons).

Full ETOPS clearance for the PW4168-powered A330 was awarded in July 1995, though this model received its 90-minute clearance on 10 November 1994 – before it entered service. The A330-300 was the first airliner to achieve this distinction. Full ETOPS clearance for the Trent 700 was gained in May 1996.

A330 deliveries in the early 1990s continued largely via ILFC. Between 1990 and 1995, however, hardly any new A330 orders were won and several operators announced their intention to acquire aircraft but deliveries never materialised. By 1 January 1992, Airbus had 143 firm orders for the A330. In 1995, the situation began to change as orders were won from Gulf Air (six A330-300s) and Philippine Airlines (eight A330-300s) in the face of stiff competition from Boeing.

1996 started well when ILFC ordered 13 A330-200s, one A330-300 and a mix of five A330/A340 options. Korean Air added two extended-range A330-200s to its existing fleet, when it signed an order in May 1996, for delivery in August and September 1998. Korean already held seven A330-300 orders with 10 options, and deliveries of these aircraft commenced on 6 March 1997. In November 1996, Emirates signed for 16 A330-200s with seven options. On 18 December 1996, Garuda took delivery of the first of a total of nine Trent 700-powered A330-300s it had on order.

The upward trend continued in 1997, as Dragonair ordered its sixth A330-300, Cathay Pacific (then Dragonair's parent company) increased its A330 tally by ordering its thirteenth A330-300, Sabena and Swissair became the first European customers for the A330-200, Thai ordered four additional A330-300s, Asiana became another new customer for the A330 and Air Canada became the first major North American airline to order the A330.

In 1998, Air Lanka signed for six A330-200s; US Airways announced seven firm A330-300 orders, seven options and 16 future reserved delivery positions for the A330, making the airline the first A330 operator in the USA; Canada 3000 became the first airline to introduce the A330-200 into service, with Austrian Airlines following on 21 August 1998 and Korean Air on 1 September.

The list of current operators and future customers of the A330 continues to grow. After a promising start, the A330 suffered a period of sales drought which placed the future of the type in doubt. However, the correction of initial problems and growing consumer confidence has rejuvenated the A330 order book and by 3 August 2005, A330 orders stood at 524, with 356 delivered and the aircraft serving as the basis for Airbus' new A350 which is being developed to rival the all-new Boeing 787 Dreamliner.

Dragonair, an associate of Cathay Pacific, currently operates a fleet of 11 Airbus A330-300s on its mainland China to Hong Kong routes.

Airbus A340
Development

Initial development of the A340 was led by the TA9 or, as it later became, the A330. However, market forces ensured that it was the four-engined A340 that was offered to customers first. This aircraft would become the first true European competitor in the prized, and US-dominated, long-range airliner market.

Like the A330, the A340 began life in the mid-1970s as a development of the A300B2. In the case of the A340, this was the 200-seat four-engined A300B11 design, redesignated TA11 in 1980. By 1982 the TA11 had become a CFM56-powered airliner with a design range of 6,830 nm (7,860 miles; 12650 km). Airbus flirted briefly with making the TA11 a tri-jet, but abandoned these plans in favour of the original four 30,000-lb (133.4-kN) class engines. The TA11 was given form at the 1982 Farnborough Air Show and though still A300-based, the new aircraft would be stretched to accommodate around 326 mixed-class passengers, or up to 410 in a single-class layout. The TA11

(and TA9) were envisaged as L-1011 and DC-10 replacements and would also provide a challenge to the 'new' Boeing 767's intended market.

Parallel development

By the Paris air show of 1983 Airbus had refined both the TA11 and TA9 concepts to the extent that it began to treat the two as one common project, built around a similar wing and fuselage design. Airbus also introduced several technical innovations in the shape of a variable-camber wing (which was later deleted from the design) and the revolutionary EFIS cockpit of the A320. January 1986 saw the TA11 officially join the Airbus product line as the A340. The A340 was defined as a very long-range

Above: Airbus unveiled the first A340 in a spectacular ceremony held at Toulouse on 4 October 1991, attended by more than 5,500 people. The first flight was made on the 25th of that month.

Top: The A340's landing gear differs from that of the A330 in having an additional twin-wheel auxiliary undercarriage unit fitted to the underside of the centre-section.

261-seat aircraft aimed at routes of 6,700 nm (7,692 miles; 12378 km). While the developed CFM56-5S1 was still earmarked as the primary A340 powerplant, Airbus was also considering the V2500 (then under development

by the International Aero Engine consortium), and even all-new ultra-high bypass designs of both engines, dubbed 'SuperFans'.

Airbus had concerns about the performance of the A340's intended engines, which were

On 26 February 1993, Air France became the first airline to receive the A340-300 variant. A340-311, F-WWCA, first flew in July 1992 and underwent a year of trial and test flying before being delivered to Air France in August 1993.

not helped by the emergence of the three-engined McDonnell Douglas MD-11 as a direct competitor – with a performance similar to that which Airbus had promised, but was perhaps beginning to doubt. The SuperFan concept, which was being driven by IAE and the V2500, offered the required thrust with much reduced fuel consumption. It would give the A340 a huge payload/range advantage and Airbus began to offer a 262-seat SuperFan-powered A340-200 and the stretched A340-300.

Based on projected performance, on 15 January 1987 Lufthansa announced that it would buy 15 SuperFan powered A340s, with 15 options. Lufthansa was soon joined by Northwest Orient, in March, with an order for 20 A340s. Then, a week after the Northwest order, IAE announced that it would not proceed with SuperFan development due to the technical risks involved. The disappearance of the SuperFan meant that Airbus had to match its performance guarantees with existing technology. The solution came in the shape of an uprated version of the CFM56, the 31,200-lb (139-kN) CFM56-5C2. Airbus also increased the A340's wingspan and added winglets. By 1995, the 34,000-lb (151-kN) CFM56-5C4 was available. With

Right: In the summer of 1991, a complete A340 airframe underwent extensive ground-based static-strength trials at the Centre d'Essais Aeronautique de Toulouse (CEAT). The front fuselage is seen here being unloaded from a Super Guppy in October 1990.

these changes the A340 was within reach of its intended performance and orders began to build slowly again.

Two A340 versions evolved after a June 1987 formal go-ahead: the 375-seat A340-300 or the short-fuselage, extended-range A340-200, normally seating 263 passengers. The first A340 to fly was an A340-300 on 25 October 1991. During the test programme, Airbus and CFM International, had to adapt airframe aerodynamics and engine parameters. Despite this, the new aircraft proved to be lighter, and to have a higher fuel load, than expected.

European JAA certification was awarded on 22 December 1992 and the first A340-200 was delivered to Lufthansa on 2 February 1993. The first A340-300 was delivered to Air France on 26 February.

Higher capacity

The standard aircraft was followed by an increased maximum take-off weight (MTOW) version. This extra available weight could be traded for fuel or payload. A growth version of the A340-300, the A340-300X, with a further increased MTOW and a range of 7,304 nm (8,400 miles; 13519 km) was ordered by Singapore Airlines. The first example flew on 25 August 1995 and deliveries followed on 17 April 1996. This variant has since been redesignated A340-300E. Since this aircraft was delivered, all A340s have been built to the same structural

standard allowing for extended-range operations.

A follow-on extended-range A340-400 development was dropped in favour of the stretched 313-seat A340-500 and 380-seat A340-600, which were launched in December 1997. The Trent 553-powered A340-500 is the world's longest-ranged airliner with a design range of 9,000 nm (10,377 miles; 16700 km). The larger Trent 556-powered A340-600 is optimised for a range of 7,880 nm (9,072 miles; 14600 km) with Virgin Atlantic its launch customer and deliveries beginning in July 2002. In August 2005 orders for the A340 stood at 384, with 239 delivered.

Above: Intended for the lucrative Boeing 747 replacement market, the A340-600 will be able to carry up to 380 three-class or 419 two-class passengers up to 7,932 nm (9,134 miles; 14700 km).

Left: Air Canada became the first North American airline to receive the ultra long-range A340-500 (foreground). The type entered Air Canada service in mid-2004.

Operational history

The A340 was launched on the understanding that the SuperFan engine option would give the aircraft outstanding payload/range capability, putting it far ahead of similar sized aircraft like the MD-11, and within reach of the larger and more expensive Boeing 747. While the SuperFan option failed, the A340 emerged with its reputation intact.

Above: The A340-200 and A340-300 were marketed simultaneously by Airbus. Egyptair ordered the -200 version in 1995 and currently operates them on the Egypt-UK-USA route.

Top: Air Mauritius operates five Airbus A340-312s which were delivered in 1994-99. This aircraft was the first delivered, and is named Paille-en-Queue.

The first expressions of interest in the A340 came from TAP Air Portugal, in 1987 and ILFC in 1988, both of which 'ordered' two aircraft. On 15 January 1987 Lufthansa announced that it had committed to 15 A340s and 15 options – though this did not become a 'real' order until April 1989 (when the firm order became four A340-200s and 11 A340-300s, followed by seven additional A340-200s in May).

Just as it had done with the A330, Northwest Orient placed a significant 'order' for 20 A340s, but again these aircraft were never delivered. Many other 'customers' signed up for aircraft that were never delivered, but confirmed customers came in the shape of Air Lanka, TAP, Kuwait Airlines and Austrian Airlines. By March 1991, Airbus figures recorded 94 orders for the A340. The failure of the SuperFan concept caused Airbus, and its customers, major concern and no doubt accounts for the vagueness surrounding the early order book.

Into service

The A340 flight test programme involved six aircraft – four -300s and two A340-200s. The first short-fuselage -200 flew on 1 April 1992 and with European JAA certification awarded, the rapidly expanding Asian and Far Eastern markets were targeted by Airbus. In 1992 important orders from Gulf Air, China Eastern, Philippine Airlines and Singapore Airlines was thus won. The first A340 entered Lufthansa service on the Frankfurt-New York (Newark) route on 15 March 1993. Air France took delivery of the first A340-300 on 26 February 1993 and Lufthansa accepted its first A340-300 on 7 December 1993. US FAA type certification was

Below: Virgin Atlantic has been one of the most important customers of the type and currently has 18 in service and 15 on order, all the outstanding aircraft being A340-600s.

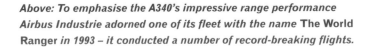

Above: To emphasise the A340's impressive range performance Airbus Industrie adorned one of its fleet with the name The World Ranger in 1993 – it conducted a number of record-breaking flights.

Philippine Airlines has operated both -200 and -300 versions of the A340. The airline opted for the most powerful version of the CFM International CFM56 engine to power its A340s. The CFM56-5C4 is capable of producing 34,000 lb (151.2 kN) of thrust.

VIP A340s

Airbus does not reveal the identities of its VIP and government customers and such sales are recorded as being made to an 'undisclosed customer'. Despite its size, complexity and price, the A340 has proved to be a popular choice for those who demand a special personal aircraft. The first VIP sale for the A340 came early, in 1993, when the Government of Qatar (Qatar Amiri Flight) took delivery of a single A340-211 in April. In 1994 the Bahrain government also acquired an A340, but this aircraft has since been passed on to the Sultan of Brunei. The Sultan's personal fleet now comprises two A340s – along with a Gulfstream V, Boeing 767 and Boeing 747-400. Brunei has operated the sole A340-8000 – a special, ultra-extended range version with three additional fuel tanks giving it a range of at least 8500 nm (9,775 miles; 15742 km). Egypt bought an A340-212 for government use which was delivered in February 1995. The example below, operated by the Saudi Arabian government, is painted in an anonymous colour scheme and carries a number of additional aerials and antennas on the top side of the fuselage.

awarded on 27 May 1993. Airbus took great delight in promoting the A340's economical long-range credentials and organised a series of high-profile flights, culminating in a world record attempt. In July, during the 1993 Paris Air Show an A340 dubbed *The World Ranger* flew around the world with only one stop, breaking many records previously set by a Boeing 747SP. Later, in November 1996, the A340 set a new non-stop distance record of 7,800 nm (8,954 miles; 14410 km) flying from Zhuhai, in China, in a flight time of 15 hours and 20 minutes.

After Lufthansa and Air France, deliveries were made to Sabena (March 1993), THY Turkish Airlines (commencing in July) and, crucially, Virgin Atlantic, which had previously operated an all-747 fleet. The first A340 for Virgin, an A340-311 named *Lady in Red*, was handed over on 26 November 1993.

Into North America

In 1994 major orders were received from Cathay Pacific, Singapore Airlines and Air Canada – the A340's first break in the North American market. In 1994 deliveries were made to Air Mauritius, Gulf Air, Air Lanka, Cathay and TAP. In February 1995 Austrian Airlines took delivery of its first A340-200. Kuwait Airlines received its first A340-300 in May 1995 and the first for Air Canada followed in June 1995. That year, sales were sluggish and, although deals were signed with Egyptair, Lufthansa and Austrian, only seven A340s were sold – while orders were cancelled by PAL and a deal with BWIA fell through.

In 1991 a vital sale had been initiated with Singapore Airlines when, in August, that company had announced that it was abandoning its plans to acquire the MD-11 and would instead opt for up to 20 extended-range, higher gross weight versions of the A340, then designated A340-300X. The first of these aircraft, now redesignated A340-300E, flew on 25 August 1995 and was delivered on 17 April 1996. New sales continued to be achieved in 1996 and in May China Eastern Airlines became the first A340 operator in China. In November of that year Egyptair also took delivery of its first aircraft.

In 1997 Airbus won A340 orders from Cathay Pacific, Virgin, Olympic, Lufthansa, Air Canada and Air France. 1998 proved to be a very successful year, with the newly-launched A340-500 and A340-600 winning the bulk of new business. This trend continued, although affected by the post-9/11 slowdown, but the A340 has continued to sell strongly. Indeed, while the A340-600 continues to impress in service after early teething troubles, the A340-500 is used by Singapore Airlines on the world's longest scheduled non-stop route, direct from Singapore to New York, in a flight time of around 18 hours.

Above: The first A340-311 for Turkish Hava Yollari is seen here during test-flying from Airbus' factory at Toulouse. The airline has a current fleet of seven A340s.

Right: Air France has been a staunch Airbus customer since the A300 was launched in the 1970s and has operated the -200, -300 and -300E versions of the A340.

Airbus A380

Europe's new Super Jumbo

With the A380, Airbus heralds a new era in commercial operations. The aircraft is the largest and heaviest airliner ever conceived and many see it as the answer to increasing airport congestion. It is also proving attractive to cargo-only operators, competing a winning against the Boeing's 747 freighters.

April 2005 saw the first flight of the giant twin-decked A380. The aircraft has continued to be used intensively on test duties, having made the type's public debut at the Paris Air Show in June 2005.

On 27 April 2005 a new era in commercial aviation began with the first flight of the largest passenger transport aircraft in the world – the Airbus A380. This event marked a major milestone following a decade of study, design and development work, and raised the stakes in the ever-escalating battle between Airbus and Boeing for the crown of the world's premier commercial airliner manufacturer.

A380 genesis

In the early 1990s almost every major civil aircraft manufacturer in the world was developing plans to produce a next generation high-capacity long-range airliner to challenge the mighty Boeing 747's dominance. As industry consolidation and the enormous cost of developing such an aircraft hit-home in the 1990s the end of the decade saw only Boeing and Airbus harbouring hopes to dominate this most prestigious of markets. In the mid-1990s the future animosity between Airbus and Boeing had

yet to emerge, as the pair co-operated on the joint VLCA (Very Large Commercial Aircraft) programme. As the study progressed, Airbus, sensing Boeing's lack of commitment, began its own independent project and, when the VLCA teaming disintegrated in 1996, Airbus integrated the work into its own efforts. Boeing, heavily committed to funding its Model 777, decided to withdraw from the race – expecting that improved versions of its 747 would suffice for what it perceived to be a shrinking market. Airbus, however, as the flagship of European industry and co-operation, was determined to press ahead.

A380 design

The mid-1990s saw Airbus consider a range of novel and

Airbus aims to offer as much commonality as possible between the cockpits of the A380 (shown here as a computer-generated impression) and the in-service A330/340 airliners.

occasionally outrageous configurations before, in 1998, settling on a twin-passenger deck, four-engined design, known as the A3XX. It was a true monster, able to carry some 550 passengers in standard and over 800 in all-economy configurations. Two full-length passenger decks, complemented by a lower cargo deck, ensured the aircraft's take off weight would exceed a mammoth 1,200,000 lb (550 tonnes) and its colossal length of 238 ft 8 in (72.75 m) and wing span of 261 ft 9¾ in (79.80 m) dwarfed anything the company had previously built. However, a multitude of strict performance, economic and operating criteria would have to be met before

Airbus could consider putting the aircraft into production.

To keep the aircraft's weight within realistic limits, reduce fatigue and corrosion problems and reinforce the company's reputation for innovation, Airbus proposed unprecedented levels of composite materials in the aircraft's structure. Some 25 per cent of the aircraft is of composites, of which 22 per cent is carbon fibre reinforced plastic and three per cent GLARE fibre-metal laminate (used for the first time on a civilian airliner). The use of these materials not only saves weight, but also leads to decreased fuel burn, fewer emissions and lower operating costs. The aircraft's powerful hydraulic system also provides a

Various exotic cabin configurations have been suggested for the A380, but it is likely that customers will opt for less ambitious configurations, choosing passenger capacity above luxury.

In an unusual move, the A380 flight-test crew cycled the aircraft's undercarriage (retracted and extended it) during the type's maiden flight, an indication of Airbus' confidence in its systems.

weight saving by allowing smaller pipes and components to be incorporated. Back-up electric systems give the aircraft the ability to land in the event of total hydraulic failure and this, combined with the triple redundancy fly-by-wire flight control system, provides the level of safety so vital on any airliner.

The A380's 'glass' two-crew cockpit builds on the successful format developed for Airbus' other products, incorporating integrated modular avionics datalinks, pull-out keyboards for the pilots and the latest in electronic flight aids, with all vital information displayed on large multi-function flat-panel displays. The commonality of the cockpit layout with that of the A330/ A340 series also reduces the amount of training needed for pilots transitioning to the type.

The range of advanced technologies is not restricted to the cockpit. The passenger cabin is equipped with an advanced fibre-optic distribution network, the first on a commercial airliner, offering an unprecedented choice of inflight entertainment. With 49 per cent more floor space than the rival 747-400, Airbus has also proposed a wide range of interior designs for its A380, including casinos, bars, sleeping areas and even onboard spa baths and massage suites.

New-generation engines

With the environmental movement making increasing demands on air travel, and customer airlines looking for unparalleled operating efficiency, the A380 could not succeed without new, efficient, quiet and lower-emission engines. After exhaustive development work two options are available for potential A380 customers – Rolls-Royce's Trent 900 and Engine Alliance's GP7200 (a joint venture between Pratt & Whitney and General Electric). Rated in the 70,000 to 80,000 lb (311 to 356 kN) thrust range, these engines not only produce a significantly lower noise footprint than those of the older 747, but also offer the fuel efficiency to allow Airbus to claim a seat-per-mile cost 17 per cent better than that of its rival.

Into the air

In December 2000, with sufficient interest from potential customers garnered, the aircraft was officially launched under its new name – A380 (the out-of-sequence '8' designation chosen to represent the shape of the aircraft's twin passenger decks). At the same time Airbus offered a dedicated freighter version as the A380F. Setting new standards in air cargo, the A380F will be able to carry in the region of 150 tonnes of payload over intercontinental distances. Launch customer for this cargo-hauling giant is Federal Express, with deliveries due to commence in 2008.

Construction of the first A380 continued apace at Airbus facilities around Europe until a triumphant first flight from Airbus' Toulouse Flight Test Centre. A further four A380s will join the test and certification programme, before the aircraft's entry into commercial service with Singapore Airlines in 2006. With 159 A380 orders and commitments received by July 2005, Airbus is confident it will exceed its 250-order break-even point and is already planning new variants, including the stretched 656-seat A380-900 and ultra long-range 'shrunk' A380-700.

With the A380 Airbus can offer a complete range of airliner capacities, a situation that is forcing Boeing to reconsider its options for a 747 Advanced development of the 747-400.

A380 Customers

Customer	Variant	Orders
Air France	A380-800	10
China Southern Airlines	A380-800	5
Emirates	A380-800	41
Emirates	A380F	2
Etihad Airways	A380-800	4
Federal Express	A380F	10
ILFC	A380-800	5
ILFC	A380F	5
Kingfisher Airlines	A380	5
Korean Air Lines	A380-800	5
Lufthansa	A380-800	15
Malaysian Airlines	A380-800	6
QANTAS	A380-800	12
Qatar Airways	A380-800	2
Singapore Airlines	A380-800	10
Thai Airways	A380-800	6
UPS	A380F	10
Virgin Atlantic	A380-800	6
Total		**154**

CASA CN-235

Multi-role airlifter

The CASA, previously Airtech, CN-235 has won a substantial portion of the international market for light tactical military transports. The joint Spanish-Indonesian design never won the airline orders it once sought, but instead its military versions have been steadily expanded and improved and it has been joined by the CASA-only, stretched C-295.

During the 1970s the state aircraft manufacturers in Spain and Indonesia – CASA and IPTN – established a long-distance working relationship that saw CASA's Aviocar light transport built under licence on the other side of the world. After a few short years of partnership the two unveiled an ambitious plan to build a new and much larger transport. In 1980 the Airtech consortium was established to handle design and production of the new 35-seat aircraft that was aimed at both the civil and military markets. Dubbed CN-235, the project received its formal launch at the 1981 Paris Air Show and was immediately hailed as a promising design. In its early stages the CN-235 was positioned chiefly as a civil aircraft, but it could not have been more different to its contemporaries such as the Dash 8, EMB-120 or the SF-340.

First and foremost, the CN-235 was optimised for operations from unprepared airstrips. Its high wing, prominent undercarriage sponsons, upswept rear fuselage and rear ramp gave it the appearance of a 'mini Hercules'. The aircraft had several military features, such as a main undercarriage housing with no doors that allowed the wheels to protrude slightly and protect the aircraft in the event of a forced landing. The air-operable rear ramp used a two-section door and two rear cabin doors were provided for paradropping.

Power was supplied by a pair of 1,760-shp (1311-kW) General Electric CT7-7 turboprops.

Above: One of the few civilian operators was Spanish carrier Binter Canarias, which received the first of four examples in December 1988. The airline withdrew the type from service a decade later.

Right: Construction of a single prototype by both manufacturers began in May 1981. CASA's example (ECT-100) is seen here at the roll-out ceremony on 10 September 1983.

Above: The French air force has acquired a total of 18 CN-235s which are used for light military transport duties. The aircraft can be configured to carry 24 stretchers in the casevac role.

Irish Air Corps CN-235MPs carry a mission fit comprising a Litton AN/APS-504(V)5 search radar, a FLIR Systems FLIR2000HP, and a two-crew operator station with datalink and air-droppable stores (including life rafts).

Production of structural components was shared between CASA (forward and centre fuselage, wing centre section, inboard flaps, engine nacelles) and IPTN (rear fuselage, tail unit, outer wings, outboard flaps), with separate production lines in each country. Later, a subcontract for elements of the tail unit was awarded to Chile's ENAER, by CASA. CASA and IPTN staged a dual roll-out ceremony of the first prototypes, held at the same (local) time on 10 September 1983. The first Spanish-built aircraft made its maiden flight on 11 November 1983, followed by Indonesia's example on 30 December 1983.

As the flight test programme proceeded, several changes had to be made to the design before joint national type certification was awarded on 19 August 1986, with approval from the FAA coming on 3 December.

Early promise

Great expectations had accompanied the CN-235 in its early years. The Indonesian government announced its intention to acquire 100 aircraft, but at the time of the Paris launch Airtech had just 54 orders and 18 options, all from civil customers. By 1985 Airtech was in serious discussions with Turkey to supply up to 50 tactical transports and other, smaller, military orders were won – but civil orders faded away. The CN-235 was never truly suited to the civil market; it was too heavy, lacked range and had a rugged appearance that tended to scare off the airlines. Commercial operators that needed the CN-235's rough field capabilities probably did not need an aircraft of its size, or cost, but gradually the military order book began to fill out.

In December 1986 the first CN-235 was delivered to Indonesia's Merpati Nusantara Airlines and that same month the Royal Saudi Air Force took delivery of the first military CN-235M. The first 30 aircraft became known as Series 10 machines (CN-235-10, CN-235M-10). The Series 100 that followed was powered by uprated CT7-9C turboprops, which remain the standard powerplant. A distinction was also drawn between CASA-built aircraft (-100) and those built by IPTN (-110). In 1990 Airtech introduced the CN-235-200/-220 which has a vastly improved range when compared to the earlier versions. The first CASA-built aircraft was certified in March 1992, but an IPTN prototype did not fly until 1996. The 200 Series and 300 Series, the latter with improved hot-and-high performance are the current basic transport variants.

Growing family

From the earliest days Airtech planned to build a family of CN-235 variants for specialist missions such as maritime patrol and Elint. Both IPTN and CASA developed different maritime patrol versions, but only CASA has placed the type in service. The Irish Air Corps was the first operator of the CN-235MPA Persuader, of which it took delivery of two in December 1994. IPTN developed a similar aircraft, dubbed the CN-235MPA Sky Guardian. This is a reflection of the slow pace of the overall IPTN CN-235 programme which won few sales outside its domestic market and was troubled with reports of poor quality control. IPTN development eventually ceased, such that the CN-235 is now considered an active product only of EADS CASA.

According to CASA in summer 2005, almost 250 aircraft were in service, although the only airline to buy new aircraft were Spain's Binter Mediterraneo and Indonesia's Mandala Airlines and Nusantara. Only the Merpati aircraft remain in service.

C-295

At the 1997 Paris Air Show CASA announced a completely independent development of the CN-235, the 'stretched' C-295. At an overall length of 80 ft 3 in (24.45 m), the C-295 is 10 ft ½ in (3.05 m) longer than the CN-235. Maximum

payload has been increased by over 50 per cent to 21,385 lb (9700 kg), allowing the C-295 to carry 78 fully-equipped troops or five standard pallets. The C-295 is powered by two 2,645-hp (1972-kW) Pratt & Whitney Canada PW127G turboprops, driving six-bladed Hamilton Standard HS0568F-5 propellers. It is fitted with the Sextant Topdeck EFIS cockpit which includes a flight management system, attitude and heading reference system, autopilot and three colour LCD screens, with associated TCAS (traffic collision avoidance system) and GPWS (ground-proximity warning system). A technology demonstrator made its maiden flight on 28 November 1997 and the first production-standard C-295 flew on 22 December 1998. FAA type certification was awarded in December 1999. In February 2000 the Spanish air force confirmed its launch order for nine aircraft, announced in April 1999. The first of these being received in 2001.

Morocco established an additional transport squadron in 1990 to operate seven CN-235Ms from their base at Kenitra. One of the aircraft is configured for the VIP transport role.

Antonov's An-12 has built its reputation on being able to deliver a hefty payload to remote regions in inhospitable conditions. Here, a tractor is unloaded from the rear ramp on a snow-covered landing strip.

Antonov An-12
Civilian 'Cubs'

As with many Soviet-era aircraft, it was often difficult to discern exactly where the An-12's civil role ended and its military duties began. In Aeroflot hands, the big transport looked like a commercial freighter, but it also served military masters, and this was true of other operators around the world.

Oleg Antonov revolutionised the design of Soviet transport aircraft. It was his creations, the An-8, An-10 and An-12, which helped to establish many of the features now seen as most desirable in a 'go-anywhere' cargo aircraft – a high wing, beaver tail, rear ramp, on-board APU (auxiliary power unit) and even rough field capability. Certainly, all these ingredients were part of the recipe for a successful military tactical airlifter, and that was Antonov's primary design goal. The same aircraft could also serve civil needs; one had only to look at Lockheed's C-130 to see the

truth in that. But the great restraint on the Antonov Design Bureau was that its primary, in many ways sole, customer was the military and no allowances were made to exploit the civil market. Outside the Soviet Union, an aircraft like the An-12 should have carved its own furrow in the airline and air cargo market (as the Hercules did).

However, as a product of the Soviet military, the An-12 entered civil service almost by default, only in limited numbers and only to very controlled customers. It took the collapse of the Soviet Union and the liberalisation of its air transport industry to place the An-12 truly on the world stage in the twilight years of its career.

The predecessors of the An-12, the An-8 transport of 1955 and 1957's An-10 Ukraina ('Cat') airliner, did serve the civil market. The An-12, on the other hand, was a military freighter. The PV-23U gun turret mounted in its tail underlined its military origins yet, like most other Soviet-era transports, it first appeared wearing the colours and civil registrations of Aeroflot. There is no doubt that Aeroflot An-12s performed many essential civil tasks – the red-painted aircraft of Aeroflot's Polar Division were just one notable group – but Aeroflot's primary purpose was to serve in the wartime transport role for the Soviet air force.

Aeroflot An-12s were seen around the world on military tasks, Aeroflot's civil identity giving it safe passage into the world's trouble spots.

Pseudo-military 'Cubs'

The cloak of respectability worn by Aeroflot's aircraft was

Based at Vnukovo 3 in Moscow, this An-12TB is operated by Kosmos, one of the many fledgling companies to emerge in Russia since 1992. Kosmos also operates an Antonov An-12 and three Tupolev Tu-134s.

Above: Vast and often inaccessible, Russia relies heavily on its air-freight network. Avial Aviation operated An-12BPs from all three of Moscow's major civilian airports until 2004.

Operated in the 1980s by Balkan Bulgarian Airlines, LZ-BAB was used as a freighter, transporting goods to destinations in both Eastern and Western Europe. The airline latterly used three An-12s in this role.

adopted by several other 'civil' users of the An-12, including Yugoslavia, Poland, Indonesia, Iraq, Egypt and Sudan. Indeed, prior to the 1990s, only a handful of legitimate airlines took delivery of An-12s, and these were all largely operating within the Soviet sphere of influence. Such customers included Air Guinea, Balkan Bulgarian and Ghana Airlines.

China and new operators

In China, things were a little different. The Chinese aviation industry worked closely with that of the Soviet Union until links were cut by Mao after the Cultural Revolution. A few An-12s had already been supplied by Antonov along with technical drawings and details. From this basis, the Chinese went on to develop a whole family of aircraft based on the

An-12, as the Shaanxi Y-8 series. The first Y-8 flew in 1975, some 18 years after the An-12 had made its maiden flight, and the basic aircraft closely resembled its Antonov counterpart. Shaanxi developed the Y-8A which incorporated an extended glass nose. Shaanxi then produced the dedicated passenger/freight Y-8B for CAAC, the monolithic state civil aviation enterprise. Y-8Bs can be distinguished from their military counterparts only by their paint scheme, some retaining the tail turret. AVIC II SAC (previously Shaanxi) still builds Y-8 variants, a further improved version with a redesigned rear ramp and a fully-pressurised fuselage. One uniquely Chinese aircraft is the Y-8F, which first flew in 1990. This aircraft is a livestock transporter, capable of carrying up to 350 sheep and goats.

The collapse of the Soviet Union allowed the many regional divisions of Aeroflot to set themselves up as independent airlines, together with hundreds of new start-up carriers – established, in many cases, with whatever aircraft could be found lying around. The An-12 was perfectly suited to operations in far-flung regions of Russia and the CIS states, but also started to appear elsewhere in the world, particularly in the Middle East and Africa. It had the advantage of being available in sizeable

numbers and was cheap to hire (if not to operate). The low-cost of aviation fuel during the mid-1990s helped the An-12 to become established in the marketplace. At one time, there were over 30 airlines or brokers in Russia and the CIS offering An-12s for cargo charters and grabbing a portion of the lucrative, if quicksilver, 'tramp' freighter market by being affordable and available. The Russian economic crash of 1998 took many of these aircraft off the market and their numbers are now much diminished.

Above: The An-10 'Cat' was the passenger-carrying forerunner of the An-12. It incorporated a pressurised fuselage, capable of carrying 84 passengers and, on entering service in 1959, was claimed by Antonov to be the most economic transport in the world.

Right: Classic transport aircraft features abound on the An-12. Clearly visible in this view are the type's rugged, wide track undercarriage and upswept beaver tail. Both attributes are equally valuable to civil and military operators.

Antonov
An-24 'Coke' family

Versatile turboprop

Tough, simple and easy to maintain, Antonov's An-24 was the Soviets' answer to the Fokker F27. Since entering service in the early 1960s, the 'Coke' and its derivatives have served with both military and civil operators around the world.

Above: Formerly part of Aeroflot's Arkhangelsk directorate, Arkhangelskie Vozdushnye Linii (AVL) is now a subsidiary of Aeroflot Russian Airlines as Aeroflot-Nord. It operates a mixture of An-24RVs (seen here), An-26Bs, An-26RBLs, Tu-134s and Tu-154s.

Of the six species of multi-bladed propellers developed in the Soviet Union in the 1980s, two were tested on An-24s. The technology has since been integrated on the An-70 and Il-114.

After World War II the 'DC-3 replacement' question bothered the USSR as much as it did the rest of the world, since the Lisunov Li-2s on Aeroflot routes were licence-built DC-3s. Ilyushin provided the first-generation replacements in the form of Il-12s and Il-14s, but by 1955 the GUGVF, the chief administration of the civil air fleet, had begun to study requirements for a replacement for all these piston-engined aircraft. For longer-range routes the An-10 and Il-18 were eventually ordered. Settling the requirement for the true mass market on the short-haul routes was more difficult.

The main reason for the delay had been uncertainty over engine type; there was great reluctance to abandon piston power.

Turboprop power

The specification drawn up did not demand a turboprop, but it was significant that a special engine, the AI-24, had in 1955 been ordered from the Ivchenko bureau. A massive single-shaft engine, it was scaled down from the established AI-20 to reduce power from 4,000 hp (2983 kW) to 2,500 hp (1864 kW). It was

deliberately made conservative in design so that it would withstand the often brutish treatment to which Soviet hardware was sometimes subjected, and still run without trouble.

From the start Antonov decided on a high-wing monoplane in order to put the cabin floor near the ground and the engines and propellers well above it, to avoid slush, stones and other material. In 1955 he had expected to use four piston engines, but with great reluctance he followed the thinking at Handley Page for the Herald and changed to two of the new turboprops. From the operating point of view this was considered retrograde: reliability was probably going to be poorer (at least initially) and costs would be slightly higher. What tipped

the scales was that in the USSR almost everything had a military angle. It was considered highly desirable, first, to train the personnel of the gigantic GVF (civil air fleet) in the rudiments of gas turbines, and to familiarise them with this type of powerplant on a daily basis, and, second, to get high-octane petrol replaced by standard turbine fuel, so that warplanes could, if necessary, refuel at all civil airports.

Thus, to Antonov's delight, the new transport was designed in 1958 as a truly modern machine, with a large, almost circular fuselage and two of Ivchenko's new AI-24 turboprops. By this time the possibility of substantial exports was also obvious.

Antonov pulled out all the stops to make the An-24, as it was

The Russian Ministry of Defence operates this An-30 'Clank' in civilian markings. The aircraft is used in the survey/mapping role and has been in service since 1977.

Above: Cuban airline Aero Caribbean was typical of the many carriers of Soviet-aligned countries that ordered examples of the An-24 family. Note the open air inlet on the starboard engine for the 1,765-lb st (7.85-kN) RU-19A-300 auxiliary turbojet on this An-26.

Below: CAAC of China operated a fleet of An-24RVs, 17 of which were delivered by Antonov, with subsequent examples being constructed by the Xian factory as Y-7s.

designated, totally modern and efficient. Very curiously, the wing was made quite small in relation to the fuselage size and aircraft gross weight. Reasonable field length was achieved by powerful, slotted, area-increasing flaps.

Thanks to the new engine, which initially gave 2,550 ehp (1902 kW), Antonov was able to exceed the specification and provide a cabin big enough for 50, even with the typically Soviet four-place flight deck. At first, however, Antonov hardly mentioned this possibility, and the first brochures did not go beyond a 40-seat 'all-tourist' version, as required. The prototype was flown at Kiev on 20 December 1959. There were no major problems, but on the second aircraft vertical tail area was increased and the engine nacelles were extended.

First delivery, to Aeroflot's Ukrainian Directorate, took place in April 1962. Flight testing was announced as complete in September, by which time regular cargo services were being flown in the Ukraine. Passenger service opened in October 1962, usually with 32 seats but from spring 1963 with nine instead of eight passenger windows on each side and 40 seats. A 44-seat version began flying from Moscow in September 1963. These initial versions were designated An-24V Srs I (NATO codename 'Coke').

By 1965 the fact that shorter field length was needed was obvious, especially in hot-and-high conditions. The An-24V Series II replaced the Srs I in production, with 2,820-ehp (2103-kW) AI-24T engines, with water injection, and with the inboard flaps extended in chord and slightly in span. Later in 1967 a further boost was added in the form of a Tumanskii RU-19-300 turbojet/APU in the rear of the right nacelle. This could give 1,985 lb (8.93 kN) of extra thrust, but was normally used to give about 480 lb (2.16 kN) of thrust and also provide all electric power, thus putting more power into the propellers. Jet-equipped aircraft were designated An-24RV. A third 1967 prototype was the An-24TV (later An-24T), with the passenger door replaced by a broader rear fuselage with twin canted ventral fins and an upward-hinging cargo door.

Now Antonov designed a complex cargo ramp door and in 1970 the An-24 so equipped was redesignated An-26 ('Curl'), and as well as being fully pressurised (which the An-24T was not), it was restressed for operation at increased weight, and had two additional fuel cells.

After 1981, production centred on the An-26B freighter. There were many special variants and over 1,000 An-24s were built.

'Clank' and 'Cline'

A variant so different that it was given a new designation was the An-30 ('Clank'), first flown in 1974. The fuselage was redesigned to accommodate a giant glazed nose for the navigator and a darkroom in the main cabin. The navigator has special precision aids for accurate positioning of the aircraft. If required, equipment for many kinds of geophysical duties can be carried.

Last of the production-derived versions, the An-32 ('Cline') achieved a dramatic improvement in the payload that can be carried in extremely adverse hot-and-high conditions. The wing is modified and the tailplane redesigned. Much more powerful AI-20 engines are fitted extraordinarily high, either the 4,195-ehp (3128-kW) AI-20M for 'normal' conditions, or the 5,180-ehp (3863-kW) AI-20DM for the most severe conditions.

Soviet production of the An-24 ended in 1978, although the type is still in production in China as the AVIC I XAC Y-7.

Turboprop family

The An-24 family has been built in huge numbers and in a wide variety of variants. Modern in appearance, the aircraft was one of the first Soviet airliners to be successfully exported. Low construction costs ensured that the unit price was far cheaper than that of its Western counterparts.

An-24 'Coke'
Typical of the civil operators of the An-24, the Polish airline LOT (Polskie Linie Lotnicze) ordered a total of 14 An-24Vs to replace the piston-engined Ilyushin Il-14 on its domestic and short-haul international routes.

An-30 'Clank'
CCCP-30022 was the prototype An-30. The type achieved modest sales, probably covering the cost of development. It uses the same basic airframe as the An-24RV, apart from the new forward fuselage.

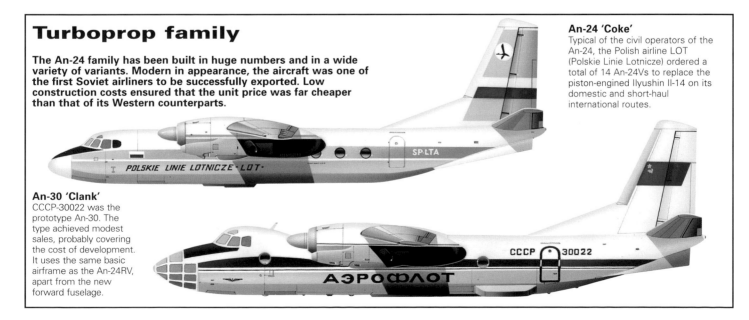

Limited availability of outsize freighters has led to the An-124 having been used by a number of Western operators, including Air Foyle at Luton and Stansted's HeavyLift Cargo Airlines (pictured).

Antonov An-124 Ruslan 'Condor'

Cargo superstar

The largest series production aircraft yet built, Antonov's colossal An-124 began life as a strategic military freighter, before finding further success in the post-Cold War era commercial heavylift market.

Designed to a specification issued following the cessation of An-22 production in 1974, the An-40 project was intended to result in an aircraft 'in the class of the C-5 Galaxy'. Revealed in 1977, Antonov's aircraft was now its designated An-400. The first prototype for the new long-range heavylift freighter made its maiden flight on 26 December 1982. Prior to the second prototype, named *Ruslan* after a character from Russian folklore, being flown to the 1985 Paris Air Show, the aircraft's designation had been changed again, to An-124.

Military operations

The Soviet V-TA (Military Transport Aviation), announced the specification of the An-124 during the developmental phase, and the resulting aircraft featured loading doors, and a fuselage cross-section and titanium floor suitable for typical military loads, together with landing gear for use from unpaved airstrips. A further stipulation insisted that the An-124 be able to fly 8,000 fully-loaded flights without fatigue problems.

Powered by four Lotarev D-18T turbofans equipped with thrust-reversal, the An-124 emerged as a world-beating aircraft, with aerodynamics superior to those of its American rivals. It also had an advanced supercritical wing. The gross weight of the An-124 is also almost 170,000 lb (77112 kg) greater than that of the C-5A, and the aircraft boasts hydraulically-powered full-span leading-edge flaps, Fowler flaps, ailerons,

inboard airbrakes and outboard spoilers. Within the wing itself, the An-124 (appropriately assigned the ASCC/NATO codename 'Condor') has capacity for 507,063 lb (230004 kg) of fuel. The An-124's flight controls are fully fly-by-wire, with hydraulic back-up. Further advanced features include the widespread use of carbon and glass composites in construction, the

engine nacelles and pylons being composed entirely of these materials.

Internal capacity

The pear-shaped fuselage section gives the An-124 a main cargo hold which is 14 ft 5 in (4.40 m) high and 21 ft (6.40 m) wide, originally designed to be capable of accepting the the currently outlawed SS-20 'Saber' mobile IRBM (intermediate-range ballistic missile) in V-TA service. Entry to the capacious 118-ft 1-in (36-m) long hold is via a rear ramp door. In order to cope with the heaviest internal loads, the hold is equipped with twin 6,614-lb (3000-kg) winches and two 22,049-lb (10000-kg) travelling cranes. A pressurised upper deck area provides seating for up to 88 personnel. In order to cope with internal payloads of around 330,668 lb (150000 kg), the An-124's robust landing gear comprises twin two-wheel independent steerable nose gear, and Hydromash main gear with five twin-wheel units retracting into low-drag fairings on each side, both of which incorporate an APU for inflight or ground auxiliary power. The wheel units can be collapsed in order to gain a nose-up or -down attitude during loading or unloading.

Production of the An-124 began at Ulyanovsk after the seventh production airframe had been completed at Kiev in late

This HeavyLift/Volga-Dnepr An-124 was used to deploy helicopters such as this No. 78 Sqn, RAF, Sea King HAR.Mk 3 from the UK to the Falkland Islands.

The An-124-102 would feature a crew reduced to just three, and the incorporation of an EFIS-equipped flight deck and dual sets of CRTs. The An-124-130 proposal would have been powered by General Electric CF6-80 turbofans. A further proposed propulsion modification would have seen the An-124 Turboprop retrofit re-equipped with four Aviadvigatel NK-93 propfans. More radical proposals have included the An-124FFR water-bomber conversion project, able to drop up to 440,917 lb (200 tonnes) of fire retardants, including 440,917 lb 154,321 lb (70 tonnes) from the centre fuel tank; and the An-124 Satellite Launcher, with, at one time, up to four An-124s earmarked for conversion in order to carry the Vozdushny Start booster, capable of placing a 4,409-lb (2000-kg) satellite into a 124-mile (200-km) orbit.

Commercial An-124 operators included Ajax (the freight subsidiary of ARIA), Polet (pictured), Titan and Trans Charter. In addition, Aviaobshchemash and Transaero both occasionally chartered examples from the Russian air force.

1985. Following a temporary interruption to Kiev production during the upheavals of 1991, both sites continued low-rate production until 1995, by which date 55 aircraft had been completed or substantially built (19 at Kiev and 36 at Ulyanovsk). By 1999, it was reported that three further examples had been built at Ulyanovsk and in 2005 Antonov and Volga-Dnepr unveiled plans to build 50 modernised An-124M-150 aircraft by 2008.

On 26 July 1985 an An-124 set a new record by lifting a payload of 377,473 lb (171222 kg) to a height of 35,269 ft (10750 m). Twenty more records followed, including a closed-circuit record which was established in May 1987 when an An-124 flew 12,521 miles (20151 km) in 25 hours 30 minutes. In January 1986 the An-124 began to be accepted into the V-TA and Aeroflot inventories. One of the first tasks for the 'Condor' was the transportation of units of 154-tonne Euclid dumper trucks

for Yakut diamond miners. Since this date, the An-124's achievements have tended to be more humanitarian-oriented.

Civil applications

The An-124-100 was granted civil certification by the Russian Interstate Aviation Committee on 30 December 1992, with civil-operated aircraft either being built to, or converted to, this new standard. The maximum take-off weight is lower than that of the standard military An-124, at 864,200 lb (392000 kg), and maximum

payload is reduced to 264,550 lb (120000 kg).

The first civilian customer for the An-124 was Air Foyle. Further civil derivatives of the baseline An-124 have been offered, comprising the An-124-100M with Western avionics. The flight crew of the An-124-100M is reduced to four, with the removal of the radio operator and the navigator. The first prototype was completed in late 1995 (the 34th Ulyanovsk aircraft), and Ajax was announced as the first customer for the derivative.

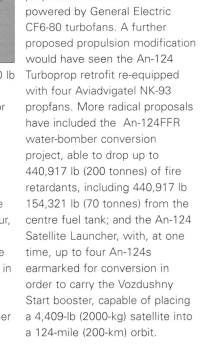

Rossiya (Russia), a division of Aeroflot, operated An-124-100s on state missions. The An-124-100 designation is applied to commercial standard aircraft. In 1996, Volga-Dnepr alone secured 64.8 per cent of the heavylift market.

In today's rationalised Russian air force, the An-124 remains an important asset for the V-TA, with around 30 examples currently in service. Here, a 'Condor' in air force livery formates with four 'Flanker' interceptors during VE-Day 50th anniversary celebrations.

Antonov An-225

Mriya 'Cossack'

Ukrainian giant

The largest aircraft in the world, the An-225 could have played an important role in Russia's space programme and the country's industrial expansion. Despite its capabilities, however, the sole 'Cossack' has long languished in the Ukraine, although there may be renewed interest in the type.

Despite making a number of appearances at international air shows and setting a collection of world records, the An-225 Mriya (Dream) is an enigma to the West. It was originally thought to have been designed to carry the Soviet space shuttle and, indeed, it did fly with *Buran* on 13 May 1989. It made its Western debut at the Paris Air Show later that year, and visited Farnborough in 1990. Since then, however, the An-225 has apparently languished in storage, many of its components being scavenged to service An-124s.

The huge twin-finned empennage was adopted so that external loads could be carried on the An-225's spine without affecting directional control. The wingspan is exceeded only by that of Hughes' immense flying boat, the Hercules.

The 'Cossack' design is firmly rooted in that of its predecessor, the An-124. Antonov had been assigned the task of designing an airframe able to carry, as a 'piggy-back' load, such enormous items as the *Buran* manned space orbiter, the Energiya space launch vehicle, and various gigantic structures needed by the expanding oil, gas and petrochemical industries, especially those in Siberia.

The main changes to the An-124 were the addition of a new wing centre section with two extra engines, the lengthening of the fuselage, and the fitting of a new twin-finned tail to a modified rear fuselage. Much thought was given to the length of the fuselage, especially in view of the aircraft's 'piggy-

With a maximum payload of some 600 tons and a wingspan of more than 260 ft (80 m), the mighty 'Cossack' lands at the Farnborough Air Show in 1990.

back' role. The first aircraft was earmarked to carry *Buran*, and two large axial beams raised above the fuselage were fitted to serve as the main load pylons. The An-225 was rolled out at the end of November 1988 and first flew on 21 December.

Record-breaker

Crowds at the Paris Air Show were impressed by Mriya's slick handling. Also impressive were details of a single flight on 22 March 1989 which broke no fewer than 106 world and class records. Taking off from Kiev at 1,126,370 lb (508350 kg), Mriya carried a payload of 344,576 lb (156300 kg) around a 1,243 mile (2000 km) circuit, at an average speed of 505 mph (813 km/h), reaching a cruise height of 40,485 ft (12340 m).

A second 'Cossack' began to take shape in the early 1990s, but it remains unfinished. There was recently talk of completing this aircraft and building more, but the 'Cossack' trail seems to have once again gone cold.

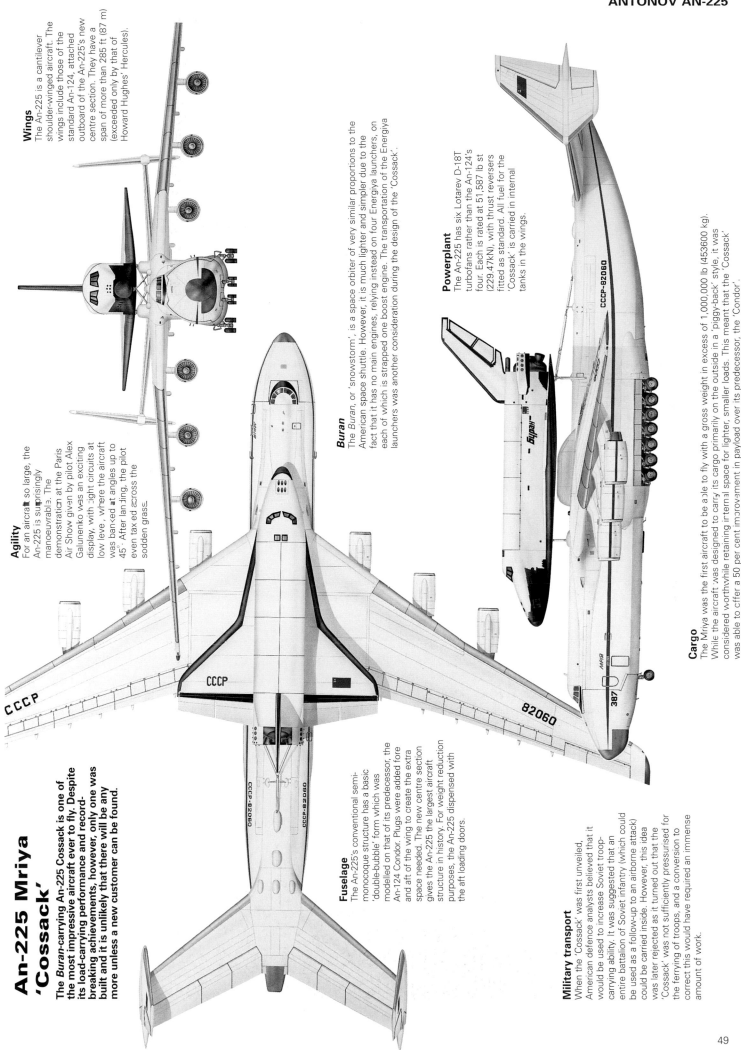

An-225 Mriya 'Cossack'

The *Buran*-carrying An-225 Cossack is one of the most impressive aircraft ever to fly. Despite its load-carrying performance and record-breaking achievements, however, only one was built and it is unlikely that there will be any more unless a new customer can be found.

Wings
The An-225 is a cantilever shoulder-winged aircraft. The wings include those of the standard An-124, attached outboard of the An-225's new centre section. They have a span of more than 285 ft (87 m) (exceeded only by that of Howard Hughes' Hercules).

Agility
For an aircraft so large, the An-225 is surprisingly manoeuvrable. The demonstration at the Paris Air Show given by pilot Alex Galunenko was an exciting display, with tight circuits at low level, where the aircraft was banked at angles up to 45°. After landing, the pilot even taxied across the sodden grass.

Buran
The *Buran*, or 'snowstorm', is a space orbiter of very similar proportions to the American space shuttle. However, it is much lighter and simpler due to the fact that it has no main engines, relying instead on four Energiya launchers, on each of which is strapped one boost engine. The transportation of the Energiya launchers was another consideration during the design of the 'Cossack'.

Fuselage
The An-225's conventional semi-monocoque structure has a basic 'double-bubble' form which was modelled on that of its predecessor, the An-124 Condor. Plugs were added fore and aft of the wing to create the extra space needed. The new centre section gives the An-225 the largest aircraft structure in history. For weight reduction purposes, the An-225 dispensed with the aft loading doors.

Powerplant
The An-225 has six Lotarev D-18T turbofans rather than the An-124's four. Each is rated at 51,587 lb st (229.47kN), with thrust reversers fitted as standard. All fuel for the 'Cossack' is carried in internal tanks in the wings.

Cargo
The Mriya was the first aircraft to be able to fly with a gross weight in excess of 1,000,000 lb (453600 kg). While the aircraft was designed to carry its cargo primarily on the outside in a 'piggy-back' style, it was considered worthwhile retaining internal space for lighter, smaller loads. This meant that the 'Cossack' was able to offer a 50 per cent improvement in payload over its predecessor, the 'Condor'.

Military transport
When the 'Cossack' was first unveiled, American defence analysts believed that it would be used to increase Soviet troop-carrying ability. It was suggested that an entire battalion of Soviet infantry (which could be used as a follow-up to an airborne attack) could be carried inside. However, this idea was later rejected as it turned out that the 'Cossack' was not sufficiently pressurised for the ferrying of troops, and a conversion to correct this would have required an immense amount of work.

ATR 42/72

Franco-Italian success

The Avions de Transport Régional family of twin-engined airliners was the result of successful collaboration between Aérospatiale and Alenia, both newcomers to the regional airline market. Despite this, the ATR 42 and 72 have been a tremendous success, notching up healthy worldwide sales.

Nord (later absorbed by Aérospatiale) had enjoyed a brief foray into the design of turboprop commuter aircraft with the Nord 262, and had played a major part in the development of the highly successful military Transall. In Italy, Alenia's experience of turboprop aircraft had been limited to the G222 military tactical transport. But during the late 1970s, it became increasingly clear that there would be a healthy market for 30-50 seat turboprop regional aircraft during the next decade, and the two companies teamed up (as Avions de Transport Régional, or ATR) to develop a

new-technology regional airliner. During much the same period, de Havilland Canada began work on the broadly similar DHC-8, Saab-Fairchild on their 340, Aero on the L-610, Fokker on the F50, and BAe on the ATP.

The ATR 42 was formally launched in October 1981, after selection of the Pratt & Whitney PW120 turboprop as the powerplant of choice, and following finalisation of the T-tail and high-wing configuration.

The first of two prototype ATR 42s made its maiden flight on 16 August 1984, and the first production aircraft followed on 30 April 1985. The aircraft carried a flight crew of two on the

Above: The ATR 72 introduced a significant fuselage stretch to seat about 30 more passengers. This, in turn, required uprated engines, a greater wingspan and strengthened undercarriage.

Top: Being built by Aérospatiale and Alenia, which have both been involved in high-tech ventures, the basic ATR 42 is available with a number of advanced features. Over complexity has been avoided, however, since the aircraft was aimed at a market that required a 'workhorse rather than a racehorse'.

modern flight deck, and up to 50 passengers. The aircraft has dynamic sound absorbers in its fuselage adjacent to the plane of the propellers, with skin damping fore and aft of the wing. Active noise control is offered as a customer option. Composites are used on the leading edges

(Kevlar/Nomex sandwich) and on control surface skins, nose and tailcone, landing gear doors and wing/fuselage fairings.

The initial production variant was the PW120-powered ATR-42-300, which gave way to the ATR 42-400 and ATR 42-500 in 1996. (The ATR 42-320 was similar to the -300, but with PW121 engines). The ATR 42-400 introduced PW121A

As a subsidiary of American Airlines, American Eagle provides feeder services across the USA. American Eagle has been the largest operator of the ATR 42/72 series, its subsidiaries still retaining an ATR 42 and some 42 ATR 72s.

Left: RFG Regional was a German commuter airline which possessed 12 ATR 42-300s, purchased from 1989 onwards. In 1993, the airline was merged with Eurowings, which went on to purchase further ATR 42s and ATR 72s and now has a fleet of 24 ATR 42/72s.

Below: Prior to its bankruptcy, Pan Am operated six ATR 42s on regional and short-range flights. This example was photographed over Toulouse prior to delivery and, although it wears Pan Am colours, it carries a French test registration.

engines and six-bladed propellers, and made its maiden flight on 12 July 1995. The ATR 42-500 remains the primary ATR 42 variant, with more powerful PW127E engines and many features borrowed from the newer ATR 72. The prototype ATR 42-500 made its maiden flight on 16 September 1994.

Other ATR 42 variants included the ATR 42 Cargo, with a 'quick-change' interior and the similar ATR 42L with a lateral cargo door. The ATR 42F was a military freighter, of which one was delivered to Gabon in 1989.

Stretched ATR

The increased-capacity ATR 72 was announced in 1985, and the first of three development aircraft made its maiden flight on 27 October 1988. The new type had a 14-ft 9-in (4.5-m) fuselage stretch, new, increased-span mainly-composite outer wing panels, and greater fuel capacity. The baseline ATR 72-200 was powered by PW124B engines. The hot-and-high ATR 72-210 had the same, more powerful, PW127 engines as the ATR 42-500. There was a further improved hot-and-high version, the ATR 72-210A, with more powerful PW127F engines driving six-bladed propellers and

these engines remain standard on the current ATR 72-500 production variant.

The ATR 42 formed the basis initially of the ATR 42MP maritime patroller and latterly the multi rolo Survoyor. Other specialised versions are available, including the ATR 42 In-flight Inspection designed for airfield and en-route navigation and landing aid calibration duties, and Corporate versions of both the AIR 42 and 72.

ATR 72-only developments include the ATR 72 ASW which combines the mission systems of the ATR 42MP with a rotary sonobuoy launcher, MAD (magnetic anomaly detector), provision for torpedoes and other equipment to provide a multi-role capability against submarines and surface vessels, as well as advanced patrol and search-and-rescue abilities.

ATR merger and beyond

In January 1997, ATR became part of the larger Aero International (Regional) or AI(R) Consortium, which included the Jetstream and BAe 146 (Avro RJ) business of DAe. Under this arrangement, AI(R) marketed, sold and supported the aircraft within the consortium. The company has reportedly held discussions with the Chinese Xian

factory and there were reports that ATR might team up with Fairchild-Dornier, but in the end no alliance was formed and the AI(R) group was dissolved.

Today ATR continues to successfully market and develop its turboprop range and with some signs of an increase in interest in turboprop commuter aircraft, the future looks bright for this successful design.

Above: The principal production ATR 42 since 1996, the -500 has more powerful PW 127E engines, reinforced wings and improved electrical systems.

Left: By July 2005 348 ATR 72s had been ordered, in addition to over 390 examples of the shorter ATR 42. Around 680 ATR turboprops had been delivered by mid-2005.

ATR 42/72 Operators

London-Gatwick based Cityflyer Express operated ATRs in British Airways' colours as a BA franchise. Both ATR 42 (above, in the older BA scheme) and ATR 72 (below in the most recent scheme) aircraft were flown.

As one of the world's best-selling turboprop airliners, the ATR has appeared in a plethora of colour schemes. A cross-section of its many operators is illustrated here.

Above: American Eagle had a large number of ATR 42 (illustrated) and 72 aircraft among its huge regional aircraft fleet. In American Eagle service the ATR 72 is known as the Super ATR.

Above: Binter Canarias flies only the ATR 72 on its regional routes throughout the Canary Islands. Seven ATR 72-500s complement six 200-series aircraft and two Raytheon 1900Ds.

Below: Norwich- and London Stansted-based KLM UK operated five ATR 72-200s, alongside BAe 146-300s, Fokker 50s and Fokker 100s. Two of its ATRs were later leased to Vietnam Airlines.

Above: Morlaix-Ploujean based Brit Air flies ATR 42-300s (illustrated), CRJs and F100s on behalf of Air France. The aircraft wear Air France colours and carry Air France flight numbers.

Left: Air Dolomiti designates its ATR 42-500 aircraft as ATR 500s and its ATR 72s as ATR 700s. Air Dolomiti operates as a Lufthansa partner airline from its base at Trieste.

Above: Kenyan registered, this **ATR 42** was one of a pair to fly briefly with Namibian airline **African Eagle**. Second-hand **ATR**s, particularly cargo conversions, are attractive to African carriers.

Left: Before it was forced to cease trading on 20 September 2001, **Gill Airways** operated a fleet of six **ATR**s. The airline had been returning to profit when finance was withdrawn by its bankers.

Above left: **Iran Asseman** (now **Iran Aseman Airlines**) fleet includes six 64-seat **ATR 72**s. In addition to its **ATR** turboprops, the airline also flies **Do 228**s, **Dassault Falcon 20**s, **F28**s, **F100**s and **Boeing 727**s.

Above: **Eurolot** flies as the regional subsidiary of **LOT Polish Airlines**. The carrier uses only **ATR**s, the second of its eight **ATR 72**s being illustrated. Five **ATR 42** were also flown in summer 2005.

Below: **Air Littoral**'s very young fleet included 10 **ATR 42-500**s at the beginning of 2002. The aircraft were finished in a striking colour scheme and flew alongside Bombardier **CRJ**s and **F70**s.

Above: Two **ATR 42-320**s flew as part of **Ethiopian Airlines** turboprop fleet. They flew alongside other turboprop types, including the de Havilland Canada **DHC-6**, Fokker **F50** and **L-100 Hercules**.

Above: **Titan Airways** offered a pair of **ATR 42-300** aircraft for charter operations. The machines could be flown in **Titan** livery, or the colours of the particular chartering company.

Olympic Aviation, a regional subsidiary of **Olympic Airways**, has been absorbed into its parent. **Olympic Airlines** now includes six **ATR 42-320**s (illustrated) and seven **ATR 72-202**s in its fleet.

BAe/Avro 146/RJ Development

Air UK was an important 146 operator, with its fleet centred around the 146-300 variant. The airline was typical of those employing the 146 intensively on regional and short-haul routes.

Having run the gauntlet of protracted development, cancellation and initially poor sales, the 146/RJ matured into a British success story.

In a world that has become increasingly conscious of noise pollution, aircraft such as the BAe 146 and Avro RJ have played an important part in commercial aviation. With four fuel-efficient and very quiet engines, the 146 can slip virtually unnoticed into any regional airfield.

After a protracted development period which initially involved Hawker Siddeley and almost brought the nationalised British Aerospace (BAe) to its knees, the 146 eventually sold well around the world and paved the way for the improved Avro RJ.

A whole series of design proposals was considered over a 20-year period before the HS.146 layout was frozen and the programme launched. Four Lycoming (later AlliedSignal and now Honeywell) ALF502 engines were chosen to power the machine and, although some critics said it was ridiculous to use four engines, the economy and performance offered in service have easily justified their use. The capital cost, fuel burn and installed weight of the

With its low noise signature, the 146 is able to operate from many airports with night-time curfews on jet operations. Based on the 146-200, the 146QT is optimised for overnight freight transport.

ALF502s were in every case better than the traditional short-haul airliner layout of two larger engines. Most importantly, the

ALF502 offered extremely low noise levels.

Bearing in mind the required field performance, the wing was fitted with powerful high-lift flaps. Contrary to all the previous proposals which had featured low-set wings, this wing was set

As the first of the 146 family, G-SSSH wore a highly appropriate registration. The aircraft was used during the flight test programme, which resulted in type certification being awarded in February 1983.

Right: Taiwan's Makung Airlines, UNI Airways Corp. from May 1996 and now Uni Air, operated a fleet of 146s, including five 146-300s as seen here. Several Asian airlines purchased the 146, many buying used aircraft from BAe's Asset Management Organisation (AMO).

Above: Three 146-100s were assessed during 800 hours of everyday cargo operations by the RAF. After this period, the original aircraft were returned to BAe, and two new machines were purchased to equip the Queen's Flight for VIP duties.

on top of the fuselage. The new configuration allowed the engines to be mounted in undisturbed air, while the wing could provide maximum lift since it was unaffected by the wide fuselage below. Coincidentally, it also allowed the fuselage to be positioned close to the ground so that passengers could embark via short airstairs. This facility opened up the possibility of operations from less-developed regional airports. The high wing also dictated that the main landing gear be fuselage-mounted.

Comfort a priority

Hawker Siddeley was determined to make the 146 as comfortable as possible. From the

Many airports which were previously the preserve of turboprop types, such as the DHC-7, benefited from the introduction of the 146. Operations from London City Airport were revolutionised, since jet services could now be offered from the city centre.

outset, a design objective was to provide five-abreast seating with a general level of comfort not less than that of the Boeing 747. Indeed, the 146 mock-up was initially furnished with actual 747 seats, and the internal cabin width was greater than that of the 146's principal competitors, the Fokker F28 and F100, and McDonnell Douglas' DC-9 and MD-80. Cabin height was also generous and, in service, the 146 has proved easily adapted to any desired seating or cargo configuration.

Programme delays

A combination of world recession and major changes in the UK aerospace industry almost destroyed the 146 before its first flight. In August 1973, the British government announced that the project would go ahead and had plans for a new nationalised aircraft company, known as British Aerospace, which would take over Hawker Siddeley. As it became apparent that the 146 was heading for a loss, potential shareholders in BAe became concerned. Thus, in October 1974, the government cancelled the 146, making Hawker Siddeley and BAe a more attractive option for investors.

A vigorous reaction from Hawker Siddeley workers led to work continuing at a much diminished rate. BAe was duly formed in 1977. One of the first tasks undertaken by its civil marketing team was to review the 146 and reassess the potential market. During the delay of almost four years, much work had been done to refine the design. Market analysis yielded positive responses, and the BAe board recommended a relaunch. This time there were no delays, and in 1987 output had to be stepped up from 28 to 40 aircraft per year, and a second assembly line was set up at Woodford.

The 146-100 prototype was flown on 3 September 1981 and Dan-Air began scheduled services on 27 May 1983. It was typical of the 146 that one of the first Dan-Air destinations should be Innsbruck, never previously served by scheduled jetliners. While production of the 146-100 continued, it became increasingly obvious that some operators would gladly trade the 146-100's amazing field capabilities for increased payload. Accordingly, the stretched 146-200 was flown on 1 August 1982 and soon became the baseline standard aircraft, only to be surpassed in turn by the 146-300 and the much-revised RJ series.

Technical details

Ignoring conventional wisdom, Hawker Siddeley dispensed with leading-edge lift-enhancing mechanisms, thrust reversal and the twin-jet layout, and achieved the fine STOL performance of the quietest jet airliner.

The 146's superb field performance is mainly due to its well-designed wing. The lift coefficent is greatly increased during landing by huge trailing-edge flaps. The petal airbrake can be snapped shut to provide instant lift in the event of an emergency.

Hawker Siddeley designed a comparatively simple, thick wing for the 146, featuring hardly any sweepback. This fits in well with the planned short field length and Mach 0.7 maximum operating speed, and enables the required high lift performance to be achieved with a plain leading edge. In addition, the flaps along the trailing edge are very powerful.

Flying controls

To keep the horizontal tail out of the wing wake, it was put on top of the vertical tail. This T-tail arrangement also made it easy to fit powerful airbrakes, which form the tailcone at the extreme end of the fuselage. These airbrakes, together with lift dumpers above the wing and powerful wheel brakes, made it possible to achieve the required landing field length without the use of engine thrust reversers.

The aircraft is cleared for ILS-coupled approaches down to Cat II minima (runway visibility down to 400 m (1,312 ft) and decision height down to 30 m (1,312 ft)). Its stall protection system, which operates with a stick shaker, takes into account the rate at which the boundary of safe flight is approached. It is doubtful if any previous large aircraft had had such safe handling qualities combined with such outstanding performance.

Key performance features

Now out of production, the 146 and RJ still offer unbeatable noise, fuel economy and field performance. In the improved RJ form, the machine is equipped for service into the next century.

1 Quiet operations: A new chapter in jet airliner operations was opened by the 146. Many airports never before visited by a jet could now be served on a regular, scheduled basis by the new machine. The accompanying diagram illustrates the ground area exposed to a 90 Perceived Noise Decibel (PNdB) sound level around the approach and take-off routes of selected types.

90 PNdB noise footprint area

Douglas DC-9-30
7.3 sq miles/18.9 km²

Fokker F100
2.4 sq miles/6.2 km²

Fokker 50
2.3 sq miles/6.0 km²

BAe 146-200
1.6 sq miles/4.1 km²

30,000/9144   10,000/3048   0   10,000/3048   30,000/9144
Distance from threshold (ft/m)   Distance from start of roll (ft/m)

BAe 146 (5.5° approach angle)

Typical twin-jet (e.g., Boeing 737) (approach angle 3°)

Comparative approach angles

2 Steep approach: With its short landing characteristics, the 146 is able to fly a very steep approach compared to other airliners. This allows it to begin its final descent much later, clearing tall obstructions close to the airport.

3 Short take-off performance: Although it is unable to offer the field performance of turboprop aircraft such as the Dash 8, the 146-100 outperforms other comparable jet airliners. Taking off in just 4,000 ft (1219 m), the 146 allows airlines to fly longer-ranged routes at jet speeds, from airports normally available only to shorter-ranged and slower turboprops. In addition, the four engines of the 146 offer much greater safety in the event of an engine failure on take-off, compared to its twin-engined rivals.

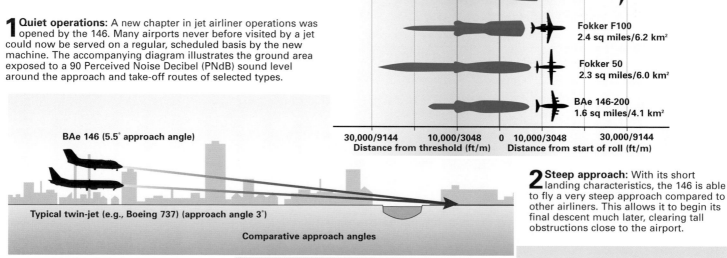

Quoted take-off distances are for aircraft at maximum take-off weight in standard conditions. In practice, at lighter weights, distances are significantly reduced.

Fokker 100
6,086 ft (1855 m)

BAe 146-100
4,000 ft (1219 m)

Dash 8 Series 100
3,150 ft (960 m)

Boeing 737-300
6,650 ft (2027 m)

Comparative take-off distances

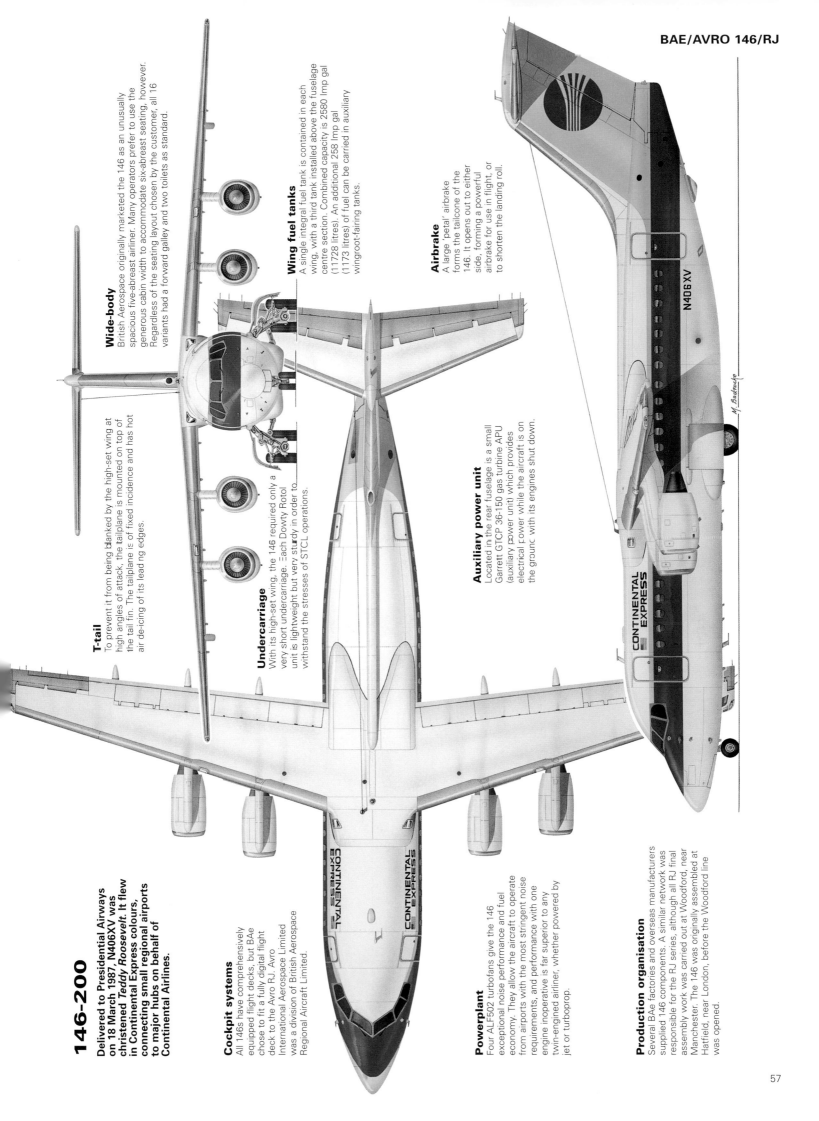

146-200

Delivered to Presidential Airways on 18 March 1987, N406XV was christened *Teddy Roosevelt*. It flew in Continental Express colours, connecting small regional airports to major hubs on behalf of Continental Airlines.

Cockpit systems

All 146s have comprehensively equipped flight decks, but BAe chose to fit a fully digital flight deck to the Avro RJ. Avro International Aerospace Limited was a division of British Aerospace Regional Aircraft Limited.

Powerplant

Four ALF502 turbofans give the 146 exceptional noise performance and fuel economy. They allow the aircraft to operate from airports with the most stringent noise requirements, and performance with one engine inoperative is far superior to any twin-engined airliner, whether powered by jet or turboprop.

Production organisation

Several BAe factories and overseas manufacturers supplied 146 components. A similar network was responsible for the RJ series, although all RJ final assembly work was carried out at Woodford, near Manchester. The 146 was originally assembled at Hatfield, near London, before the Woodford line was opened.

Wide-body

British Aerospace originally marketed the 146 as an unusually spacious five-abreast airliner. Many operators prefer to use the generous cabin width to accommodate six-abreast seating, however. Regardless of the seating layout chosen by the customer, all 16 variants had a forward galley and two toilets as standard.

T-tail

To prevent it from being blanked by the high-set wing at high angles of attack, the tailplane is mounted on top of the tail fin. The tailplane is of fixed incidence and has hot air de-icing of its leading edges.

Wing fuel tanks

A single integral fuel tank is contained in each wing, with a third tank installed above the fuselage centre section. Combined capacity is 2580 Imp gal (11728 litres). An additional 258 Imp gal (1173 litres) of fuel can be carried in auxiliary wingroot-fairing tanks.

Undercarriage

With its high-set wing, the 146 required only a very short undercarriage. Each Dowty Rotol unit is lightweight but very sturdy in order to withstand the stresses of STCL operations.

Airbrake

A large 'petal' airbrake forms the tailcone of the 146. It opens out to either side, forming a powerful airbrake for use in flight, or to shorten the landing roll.

Auxiliary power unit

Located in the rear fuselage is a small Garrett GTCP 36-150 gas turbine APU (auxiliary power unit) which provides electrical power while the aircraft is on the ground with its engines shut down.

146-300 and RJ

Avro family: all the RJ variants fly in formation. The short-fuselage RJ70 left production first, while the RJ85 and RJ100 remained as equivalents to the 146-200 and 146-300, respectively. The RJ115 had the same dimensions as the RJ100, but higher weights.

Updating its already successful 146 series as the RJ family – with standard five-abreast seating, glass cockpits and uprated engines – BAe (now trading in the regional airliner market as Avro) was guaranteed to find success.

The 146 entered service during 1983, initially as the 88-seat 146-100 with Dan-Air, followed by the 100-seat Series 200 for Air Wisconsin. Both versions used a six-abreast seating standard which, with a reasonable load factor, enabled the aircraft to offer a sound return.

As Pacific Southwest Airlines (PSA) built up its fleet from mid-1984 onward, it became apparent that this layout was too tight for generously-built Californians and the airline decided to adopt five-abreast seating, thus offering a much larger seat and enhanced comfort. BAe, which had been considering a stretched version of the aircraft, quickly recognised the need to restore 100-seat capability as soon as possible, believing that, in many parts of the world, a fare structure to support a maximum of 85 seats would be untenable. Initial project studies showed that a

significant stretch could be achieved with only minor changes to the basic structure and that the existing engines would not require an upgrade.

To reduce the development costs of what would become the 146-300, aircraft 1001 was withdrawn from service and its nose and rear fuselage were separated from its centre section and moved out to allow two fuselage drums to be inserted. The 8 ft 1-in (2.46-m) forward plug and 7 ft 8-in (2.34-m) rear plug resulted in an increase in length to 101 ft 8⅛ in (30.99 m). This more than restored the seating capacity; 103 passengers could be accommodated in five-abreast comfort while (subject to the insertion of additional emergency exits) high-density seating could be provided for a maximum of 128 passengers.

Fears that the increased maximum weight would erode short-field performance – which

The shortest of the RJs, the RJ70 fell by the wayside as operators realised the limitations of its smaller capacity. Many RJ customers continue the tradition of the 146, by flying into inner city airports.

was so much a selling point for the type – proved groundless. The new version soon joined the earlier series in gaining approval to operate from London City Airport.

The first order for the longer aircraft came from the airline that had initially put the type into service in the US – Air

Wisconsin. Five aircraft were delivered between December 1988 and November 1989, and all are still in service with the airline today.

Avro RJ series

The first Woodford-built 146 emerged in March 1988,

intended at first to bolster the Hatfield assembly line, although it would later supplant it. The last Hatfield-built aircraft was the prototype that was to lead to the RJ series.

Hatfield had extensive experience of glass cockpits through its work on the BAe 125 executive jet, and applied this knowledge to the 146 in stages. Honeywell supplied the complete avionics suite which included a flight management system which vastly reduced the crew's workload. European regional carriers were now becoming customers, with Crossair and Sabena DAT in the lead, and the RJ was turning into the aircraft of choice for major airlines seeking its capacity.

Improvements

With this new emerging market, Avro concentrated on further improving cabin comfort. An irritating 'hoot' that accompanied the up or down movement of the flaps was eliminated by sealing the wingroot flap tracks, extra width was found inside the cabin by reaming the fuselage frames, the overhead bins were refined and changes were made to the cabin lighting – all these improvements allowing the aircraft to offer the most comfortable ride available in regional air transport.

While the RJ specification was firming up, another outstanding irritant was being dealt with. Right from the first flight, it had been

Freighter variants

In March 1986, airframe c/n E2056 left Hatfield as a 'green' airframe for Dothan, Alabama, where Pemco carried out the first 146 conversion to freighter standard. Rather than just cutting a large door in the rear fuselage, this involved the installation of a heavy-duty floor with built-in rollers, crash protection for the flight-deck (preventing the intrusion of cargo) and a comprehensive fire-detection system. The aircraft's operating weight turned out to be around 2,000 lb (907 kg) less than that of a comparable passenger aircraft. The Series 200QT (QT – Quiet Trader) could carry a 22,500-lb (10206-kg) payload; the Series 300QT (below) increased this to 25,380 lb (11512 kg).

The prototype returned to the UK just in time to appear at the 1986 Farnborough Air Show where

it excited the interest of the TNT Group, then in the throes of setting up an overnight operation centred on Birmingham. A highly successful two-night trial led to the optimistic announcement of an order for 72 freighters from TNT for worldwide use. While this did not materialise in full, the type was used for a sophisticated overnight European network, taking advantage of its quietness to operate where other aircraft were excluded by curfews. One Series 100 was converted as a possible military variant, but this was not accepted and the aircraft was later sold on the civil market. Several aircraft were made into QCs (Quickly Convertible) – able to make a rapid transition from the freighter to the passenger-carrying role. The QCs retain cabin trim and have seats mounted on pallets for quick installation.

apparent that neither the APU nor control of the cabin air-conditioning were up to the task. The result had been that passengers would occasionally be faced with an oily smell in the cabin. A new APU supplier was found, and the air-conditioning and

pressurisation programmes were rescheduled.

Performance enhancements were achieved in two ways. A weight-saving programme resulted in improvements to both payload and range, but of greater significance to most operators

was a redesign of the engine to incorporate full-authority digital engine control (FADEC) and an additional supercharger stage, resulting in the engine running cooler, so retaining performance at higher altitudes. The new engine was designated LF507.

Above: Turkey's national airline, Turkish Airlines, was one of the first carriers to receive the RJ100. The airline ordered nine RJ100s and four RJ70s, of which six and three, respectively, remain in service.

Left: Ansett New Zealand received nine 146-300s (illustrated) and one 146-200QC. The quietness of the 146 was appreciated by both Queenstown and Wellington airports, which have noise restrictions.

British Aerospace ATP/Jetstream 61

Manx Airlines became one of a number of British Airways partner airlines to be absorbed into British Regional Airlines, now British Airways Citiexpress. A fleet of six ATPs remains on strength.

Underachieving turboprop

The ATP is widely regarded as an unsuccessful aircraft – a mid-1980s regional turboprop airliner that was killed off by heavy competition and its own unremarkable performance. Just over 60 aircraft were built before the production line was closed down, but today demand for the surviving ATPs remains strong, with freighter conversions the way for the future.

On 1 March 1984 BAe announced its intention to develop a larger advanced turboprop (ATP) regional transport, to succeed the Super 748 (HS.748). The BAe ATP design that emerged had the same cabin cross-section as the Super 748, but a longer fuselage to accommodate 64 passengers in a standard configuration, with up to 72 seats possible. An important change was the aircraft's longer nose gear, which effectively raised the sill-height of the main cabin door and allowed it to be used with conventional airport jetways. New, fuel-efficient, 2,150-hp (1604-kW) Pratt & Whitney Canada PW124 turboprops, driving slow-turning propellers with six composite blades were fitted, but later replaced by the more powerful PW126A engine.

Other significant improvements included the installation of the most modern equipment, including an advanced flight deck with a four-screen Smiths SDS-201 EFIS cockpit. The ATP also introduced separate forward and rear passenger doors, with integral airstairs in the forward door, and separate forward and rear baggage doors.

Maiden flight

The prototype ATP flew for the first time on 6 August 1986 and was joined in the air by the first production aircraft on 20 February 1987. The ATP obtained its European JAR 25 certification in March 1988 and US FAR 25 certification in August 1988. The launch customer for the type was the Airlines of Britain (AoB) group and British Midland Airways put the first ATP into revenue service on 9 May 1988. The AoB ATP order was initially for eight aircraft, but was later increased to 13. Other early ATP customers included Air Wisconsin (14), British Airways (14), Biman Bangladesh (two), SATA (three),

Launched in March 1984 as a modern, quiet, fuel-efficient development of the HS.748, the Advanced Turboprop (ATP) first flew in prototype form on 6 August 1986.

Merpati Nusantara (five) and THT (four).

In spite of good operating economics and figures that showed the ATP to be the quietest aircraft in its class, its slow speed and repeated early technical reliability problems kept sales sluggish. By December 1993 just 58 had been ordered and prospects were virtually non-existent. In a last-ditch attempt to stimulate interest in the ATP, on 26 April 1993 BAe announced

SATA Air Açores owns two ATPs and leases a further two examples. The aircraft are operated on inter-island services in the Azores and are configured to carry 64 passengers.

Right: In the early 1990s, BAe proposed the BAe P132 ASW/ASuW variant with equipment to include a 360° maritime radar, FLIR, MAD and six weapon hardpoints – no orders were forthcoming.

*The ATP was relaunched in 1993 as the Jetstream 61 with **G-JLXI** being the sole example to fly. It is seen here in promotional livery prior to the 1994 Farnborough Air Show.*

an improved version which it dubbed the Jetstream 61 Adopting the Jetstream name neatly did away with the unpopularity associated with the ATP and aligned the new aircraft with the more successful Jetstream 31/41 family.

The Jetstream 61 was powered by more powerful 2,750-hp (2051-kW) Pratt & Whitney PW127D engines, providing improved airfield performance, especially in 'hot-and-high' conditions. A completely new interior with new-style seats, better underseat stowage and larger overhead bins was also added to enhance passenger appeal. The aircraft would also be certified to operate at higher weights.

Despite an aggressive marketing campaign, the ATP never made the impact on the lucrative North American regional airliner market that it needed to become successful. This example was painted in American Eagle colours, but the airline purchased ATR 42s and 72s instead.

However, the relaunch failed to attract any meaningful new orders and production was finally halted at a total of 65 aircraft. The aircraft dubbed as the first Jetstream 61 was, in fact, the 64th ATP to fly. Both it and the 65th aircraft were later broken up (along with several unfinished aircraft on the production line).

The last ATP customer delivery came in 1995, with an aircraft built in 1993. However, the fortunes of those that remain in service have undergone a renaissance in the hands of BAE

Systems Asset Management – demand for them is solid with nearly all are in regular service. Today the aircraft is referred to only as the ATP. ATP operators have included Air Europa Express, British Regional Airways, West Air Sweden, British World Airlines, SATA, Sun Air, Biman Bangladesh, BAE Systems (as a corporate shuttle).

Freighter ATP

On 28 June 2000, BAE Systems and West Air Sweden AB announced a 50:50 joint venture agreement to develop and market a freighter version of the ATP. Together, the two co-operated in the design and development of a side cargo door (SCD) modification. The new sliding door is been sized to accommodate a standard LD3 container and mounted on the port rear fuselage. Up to eight LD3s can be carried, plus one additional LD346 (the cut-down version used by the Airbus

A320). In this configuration the ATP freighter has a range of approximately 1,000 nm (1,150 miles, 1850 km). With BAE introducing an increased maximum weight limit for the basic ATP, the freighter has a maximum gross structural payload of 18,560 lb (8237 kg).

West Air (which already had a fleet of 11 HS.748 freighters), acquired six of the nine ATPs formerly operated by United Feeder Services in the USA, and placed options on the others. The first aircraft was immediately operated in the all-freight role – the first time that ATPs had been used in this way. The SCD modification was then planned to produce the first ATP freighter proper, with West Air initially having the capacity to undertake four conversions per year, with a maximum of six possible. By August 2005, the carrier had five ATP freight conversions in service, alongside nine unconverted aircraft.

Boeing 707

When it first appeared, the Boeing 707 offered unrivalled speed on US transcontinental routes, but could barely span the Atlantic. The arrival of the Series 300 allowed the 707 to become a true intercontinental classic.

Introduction

Although it was not the first jetliner in commercial service, nor the best performing or most cost-effective, the Boeing 707 was, nevertheless, the first aircraft to introduce the concept of jet air travel for the masses. It was built in large numbers and in several different variants. Many remain in service.

Prior to the 1950s, the biggest contenders in the US airliner market were Douglas and Lockheed. Boeing by contrast, remained largely a minor player, its Model 377 Stratocruiser, despite being technically advanced, selling only in modest numbers.

In 1954, the company rolled out a single prototype from its Renton assembly plant. Built as a private venture and at huge cost, this aircraft spawned two distinct families, the 717/C-135 military tankers/ transports, and the commercial 707 airliner which became the jetliner of choice throughout the 1960s. During the development of the 707, Boeing had to fight arch rival Douglas, every step of the way and, initially, it appeared that the DC-8 would find favour with the airlines.

Design flexibility

The fuselage of the prototype, known as the Model 367-80 (or Dash 80), had been criticised by the airlines as being too narrow. In order to outflank Douglas and satisfy the critics, Boeing completely redesigned the fuselage, making it both longer and wider and able to seat as many as six passengers abreast, whereas the DC-8 could manage only four. This tactic worked, and demonstrated the enormous potential which existed in the basic 707 design. The aircraft entered service in 1958 and, at the time, caused quite a stir. The 707 was bigger, heavier and noisier than any airliner in service at the time and was able to carry many more passengers over greater distances than ever before. It had started a revolution

Boeing's privately funded Model 367-80 was built at huge risk to the company. This revolutionary aircraft spawned one of the greatest jetliner dynasties in the world.

in air travel and it was not long before other US manufacturers began developing their own jet airliners, eager to obtain a slice of the very lucrative market uncovered by the 707. By 1965, Boeing had sold 430 707s, making it the most popular airliner since the pre-war Douglas DC-3, and still the orders kept coming in. As production continued apace, Boeing introduced improvements such as a taller tail and more powerful engines, plus an increasing number of sub-variants tailored to specific requirements. These included the intercontinental series 300 and 400, convertible/ freighter variants, and the

derivative 720, designed for high-capacity US domestic services.

Far from perfect

Although it was proving tremendously popular with airlines, the 707 did have noticeable shortcomings. The Pratt & Whitney JT3 turbojets which powered early aircraft were noisy and required water injection for take-off, resulting in huge clouds of black smoke. Early 707s were also not really capable of intercontinental flights, requiring pilots to fly the aircraft gingerly on long distance services in order to conserve fuel. Furthermore, during the early days of 707 operations, stopovers on long-haul routes

Designed to introduce the world to the convenience of regular, high-speed, transcontinental jet travel, the 707 exhibited greater versatility than could ever have been expected. Aircraft were initially operated only by the major carriers, passing to smaller operators later in their careers. This Western Airlines 707 is typical; it was delivered on 13 May 1960, and later flew with Pan Am, Mandala Airlines and Egypt Air.

Above: World Airways was one of the smaller US carriers to adopt the 707 – and this 707-373C was one of the very first -300s to be delivered.

Initially criticised for having too narrow a fuselage, the Boeing 707 was redesigned – Boeing took great trouble to ensure that the aircraft had the widest cabin available on the market. This early publicity shot shows a five-abreast layout, although a six-abreast arrangement was often specified.

were mandatory and, compared to contemporary propliners, the aircraft was thirsty and required excessive runway lengths from which to operate. The 707 also proved to be less profitable than other jetliners and, initially, was expensive and difficult to maintain. In addition, the world's major airports had to embark on expensive projects to extend and strengthen their runways and improve facilities in order to accommodate the new Boeing jet. Although these drawbacks were quick to be exploited by traditionalists and propliner aficionados, the new airliner was welcomed with open arms by others, who foresaw a future of airline operations without government subsidies, and a proliferation of routes.

Boeing supreme

Despite the flood of orders from airlines eager to acquire Boeing's latest, the competition had not been standing still. Besides Douglas, Convair had begun development of its own four-engined jet, the 880 and, in the UK, Vickers introduced the technically advanced VC10.

Both the 880 and the VC10, however, failed to find sufficient orders, but sales of the DC-8

remained strong and, in an attempt to attract orders from overseas, Boeing launched the 707-320, which offered true intercontinental range. BOAC, which was under political pressure to 'buy British', displayed much interest in the 707 and managed to win approval for an order by specifying that its machines used Rolls-Royce Conway engines. Orders from Lufthansa and Sabena soon followed and, by 1965, it was clear that the 707 was proving more popular than the DC-8, despite the fact that Douglas was introducing stretched variants of the latter. Furthermore, with the 707 selling so well, Boeing began developing a family of new models, using many components already proven on the 707. The first of these new aircraft became the 727, and so began the familiar pattern for Boeing civil designations which continues to this very day.

In addition to the acquisition of 707s by an increasing number of new airlines, original customers like Pan Am and TWA remained faithful, and placed further orders for series 300 aircraft.

Not only was the 707 the first mainstream commercial jet, it

also introduced a number of features which are airline 'benchmarks'. For example, in the 1950s, new aircraft were often used to transport first-class passengers, while older and slower types were used to carry the tourist class. The 707 was the first aircraft to accommodate two or three different classes of passengers on the same aircraft. Moreover, on the 707, the passenger entry/exit doors were located fore and aft on the port side of the fuselage, with the cargo deck hatches located to starboard – a feature standardised on subsequent Boeing jetliners.

Record production

By the dawn of the 1970s, early 707s had begun to find their way on to the used airliner market, as larger and more efficient types became available. Used examples were quickly snapped up by smaller airlines and often employed on holiday charter flights. Still more were converted into dedicated freighters – as which the majority of 707 survivors continue to serve today. By 1982, when the last civilian model 707 was delivered to the Government of Morocco, a grand total of 916 examples had been delivered.

Above: American Airlines was typical of the big US carriers in adopting the Boeing 707 for its New York to Los Angeles route, on 25 March 1959. It bought the aircraft in large numbers, operating it until 1983 when the last of the type were retired.

Left: Air Mauritius received this 707-400 from BEA Airtours, to which it had been handed down by BOAC. The -400 was an anglicised variant of the intercontinental 707-300. The aircraft featured Rolls-Royce Conway engines as part of the offset package agreed by BOAC and Boeing when the aircraft were ordered.

707 Development

One of the most influential aircraft in history, Boeing's Model 367-80 prototype not only spawned the huge C-135 tanker family, but gave rise to the 707/720 airliner dynasty. Its design was also the basis of subsequent Boeing airliners.

N70700 lifted off from Renton on 15 July 1954 to inaugurate a worldwide era of jet transportation. After many years flying as a research platform for Boeing, this historic aircraft was rebuilt in its original form.

Boeing was convinced that both the airlines and the US Air Force would buy jet transports, and that the same design could basically be used for both tankers and civil liners. But Boeing had to do it the hard way. It had to tighten its belt and produce a prototype with its own money at an estimated cost of no less than $15 million.

One essential ingredient was the Pratt & Whitney JT3 engine, the lightweight commercial version of the fuel-efficient J57 used in the B-52. The transport would use four JT3s, hung in pods below and ahead of the 35°-swept wing. Gross weight worked out at 190,000 lb (86184 kg) and, although the military model would have an interior configured for cargo and fuel, the commercial passenger

aircraft could seat 130. Because it could fly at 600 mph (966 km/h), the jetliner promised to do three times the work of the military KC-97 or contemporary propliners.

707 emerges

Boeing's model number for the prototype was 367-80, although it was more popularly known as the Dash-80. When the Model 367-80 finally became a flyable aircraft, it was given the new designation Model 707. Boeing deliberately capitalised on this memorable sequence by naming its

subsequent jet transports Models 717, 727 and so on through to the Model 787. There was still nothing certain about the 707's development when it was rolled out on 15 May 1954. During early taxi tests six days later, the left main gear smashed its way up through the wing and left the prototype crippled on its left outer engine pod. It was not, therefore, until 15 July of that year that the

aircraft flew for the first time.

By now, the USAF had told Boeing that it wanted a new-build jet tanker. In October 1954 the first tanker order came through, for 29 aircraft, launching a large programme for the Model 717 (military KC-135 and C-135).

However, Boeing failed to win any orders of a major nature, losing to its great rival Douglas with its DC-8. To compete with this aircraft, Boeing undertook one of the costliest modifications possible: it changed the body cross-section. The 707 retained

Above left: Aviation history was made on 26 October 1958 when a PanAm Boeing 707-121 opened the 'Big Jet' era with a scheduled service from New York to Paris.

Left: Boeing produced five 707-220s with JT4A-3 turbojets in response to a request from Braniff for its South American services. These engines improved take-off performance at high altitude.

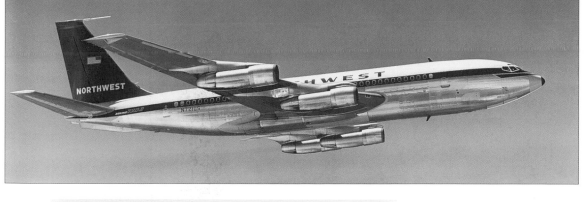

Special-purpose military developments

The USAF Military Air Transport Service was quick to introduce the 707 into military service. Illustrated above is a 707-153, one of the first of many military examples, which was delivered on 4 May 1959 to the service as a VC-137A. It was equipped with a convertible interior able to seat either 22 VIPs or to serve as an airborne command post.

its figure-of-eight fuselage with smoothly faired sides, but the upper lobe was increased in width to 140 in (3.56 m), beating Douglas by 2 in (5.08 cm) and enabling a triple seat unit to be installed on each side of the aisle for up to 150 passengers. In addition, fuel capacity was increased and the first models offered were the Model 707-120 series and the special Model 707-138 which was 10 ft (3.048 m) shorter. The standard launch engine was the JT3C 6 rated at 13,500-lb (60.02-kN) thrust with water injection, and fitted with a large noise-suppressing nozzle.

The first airline customer was Pan American, which bought 20 Model 707-112s; but the airline also signed for 25 Douglas DC-8s on the same day, so souring any accomplishment that Boeing might have felt. Following this, Douglas announced its development of a longer-ranged DC-8 equipped with the JT4A

engine. Boeing responded by developing a larger, long-ranged model, the Model 707-320 Intercontinental.

BOAC, like PanAm, was interested in Boeing's bigger and longer-range model. This had a new high-efficiency, longer-span wing, a longer fuselage seating up to 189 passengers and much greater fuel capacity. The launch engine was the JT4A at the increased rating of 16,800 lb (74.68 kN), but Rolls-Royce's Conway bypass turbojet fitted perfectly and offered greater power, lower installed weight and much better fuel consumption, and was selected by a small minority of airlines. The considerably greater capability of the Intercontinental quickly made this the standard Model 707, while the original aircraft was

developed into the Model 720.

The first production Model 707 was flown at Renton on 20 December 1957, but was actually numbered as the second of the initial batch of 20 Model 707-121s for PanAm. FAA certification was awarded on 23 September 1958.

PanAm opened services between New York and Paris on 26 October 1958. On these routes, the range of the Model 707-121 was marginal. It had not been designed for the North Atlantic, and the flight crews had to learn the correct take-off procedures and how to obtain the maximum number of air-miles per pound of fuel.

Spurred by the competition from the DC-8 and CV-880, Boeing embarked on a programme to build an even better jetliner. Pratt & Whitney met the competition of the Conway with a startling modification to the JT3C, which replaced the first three stages of the compressor with two stages of enormous blades called a fan – it dubbed this the turbofan. The new engine, known as the JT3D, offered better fuel economy and a considerable reduction in noise levels over the JT3C.

Before this was available, the big Model 707-320 Intercontinental flew as the

sixteenth off the Renton line on 16 January 1959. The introduction of the -320 into service was not without problems, however, the most significant concerning the aircraft's handling in adverse weather. Eventually, a taller fin was retrofitted to the type and was later introduced on all civilian and military 707 models.

The first model to have the JT3D fan engine was the Model 707-120B. Based on the Model 720, it first flew on 23 November 1959, with a revised lightweight airframe, along with aerodynamic improvements to the wing which allowed for a higher cruising speed.

The last of the major variants was the Model 707-320C. Boeing had already fitted the fan engine to the 707-320B, and with it came a host of aerodynamic improvements including longer-span curved wingtips giving reduced drag. The 707-320B entered service in June 1962 with PanAm which, a year later, pioneered the use of the Model 707-320C, a mixed-traffic version able to carry a total of 202 passengers or 96,126 lb (43603 kg) of cargo. This variant soon became the standard 707 and the orders kept rolling in for the revolutionary airliner.

Operational history

The innovative Boeing 707 was eagerly snapped up by a host of airlines and, within a few years, was operating out of airports worldwide. Years later, even with the advent of more economical types, the 707 is still being operated by several airlines.

Many might be surprised to learn that Boeing only built 725 commercial 707s, plus 154 720s. But the total number of aircraft built does not reflect the type's enormous importance. The pace of aeronautical development in the late 1950s and early 1960s was such that no aircraft could expect to remain in production for long before being superseded by new and more advanced types. This contrasts with today, when a jetliner will remain in production for decades with minor 'tweaks' to produce new versions of the same basic design. And, in its time, the 707's lead was unassailable. The primitive Russian jet airliners of the time were good, as long as only minimal profits were required, and the VC10 was

unmatched from short runways or in hot-and-high conditions, but it was assumed (wrongly, as it now transpires) that operating costs would be higher than those of the 707. Convair's 880 and 990 were plagued by a host of technical and industrial problems. But the Boeing 707 did not succeed only by default, since it competed directly with the DC-8, which was an excellent aircraft in every respect.

Launch customer for the commercial Boeing 707 (originally known as the Jet Stratoliner) was Pan Am, an airline which then amounted to America's 'flag-carrier'. This was thus a useful and high-profile order for Boeing. Series 100s were also purchased by American, Continental, TWA and Western. QANTAS ordered a

Above: The original 367-80, seen here with a KC-97, marks a milestone in American aviation history and has, accordingly, been honoured with a place in the National Air and Space Museum.

Top: During the mid-1960s, Flying Tiger leased four -300Cs from Aer Lingus, El Al and Caledonian for short periods, using them as cargo aircraft in North America.

shortened version for long-range use, with provision for a streamlined engine ferry pod under the port wingroot. Some basic 707-100s were delivered with the turbofan engines

associated with the Model 720, and with that aircraft's increased-span tail, and Krüger flaps on the leading edge and wingroot. These aircraft were operated by American and TWA, and

Below: N709PA was the third 707 delivered to Pan Am, which was instrumental in the continued development of the aircraft.

Above: Trans World Airlines put its first jet airliner, the Boeing 707, into service on domestic routes in March 1959 and retired the last in 1982. This short-fuselage -131B was delivered in March 1962 and was operated by TWA until April 1982, when it was traded back to Boeing.

QANTAS had some similarly modified 'short' 707s.

Boeing's willingness to provide modified, specialised variants for customers paid off with Braniff, which received five 707-227s in 1959. These aircraft had uprated JT4A-3 engines (equivalent to the military J75) to allow improved hot-and-high performance.

Boeing also developed a dedicated long-range, trans-oceanic version, the 707-300 Intercontinental, though many operators were already using the basic 707-100 on transatlantic services. The 707-300 had a lengthened fuselage, a wing of increased span and root-chord, an increased-span tail and JT4A-3 engines. The new variant had increased internal fuel capacity and could carry more passengers. Pan Am was the first customer for the 707-300, which became the most popular 707 model, although principally in the form of the improved -300B and -300C.

Further improvements and the fitting of JT3D turbofans resulted in the 707-300B, delivered to

Right: BOAC began to operate Conway-engined 707-400s from April 1960 and they initially flew the London to New York route. Later, they were used to develop new routes for the airline.

Aerolineas Argentinas, Air France, Air India, American, Avianca, El Al, Lufthansa, Malaysia, Northwest, Olympic, Pan Am, SAA, TAP and TWA. The 707-300C was essentially a -300B with a cargo door in the port forward fuselage. Customers for the -300C included Aer Lingus, Air France, Air India, Airlift International, American, BOAC, Braniff, British Airways, British Caledonian, British Eagle, China Airlines, Continental, Egypt Air, El Al, Ethiopian, Executive Jet, Flying Tiger, Iranair, Iraqi, Kuwait, Lufthansa, MEA, Northwest, Olympic, Pan Am, PIA, QANTAS, SAA, Saudi, Seaboard World, TWA, Varig, Wardair and World Airways.

The final major service variant was the 707-400, with Conway turbofan engines. These were actually the first turbofan-engined 707s and proved very successful in service, although only 37 were built. The aircraft were delivered

principally to BOAC, but others went to Cunard Eagle, Air India, Lufthansa, El Al and Varig.

When the original Model 367-80B prototype was finally retired to the National Air and Space Museum in 1972, it was designated (by the Smithsonian) as one of the 12 most significant aircraft designs of all time. It was then still the jetliner produced in the largest numbers, and very large numbers remained in use as the flagships of some of the world's major airlines, although the age of the Jumbo was by then beginning to dawn. The 707's production total was finally overtaken (by the 727) in 1973. The type remained in service with TWA and Pan Am until 1983, when a slow decline began. With tougher noise legislation coming into force in 1985, 707s operating in the USA had to be hush-kitted but, elsewhere, 707s retired by major

airlines were usually eagerly snapped up by smaller operators. Large numbers of fan-engined passenger 707s were broken up in the 1980s, with engines and wide-span tailplanes being donated to the KC-135 re-engining programme.

End of the line

Boeing never modernised the 707 or 720 in the way that Douglas did with the DC-8 and, as a result, the aircraft is now a less common sight today than its old rival. The 707 is now used almost exclusively in the freight role, or as a corporate transport. There are around 80 707s still operational, mainly operated in ones and twos, many of them based in Africa and the Middle East. A handful in passenger/VIP configuration are in corporate or government use. Some 707s were even hush-kitted as Comtran Q707s to meet Stage 2/Chapter 2 noise regulations. But time is now finally running out for the 707, which fails to meet the most stringent Stage 3/Chapter 3 noise regulations, and which is thus certain to disappear from service in the next few years. With the downturn in airline fortunes following 9/11, and with large numbers of more modern and more economical airliners already sitting in desert 'boneyards' (available at bargain prices), the 707's survival so far looks little short of miraculous.

Left: Originally a CIA 'front' organisation, Southern Air Transport began operating 707s from 1985 and continued to do so until 1992, when the type was retired. This particular aircraft was later sold on to Air Afrique and crashed while landing in Mali in 1996.

Variants

The Boeing 707 established Boeing's dynasty as 'plane-maker to the world'. It shrugged off competition from Britain's Comet and the DC-8 to spawn a family of similar-looking, but quite distinct variants over its 21-year production life.

Boeing Model 707-200

To provide improved take-off performance at high-altitude South American airports, Boeing produced just five examples of the JT4A-3 turbojet-powered 707 for Braniff Airways.

Boeing Model 387-80 prototype ('Dash 80')

On 15 July 1954, the age of Boeing jetliners arrived when the Model 387-80 prototype first flew at Renton, Washington. Also known as the 'Dash 80', the Model 387-80 was aimed chiefly at the US Air Force's emerging requirement for a jet transport/air-to-air tanker. Structurally, it was very different to the civil Model 707, but it set the pattern for all that followed. Here it is illustrated flying engine test duties.

Boeing Model 707-100 'Short Body'

Australia's QANTAS asked Boeing for a special version of the basic 707-100 to handle the extreme long-range requirements of its Sydney to London service. As a result, Boeing built seven short-fuselage 707-138s, which were 10 ft (3.05 m) shorter than the other 707-100s. The 707-138 was certified in June 1959. In 1961, the 707-138s built for QANTAS were replaced by six turbofan-powered 707-138Bs. The -138s all had the same maximum take-off weight as the standard -100s, but a reduced maximum landing weight.

Boeing Model 707-100

The initial production version of the 707, the Pratt & Whitney JT3C turbojet-powered 707-100, was chiefly intended for the US domestic market and had only marginal transatlantic capability. It was wider and longer than the Model 387-80 and had a greater wingspan. The 707-100B introduced more fuel-efficient JT3D-1/3B turbofans, and some of the airframe refinements developed by Boeing for the Model 720. A total of 56 -100s and 78 -100Bs was delivered up to 1969, when production switched to the definitive 707-300.

Boeing Model 707-300

Designed for trans-oceanic flights, the 'Intercontinental' 707-300 was larger than its predecessors. The fuselage was stretched by 6 ft 8 in (2.07 m) to 145 ft 6 in (44.37 m), wingspan was increased by 11 ft 7 in (3.53 m) and fuel capacity was increased to 21,200 US gallons (78552 litres). Basic -300s were powered by JT4A-11s and 69 were built.

Boeing Model 707-300B

The 707-300B was based on the -300 but featured a longer wing, an increased maximum take-off weight (MTOW) and four 18,000-lb (80.1-kN) JT3D-3 turbofans. A total of 176 -300Bs was built, including a number of Advanced Series 300Bs (or -300BAs), which had three-segment leading-edge flaps. Some of these aircraft were built as 707-300BA-H with a further increased MTOW.

Boeing Model 707-300C (all-freight)

When the -300C Combi version of the 707 was produced, a few customers, such as American Airlines, opted for a pure freighter ('707-300F') variant which had most of the cabin windows blanked out, all passenger seating facilities removed, and a large (91-in x 134-in/231-cm x 340-cm) cargo door inserted in the port fuselage side.

Boeing Model 707-300C Combi

The 707-300C passenger/cargo convertible (Combi) variant of the -300B had a side-loading freight door in the forward fuselage with an associated Boeing-developed cargo loading system. A maximum of 215 passengers could be carried in the all-passenger configuration. A total of 337 -300Cs was built until 1979.

Boeing Model 707-400

The 707-400 was very similar to the early 707-300 series but was fitted with British Rolls-Royce Conway 508 turbojets, rated at 17,500 lb (77.84 kN). Only 37 Conway-powered 707s were built, even though they proved to be more economical to operate than the rival US turbojets. By the time the 707-400 appeared in 1960, turbojets were being replaced by far more cost-effective turbofans. 707-400s were operated by BOAC, Air India, El Al, VARIG and Lufthansa.

Boeing Model 707-700

This aircraft was used as a test-bed for the CFM56 turbofan developed by CFM International and SNECMA. The CFM56 was designed to have a much reduced fuel consumption and lower noise levels than any existing engine. It was planned that CFM56s would equip existing and new 707s, but the idea was later scrapped to avoid competing with the 757. However, CFM56s were used extensively on late model military 707s, E-3s and E-6s and for the USAF's KC-135R programme.

Boeing/McDonnell Douglas 717/MD-90

The MD-90 series was an ultimately unsuccessful attempt by McDonnell Douglas to further extend the life of the DC-9/MD-80 family. However, the smaller MD-95 survived the takeover by Boeing to be marketed as the Boeing 717.

Last of the MD line

Intended as an advanced-technology follow-on to the MD-80 series, the MD-90 was distinguished by the use of IAE V2500 turbofans, in place of the Pratt & Whitney JT8Ds that have powered every DC-9 and MD-80. The programme was launched in November 1989, with an order for 50 from Delta Air Lines plus 115 options (numbers that were soon revised downward). McDonnell Douglas decreed that the aircraft should be referred to as the MD-90, but when dealing with specific sub-types the hyphen was omitted. The baseline MD90-30 has an MD-80-type fuselage stretched by 4 ft 9 in (1.45 m), combined with the enlarged tail of the MD-87. It can carry a maximum of 172 passengers and is powered by V2525-D5 turbofans. A developed version of this aircraft, the MD90-30ER, was subsequently introduced with an order for two aircraft from Egypt's AMC Aviation. The first of these was delivered on 24 September 1997.

Above: Delta Air Lines was the launch customer for the MD-90 and currently operates 16 of the baseline -30 variant. The aircraft were delivered between February 1995 and December 1996.

Top: This Japan Air System MD-90 wears one of seven colourful paint schemes designed for the airline's fleet by the famous Japanese motion picture director, Akira Kurosawa.

Unbuilt variants

McDonnell Douglas also planned, but did not build, the MD90-50, an extended-range version of the -30 carrying fewer passengers but powered by more powerful V2528-D5 engines and the MD90-55, identical to the previous model, but with additional exits fitted for up to 187 passengers.

The first MD-90 flew on 22 February 1993 and two aircraft were engaged in the flight test programme that led to certification on 16 November 1994. Assembly of the first production example began at Long Beach in February 1994,

and the first aircraft was handed over to Delta on 24 February 1995. It entered service on 1 April. The first European MD-90 operator was SAS, which placed its first aircraft into service on 11 November 1996.

From April 1986 the Shanghai Aircraft Manufacturing Factory (SAMF) assembled MD-82s and MD-83s for the Chinese airline market and in 1992 SAMF and McDonnell Douglas announced the Trunkliner agreement, to develop the MD90-30T Trunkliner with dual main landing gear for operations from rough Chinese airfields. The terms of the deal were re-negotiated several times

Saudi Arabian operates the largest fleet of MD-90s, having received the last of its 29 examples in the spring of 2000. The aircraft are configured with 18 first-class and 103 economy seats.

Right: When it took over the MD-95 programme, Boeing predicted a 2,600-aircraft market for the 80- to 120- seat short-range airliner market over the next 20 years. Hopes that the 717 would capture a significant percentage of these sales proved unfounded.

and finally called for the delivery of 20 MD-90s from the US (beginning in 1996) along with 20 built in China. Construction of Chinese-built MD-90s began in 1995, but no deliveries were ever made.

Following the August 1997 acquisition of McDonnell Douglas by Boeing, Boeing announced in June 1998 that MD-90 production would cease in 2000. By early April 2000 MD-90 orders totalled 114. Current operators include, China Eastern Airlines (9), China Southern Airlines (13), Delta Air Lines (16), Japan Airlines Domestic (16), Saudia (29), SAS (8) and Uni Air (13).

Boeing 717

What we know today as the Boeing 717 actually began life at Long Beach as the McDonnell Douglas MD-95. The aircraft was announced by McAir in June 1994 after a long series of design studies for new 100 to 130-seat aircraft. The MD-95 was conceived as an MD-80 'shrink' (dubbed MD-87-105), powered by the MD-80's JT8D-200 engines, or perhaps Rolls-Royce Tays. The aircraft that emerged owed far more to the DC-9, using the wing and empennage

of the DC-9-34, the enlarged fin of the MD-87 and new-technology BMW Rolls-Royce BR700 turbofans. It was intended to assemble the MD-95 in China as part of McDonnell Douglas's MD90-30 Trunkliner programme, but this deal was never signed and, after several changes of mind, production reverted to the line at Long Beach, California.

After the August 1997 takeover, the historic family of Douglas airliners was rechristened as Boeing's and, in January 1998, the MD-95 became the Model 717. This decision was greeted with surprise as Boeing had already devoted the Model 717 designation to the huge C-135 family. The production version became the 717-200, with Boeing reserving the 717-100 designation for a possible future 85-seat version.

The 717 was aimed at the 100-seat 'regional' market, over routes of 1,500 miles (2414 km). Two versions were planned – the basic gross weight (BGW) and high gross weight (HGW) 717. McDonnell

Douglas struggled to find a launch customer but finally announced an order for 50, with 50 options, from Florida's ValuJet (now AirTran Airways), on 19 October 1995. By summer 2005 Boeing had accumulated just 169 orders for the aircraft. Against this background of sluggish demand, suggestions grew that Boeing would terminate the programme even from its earliest days. In fact, Boeing remained committed to the 717, reportedly studying closely the 85-seat 717-100X and 130-seat 717-300X concepts.

The first 717-200 was rolled out on 10 June 1998 and made its maiden flight on 2 September. Four aircraft were dedicated to the nine-month flight test programme. After joint US and European FAA/JAA certification AirTran took delivery of its first aircraft on 23 September 1999. The first European customer was Bavaria International Aircraft Company, a leasing firm. Bavaria took delivery of its first four aircraft on 29 December 1999. Its first

client was Greek start-up carrier Olympic Aviation, which received two aircraft on 7 January 2000. Bavaria's next customer was new Australian regional operator Impulse Airlines, which took delivery of two aircraft at the end of April 2000 amid plans to acquire three 717s from Bavaria and two from Irish-based Pembroke Capital. Pembroke also announced lease deals with Bangkok Airways (two aircraft) and accepted its first aircraft from Boeing in August 2000. TWA took delivery of its first Model 717 on 18 February 2000.

However, the hoped for increase in demand for the 717 never materialised, in spite of the quality of the airframe. Added to this, the type offered a passenger capacity uncomfortably close to Boeing's own Next Generation 737 and as such, in 2004 the company announced is decision to cease 717 production in 2005. Aircraft were being delivered as late as June 2005, but with the deletion of 14 orders, the line has closed.

Below: Low-cost airline AirTran was typical of the operators at which the 717 was aimed. In the summer of 1999 the 717 undertook a major tour of Europe, seen as a key market for the type.

Above: The 717's economy over short sectors influenced Hawaiian Air's decision to purchase 13 Series 200s for operating its inter-island services in the Hawaiian Islands.

Boeing 727
Seattle's trijet

This early Boeing 727-100 demonstrates the type's key features to good effect. The three rear-mounted engines are immediately obvious, but the aircraft also has its advanced leading-edge slats and flaps deflected.

Left: N7006U, a 727-122 (a designation often shortened to 727-22), was delivered to United Air Lines in November 1963. In a superb demonstration of the type's reliability and longevity, the aircraft remained with the airline until 1992, when it was sold and broken up for spares.

Boeing took significant components from its Model 707 and combined them with a trijet layout and an advanced high-lift wing to produce a market-leading short-/medium-haul airliner.

Well before the introduction of its Model 720, Boeing was engaged in the preliminary design of a short-/medium-range and medium-capacity airliner to suit the growing needs of the US domestic and inter-city markets on routes unsuitable for the 720. The intention was to produce a high-performance utility jet transport with low approach speeds and short-field properties, combined with independence from ground support services. The market for such an aircraft was certainly there, but as always the go-ahead for production was dependent on securing orders.

In addition to the needs of the US domestic market, there was also an opening for high-performance, medium-range air transports abroad. And here, noted Boeing, the new de Havilland DH.121 Trident, with its unique trijet configuration, promised to be a keen and determined contender. By the late 1950s, the commercial aviation market was on the upsurge; the cry was for extra seating capacity on aircraft plying high-density routes in the US and Europe. The old piston-engined DC-3, DC-6 and L-749, and the turboprop L-188 (although relatively new) were cheap to operate but too slow, while the Caravelle was too small.

Design of the Model 727, as the new type was designated, started in February 1956, and the parameters laid before Boeing's preliminary design group were exacting. Other companies, notably de Havilland, were vying for high-cruise Mach numbers to reduce seat-air mile costs. Boeing wanted this factor on its Model 727, but combined with short-field characteristics that required a high power/weight ratio and a highly adaptable and efficient wing.

Wing technology

The 727 wing design broached new horizons, and its unique system of flaps and slats allied with spoilers also became the format for the 747. The basic 727 wing was actually of routine design, but its high-lift and lift-dump devices most certainly were not. On the trailing edge of the wing, massive triple-slotted flaps were combined with four leading-edge slats on the outer two-thirds of the wing, and three Krüger leading-edge flaps on the inner portion. These were joined by seven spoilers on each upper wing surface which doubled as airbrakes and/or roll augmentation spoilers.

Taking shape

Allied to its excellent field performance, the 727 had lively performance and good fuel economy with the adoption of

Air France's second 727-228 was delivered in 1968. In recent years, stringent noise regulations have forced the retirement of many 727s. However, hush-kitting extended the service lives of many, including this aircraft, which went on to fly with UPS.

Right: Boeing's 727 test aircraft, including this 727-22, usually adopted house colours. Early on in the type's development this saw the application of the distinctive pale yellow (or cream) and brown scheme of the pioneering 'Dash-80'.

Below right: With the stretched 727-200, Boeing increased the 727's maximum passenger capacity to 189. Two fuselage plugs, each 10 ft (3 m) in length, were added to the 727-100 fuselage fore and aft of the wing to achieve the stretch.

the 14,000-lb st (62.2-kN) Pratt & Whitney JT8D-1 turbofan in August 1960. The fuselage upper portion was identical to that of the Model 707/720 series. In addition, much stress was laid upon independence of operation: the Model 727 needed nothing on the ground if a stop-go transit were required, having a Garrett-AiResearch GTC85 APU, an airstair and a ventral staircase to the rear. With a very high maximum landing weight, as a result of wing stressing and landing gear strength, the 727 could take on fuel at the originating station, fly several transits, and gain quick turnarounds and the on-schedule departures that are so vitally important. All these facets were built in during the course of very thorough research and design.

Construction go-ahead was given in August 1960, with Boeing acting on the good faith of United Air Lines and Eastern Airlines. In fact, it was not until 5 December 1960 that these operators placed their orders: 20 for United with another 20 on option, and 40 for Eastern.

At 11.33 (local) on 9 February 1963 the first flight was made from Renton, when Lew Wallick, Boeing's senior experimental test pilot, lifted N7001U off. N7001U weighed in at 130,000 lb (58968 kg) and flew for 2 hours

1 minute before Wallick put it down in 2,000 ft (610 m) on Paine Field's limited concrete. To the assembled press, Wallick said that, 'She behaved as expected, even better than expected in many respects.' Indeed, few problems cropped up during subsequent testing. The second Model 727 (N72700) flew on 12 March, and by the end of the month tour Model 727s were undergoing thorough flight trials from Paine, Seattle, Edwards AFB, Denver and Albuquerque. By mid-May

N7001U had completed 430 hours on flutter and structural damping tests up to Mach 0.9; N72700 had completed 320 hours on systems and braking; 180 hours on 727 No. 3, including handling high-g pull-ups, side-slipping and even barrel-rolls; while 313 hours had been completed in furnishing and air-conditioning on Model 727 No. 4. The order book was filling: 25 to American Air Lines, 40 to United, 10 to TWA, 12 to Lufthansa, and four to Australia's TAA and Ansett-ANA.

Left: With increased capacity came the need to provide additional escape exits. The 727-200 (illustrated) therefore introduced a second emergency exit over each wing.

Right: The facts that Lufthansa had adopted an all-Boeing policy at an early stage in its post-war incarnation, and that the carrier had become the first outside the US to operate the 727, were both major achievements for Boeing.

Success in service

Showing an economy of performance that exceeded the predictions of even Boeing's own engineers, the 727 dominated sales of medium-range airliners. Become the world's best selling jet airliner (until overtaken by the Boeing 737), the 727 finally went out of production in 1984 after 1,832 had been built.

Most of Alaska Airlines' fleet of 23 Advanced Boeing 727-200s were delivered second-hand in 1980-89. The aircraft were replaced in service by the even more successful Boeing 737-400 in the early 1990s.

Inset: The initial sales success of the 727 in the early 1960s to domestic customers such as TWA (seen here), Eastern, United and American provided the platform for its outstanding sales performance over the following two decades.

When FAA certification for the production Model 727-100 was received in December 1963, Boeing had already launched an aggressive sales campaign to clinch export orders ahead of its main contemporary rival, the Hawker Siddeley Trident 1.

Emphasising the aircraft's excellent fuel consumption and superior performance from hot-and-high airfields, the 727 embarked on a world tour in September 1963. By the time the aircraft returned to the US, domestic carrier Eastern Air Lines had placed a significant order, its services commencing in February 1964. Lufthansa's first 727-100 was rolled out in January 1964 and the first of its Europa-Jet scheduled services commenced on 16 April 1964.

The highly successful world tour began to bear fruit in 1964

Production of the Boeing 727 was undertaken at Boeing's Renton facility near Seattle, Washington. Production peaked between 1967 and 1968 when 315 aircraft were delivered. After a lull in the early 1970s, deliveries again reached over 100 per year during 1978-80.

Right: Small numbers of 727s found their way into military and government service. The Royal New Zealand Air Force operated two 727-22QCs.

Below: Iberia was the last major European operator of the 727. Its fleet of Advanced 727-200s was replaced by the Airbus A319/320/321 and Boeing 757.

with Japan Air Lines and All Nippon's decision to order the aircraft for their domestic routes. Both airlines initially favoured the Trident, but required the higher-capacity Trident 1F which was not scheduled for certification until 1966. With both airlines intending to start services in April of that year, the alternative of ordering the 727, which would be ready for delivery in October 1965, became increasingly attractive. The balance was tipped in the 727's favour by its performance from Osaka's short runway. In temperatures exceeding 95°F (35°C), the Trident was unable to operate with an economic load, while the 727 was able to carry a full complement of passengers. In July 1964 JAL signed a deal for six Model 727-100s and All Nippon soon followed suit.

By mid-1964, 727 orders were increasing, but were still 100 short of the break-even mark. To capitalise on an expanding air

Although now rarely seen at European or Asian airports, the 727 remains in limited use with smaller operators in the United States. Champion Air currently operates the Model 727-200 Advanced on domestic routes.

cargo market therefore, Boeing introduced the 727-100C convertible cargo/passenger derivative in July 1964, able to carry 30,000-lb (13608-kg) loads over a distance of 1,900 miles (3058 km). The aircraft could fly passengers by day and freight by night, something that was particularly attractive to US domestic customers. Northwest Orient signed as the first customer and 727 orders quickly surged past the 300 mark.

Many European and Far East airlines had now placed orders and by April 1967 the 727 was

the most widely used jet airliner in service. Later 727-100 versions included the 727-100QC with palletised passenger seats and galleys and advanced cargo-loading technology, and the 727-100 Business Jet.

New variant

In November 1967 certification was granted to a stretched 727. Capable of carrying up to 189 passengers, the 727-200 became the standard model for the remainder of the production run, with over 1,000 being produced. Featuring JT8D-9s or uprated JT8D-11s or -15s, the 727-200 featured a 10-ft (3.05-m) fuselage extension and localised structural strengthening to cope with its higher weights.

Boeing's grip on the medium-haul market was strengthened in the early 1970s with the introduction of the 727-200 Advanced which, with increased fuel capacity and weight and extended range, continued the outstanding sales success into the early 1980s.

In the late 1970s the availability of a new generation of efficient turbofans prompted Boeing to start designing a 727 replacement. By this time the aircraft had become the best-selling jet airliner of all time and had established Boeing's position as the world's premier airliner manufacturer.

The last of 1,832 Model 727s, a 727-200F freighter, was delivered to Federal Express in August 1984.

Boeing 737
Introduction

The 737 capitalised on design work done on the 707/727, retaining the same cabin cross-section. As shown here by the prototype, the original 737-100 model featured a short fuselage.

Boeing's superlative 737 is by far the world's best-selling airliner. Indeed, it seems unlikely ever to lose this title, since the most recent incarnations of the 1960s-vintage basic design utilise the very latest in airframe, avionics and engine design, to propel the 737 into the next century.

On Friday 19 February 1965, Boeing's international sales manager was biting his fingernails as he sat in an outer office at the headquarters of Lufthansa. He was hoping that the carrier would place an order that would launch a brand-new jetliner, the Model 737. Boeing was not yet committed to building it, but was already losing out to its competitors in the important short-/medium-range airliner market, and knew that it must go ahead with the programme if its own airliner business was to survive.

Many of the major airlines had already bought small twinjets, although Eastern, United and Lufthansa had yet to choose their aircraft. Boeing needed all three airlines to order 737s before it could invest in the type. It was therefore the worst possible news when Boeing's

chief executive announced that Eastern was buying the DC-9.

Pressing on regardless

In spite of Eastern Airlines' decision, Boeing decided to continue with development of the 737. It was launching the aircraft with an order for just 21 machines from a foreign airline!

However, despite its verbal promise to Lufthansa, Boeing did not commit itself to the 737 on the strength of that single order. Instead, it strove to present the best possible case to United, trying to overcome the late arrival of the first 737s by offering large numbers of 727s on almost giveaway lease terms to bridge the gap.

Boeing went through a second nail-biting day on 5 April 1965. United held a board meeting, after which the airline gave a press conference. It was going along with Boeing's big 727 deal

and, on top of that, was buying 40 of the new 737s, as well as signing options for another 30.

The 737 was to be in the 100-seat class, which saved weight compared to its rivals – the rear-engined DC-9, Caravelle and BAC One-Eleven – by putting the engines under the wings. Boeing saved money and attempted to keep the unit cost down by using the same cabin cross-section as on the 707 and 727. From that instant, Boeing worked flat out on the small twinjet. Even coming from behind, Boeing hoped that the aircraft's qualities would eventually bring about enough orders for the programme to show a profit. Nobody ever expected the 737

to become the best-selling airliner in history, with total sales exceeding 5,750 and continuing to rise.

As far as possible, Boeing made use of parts and experience from previous programmes, especially that of the 727. The fuselage, including the nose and cockpit, was almost identical, although it was much shorter and had a totally different tail section. United, in fact, had ordered a slightly longer aircraft than Lufthansa, and Boeing designated this as the 737-200. Its cabin was normally configured to seat 115 passengers in triple seats on each side of the central aisle. Lufthansa's Dash-100 seated 103.

Inauspicious start

Although the new product obviously had many good features, its early history was not auspicious. From the first flight, on 9 April 1967, measured drag was significantly higher than predicted. This was the opposite of what had happened with the 727, and it hurt both Boeing's pride and the 737's image. The cures, which took months, included a new nacelle/wing

As the 737's popularity grew, it found purchasers all over the world. Sales were initially slow, but the brilliance of the design inevitably won through.

As the single most popular airliner type, the 737 has been, or continues to be, a part of the majority of airline inventories. It also serves with a number of government and military units.

All three members of the 737-300/-400/-500 family fly in formation. The -400 (top) is the largest of the three, while the -300 (lower) and -500 (leading) have smaller capacities.

fairing and vortex generators on the rear fuselage. It was also found that the engine thrust reversers were not very effective, and the cure here was to extend the jetpipes well aft of the wing, and use target buckets hinged straight up and down.

Not least of the problems was the Air Line Pilots' Association's (ALPA) totally negative ruling that the 737 must have a three-man crew, adding 50 per cent to crew costs by comparison with the rival McDonnell Douglas DC-9. Eventually, ALPA let sense

prevail, but not until it had lost Boeing several potential sales.

Advanced 737

United's 737-200 immediately became the standard aircraft. Apart from those ordered by Lufthansa, only seven more 737-100s were sold. The 737-200 gradually began to pick up a number of small orders, although the process was a slow one, and five years had elapsed before the superiority of the Boeing product had been realised and had allowed Boeing

to start matching the DC-9 on equal terms. This gradual penetration into the marketplace was aided by the introduction of 737-200C convertible passenger/cargo and 737-200QC quick-change convertible models. In addition, a 'gravel kit' was offered, allowing operations from semi-prepared runways.

The major change, however, came with the 737-200 Advanced. The new machine featured a remarkable 81 per cent increase in fuel capacity, largely thanks to the higher take-off weights made possible by the increased power of its uprated JT8D turbofans Weight-saving graphite composite control surfaces were also installed, along with a new interior, offering seating for 130 passengers, while improved flaps and brakes meant that the aircraft could use smaller airports. With the Advanced 737, Boeing began

to win almost every competition with the DC-9.

However, the 737 was beginning to suffer from having outdated engines. This became particularly apparent when Boeing produced an even longer-ranged High Gross Weight version. It was clear that major changes had to be made.

CFM56 power

Boeing looked to the next-generation CFM International CFM56 turbofan, mounted in a new nacelle held ahead of the wing. The new engine offered not only increased thrust, but also improved fuel economy, enabling Boeing to produce the even more successful 737-300/-400/-500 family. Responsible for 1,936 737 sales, this series has now made way for the next-generation 737-600/-700/-800/-900, which seem set to extend the stunning success of the Boeing 737 well into the 21st century.

A key feature of the Next Generation 737 is its all-glass cockpit. Modern avionics improve economy and safety.

Below: With the first-generation 737 Higher Gross Weight version and the 737-400 (illustrated), Boeing moved its short-ranged 737 into the medium-haul sector.

737 Development
Building the 'baby'

Boeing was a late-comer to the small medium-range jet airliner market and the success of its first design, the 737, was once far from assured. Despite its initial troubles, however, the 737 went on to be the best-selling jet airliner in history.

Studies of what would today be termed a 'regional airliner' had begun at Boeing in 1962, but it was not until November 1964 that the 737 emerged as a firm project. At that time, Boeing designers had conceived an aircraft approximately 85 ft (25.90 m) in length, with a wingspan of 75 ft (22.86 m). Versions of the JT8D engine were slated to power the new aircraft, which would have a maximum take-of weight of 79,000 lb (35834 kg). Adopting a low-winged design with underwing engines allowed the airframe to be lighter, but crucially permitted many common parts and structures to be incorporated from the Model 727 production line.

The 737 had its engines fitted snugly against the wings, not in pods on pylons as on the 707

Indonesia continues to operate three 737-2X9 Surveillor maritime patrollers. They carry side-looking radar above their rear fuselages.

Lufthansa was the launch customer for the 737, initially ordering 21 Series 100 aircraft. The airline added a further 737-100, and later signed up for a batch of the definitive early-generation Series 200.

and the 747. This allowed the aircraft to be even lighter and also kept the cabin floor as close to the ground a possible. The 737 had a wider cabin than the DC-9 or One-Eleven. The design was undergoing constant revision and, under pressure from the market, began to grow in size. On 19 February 1965 the 737 received its formal go-ahead with a launch order from Germany's Lufthansa for 21 aircraft. This marked the first time that a Boeing programme had gone ahead without a firm commitment from a US airline. Lufthansa, already a 727 operator, had told Boeing that if it did not offer the 737 as a firm project, then the airline would buy the DC-9 instead.

Fuselage stretches

The aircraft that was delivered to Lufthansa became known as

the 737 Series 100 (737-100) and was larger than originally planned. It was 94 ft (28.65 m) long and had a maximum take-off weight of 97,000 lb (43999 kg). This growth, however, was not enough and to win the 737's next critical order, from United Airlines, the design had to change again. United demanded a longer version of the 737, with a 6-ft 6-in (2.01-m) fuselage stretch. This allowed the 737 to accommodate two extra rows of seats, and with these changes in place United ordered 40 aircraft in 1965, with options on another 30 machines.

This revised design was the 737-200 and it would prove to be the definitive 737 for the next 20 years. But before this aircraft could write itself into the history books, the 737 encountered some serious teething troubles. The prototype 737 made its first

flight on 9 April 1967 with first deliveries set for just nine months later. The aircraft proved to be much more 'draggy' in the air then its designers had anticipated, and the engine nacelle fairings had to be completely redesigned. A problem also arose with the thrust reversers, which were too close to the wing trailing edge, and so the rear of the engine nacelles had to be extended by 40 in (102 cm). These problems seriously affected the 737-100's sales and only 30 of this version were built. However, the 737's troubles had been cured by the time the 737-200 was ready for airline service.

The 737-200 was a far more economical version of the aircraft to operate – chiefly because of its improved passenger capacity, but also because of its higher fuel load and improved Pratt & Whitney JT8D-7 engines. The 737-200 could be powered by 14,500-lb (64.5-kN) JT8D-7/9As, 15,500-lb (69-kN)

Lufthansa ground crew load cargo 'igloos' into a 737-230C at Frankfurt. This versatile version had a side cargo door and could also be fitted with non-palletised seating for passenger operations.

Left: An option offered on the 737 was a kit for gravel strip operations. To prevent damage from debris thrown up by the nosewheel a retractable guard was added.

Above: Boeing's rough-field demonstrator is seen operating from a dirt strip high in the Andes.

Right: An important part of the rough-field modification kit was the addition of an air blower below the intake lip to reduce the amount of debris sucked up by the low-slung engine intake.

JT8D-9/-15/-15As or the 16,000-lb (71.2-kN) JT8D-17/-17A. This array of engines was required to cope with the 737's range of take-off weights which stretched from 100,000 lb (45360 kg) to 128,100 lb (58106 kg). With 115 passengers, a 737-200 had a typical range of 1,800 nm (2,066 miles; 3325 km).

After the first 280 aircraft had been delivered, Boeing introduced the 737-200 Advanced which became the main production version from May 1971 onwards. This aircraft had an aerodynamically refined wing with many changes made to the engine nacelle fairings, leading-edge, trailing-edge, slats and flaps. The first 737-200 Advanced first flew on 15 April 1971 and it was this version which took the lion's share of 737-200 sales.

Boeing built a military version of the 737-200 Advanced, the T-43A, which served with the USAF primarily as a navigation trainer. These distinctive aircraft had only nine cabin windows and two cabin doors. They had a strengthened floor to carry the required avionics consoles and view ports in the cabin roof for sextant alignment/astro navigation training. A total of 19 aircraft was delivered between 1973 and 1974 and several were later adapted to serve as VIP and staff transports.

Another military development of the 737-200 was a maritime patrol/surveillance version fitted with a Motorola SLAMMR (side-looking airborne multi-mission radar), which was announced in 1981. Three of these aircraft were delivered to Indonesia in 1982/1983.

Rough-field operation

Boeing also developed a rough-field kit for the 737, allowing the aircraft to operate from unpaved runways. On these aircraft, the underfuselage surface was given a protective coating to reduce gravel damage and the antennas were all strengthened to avoid being broken off. The landing gear and flap sections were also given reinforced protection and the main landing gear tyres were increased in size. A deflector plate was fitted to the nose gear, which did not retract into the wheel well but remained outside, flush with the fuselage. An air blower was fixed to the front of each engine inlet, to bleed off engine pressure and to reduce the chances of debris being sucked into the (low-slung) engines. This kit was fitted by several 737 operators, particularly in Africa and Alaska.

Cargo versions of the 737-200 were also developed by Boeing, allowing the aircraft to be operated in all-freight or Combi (with passengers and freight on the same deck) layouts. An 84.5-in x 134-in (214.6-cm x 340-cm) cargo door was fitted to the front forward fuselage and the aircraft was given a reinforced floor, with cargo-handling equipment, restraint netting, etc. Two versions were offered, the 737-220C which used conventional non-palletised seats (taking approximately 5.7 man-hours to convert from freighter to passenger configuration), and the 'quick change' 737-200QC with palletised seating that could be removed/refitted in just 0.92 man-hours.

Canada's Pacific Western flew this aircraft, a 737-275 Advanced delivered in 1982, as part of its large domestic fleet. The aircraft is now with Air Canada.

Operational history

The 737 became an airline workhorse during the 1970s and 1980s. The basic aircraft changed little over its service life and a large fleet of 737-200s is still in everyday use around the world.

Top: Aer Lingus was the third European customer for the Boeing 737, receiving this, its first example, on 28 March 1969. The airline slowly acquired a sizeable fleet, finding the type ideal for its major Dublin-London route.

Lufthansa launched the 737 programme on 19 February 1965, acquiring the largest fleet of 737-100s. Lufthansa placed a follow-on order for three aircraft in August 1967, but only one of these was ever delivered. Further 737-100 customers included Colombia's Avianca (two ordered in January 1967) and Malaysia-Singapore Airlines (five ordered in May 1967). An order for two aircraft from Mexicana was cancelled. The last 737-100 (of 30 built) was delivered to MSA on 31 October 1969. Most of these aircraft soldiered on, if not with their original owners, into the 1990s – though the bulk of them have now been retired. The very first prototype 737 was acquired by NASA in 1973 and remained in service with NASA until September 1997, when it was donated to the Seattle Museum of Flight.

Soon after the launch of the 737, Boeing had gathered 86 orders – chiefly for the much-improved 737-200. The first 737-200, a 737-222 destined for United Airlines, flew on 8 August 1967. FAA type certification was awarded on 21 December 1967, only a week after the 737-100, and the first 737-200 entered service on 24 April 1968. This aircraft remained in daily use with United until it was withdrawn in 1996. The first European customer for the 737-200 was Braathens SAFE which took delivery of its first 737-205 on 31 December 1968, followed closely by Aer Lingus in March 1969.

Three-person crew

The Boeing 737 was initially hit by a US pilot's union ruling that dictated the aircraft had to be flown by a crew of three – even though the DC-9 had already been accepted as a two-crew aircraft. This badly affected sales in the American market and Boeing was also beaten to several important European orders by Douglas and the DC-9. By the early 1970s Boeing was on the verge of a major crisis as the massive investment it had made in the 747 had yet to be repaid. Neither were its other aircraft doing as well as it expected – in 1972 just 14 737s were sold. In later years the aircraft became a consistent seller but only in moderate numbers – approximately 40 aircraft per year were sold until the late 1970s. In 1978, however, the potential of the US market was unleashed when the laws governing the US airline scene were changed and the market was 'deregulated'. This made it

much easier for smaller airlines to expand and for new airlines to be established. The 737 was ideal for this market. A total of 145 Boeing 737 orders was won that year, from airlines such as USAir, Southwest and Frontier, and from British Airways and Lufthansa which began to replace their existing medium-haul fleets with the 737-200. From then on, the 737, 'Boeing's baby', became a consistent seller and established itself as the best-selling airliner of all time.

A total of 249 basic model 737-200s was built before the 737-200 Advanced was introduced (a 737-281 for ANA), in May 1971. The 737-200 remained largely unchanged from then until early 1984 when Boeing began to integrate composite materials into its structure to save weight. The last 737-200 was ordered by the (then) Chinese state airline CAAC, in December 1987 and was delivered on 2 August. In all, a total of 865 Advanced 737-200s was built, bringing the total of JT8D-powered 737s built

Apart from Lufthansa, only Avianca and MSA bought short-body Series 100s from new. Both Avianca aircraft were delivered in November 1968, but served only briefly before being sold to the Luftwaffe in 1971.

Norwegian operator Braathens SAFE was the first 737-200 customer in Europe. The type later became a common sight on the continent as large numbers were adopted by British Airways, Air France, Lufthansa and numerous smaller airlines.

to 1,125. By that time the next-generation of CFM56-powered 737s had been introduced and, as a result, the 737 exceeded the Boeing 727's record sales figure of 1,832 aircraft in June 1987.

Today, a large number of 737-200s remains in service, the type's low acquisition price and affordable operating costs, coupled with a generally excellent track record makes it a desirable aircraft, but the biggest

obstacles to 737-200 operations are its noisy JT8D engines.

Most existing 737-200s were built with the 'quiet' nacelle, but none meets current noise requirements without the addition of hushkits. Several firms offer JT8D hushkits for the 737-200 and hush-kitted aircraft are in service with several operators. The availability of second-hand 737-300s and 737-400s made and -200 re-

engining effort unlikely. In 1991 and 1994 two unexplained crashes shook the confidence of the Boeing 737 community and concerns were expressed about the possibility of uncommanded rudder movements which may have fatally destabilised the aircraft. In March 1997 the FAA issued a directive ordering

modifications to be made to the rudder power-control units of all in-service 737-200s. Boeing was given just two years to make these changes, a schedule which the manufacturer announced it would meet. The cost of these repairs was estimated at $126 million, or about $50,000 per aircraft.

Below: Despite the major first order from United, US domestic sales of the 737 were slow in getting started. N310AU was the first 737-2B7 of a large order for USAir which began delivery in November 1982.

Boeing 737-200

Based in Texas at Dallas and Houston, SWAL has built up a huge fleet of Boeing 737s which it operates on low-cost economy operations across the southern United States. The airline operates only 737s, now with just Series 300s, 500s and 700s on strength.

N24SW
This aircraft was from SWAL's early batch of deliveries, first flying on 9 September 1974 and being delivered to the airline nine days later. Southwest Airlines began 737 operations in 1971.

Cabin configuration
In keeping with the low-cost fare strategy of the airline, Southwest's 737s are all configured in a single-class high-density seating arrangement. The passenger load for the Series 200 was the same as that for the 500 at 122; the Series 300 and 700 aircraft accommodate 137. In a standard two-class arrangement, as favoured by most scheduled operators, the capacity of the Series 200 falls to around 110 passengers.

Cockpit
Boeing capitalised on design work already completed for the 707/727 by using a similar front fuselage and cockpit for the 737. The 737 could be flown by two pilots only, with an optional position for a flight engineer.

Powerplant
Southwest's 737-2H4s were powered by the JT8D-9A, one of many powerplant options offered to cater for individual customer requirements.

Nacelles
Boeing mounted the engine nacelles directly under the wings, rather than on pylons. This reduced the required length of the landing gear, with a considerable saving in weight.

Boeing
737 Series 300/400/500

Building on the 'baby'

The best-selling airliner of all time was rejuvenated in the 1980s and fitted with the revolutionary and highly efficient CFM56 engine. Produced in three variants, the aircraft was a hit around the world.

Above: The first Series 737-300, appropriately registered N73700, made its maiden flight in February 1984. After 14 months of test and evaluation flights, the aircraft was delivered to US Air.

Top: An early export customer for the 737 Series 300 was Australian Airlines, which eventually acquired 16 737-376s. In October 1993 the airline became part of QANTAS.

The arrival of a new 737 variant allowed the 737-200 production line to close in the summer of 1988. This was the Series 300, which spawned variants to cover the short-/medium-range, low- to medium-density requirements.

By the late 1970s, it had become obvious to Boeing that to tackle the increasing problems of fuel economy and noise pollution would require the use of high-bypass ratio turbofans. However, at the time, the smallest new-technology engines were far too powerful for an airliner in the 737 class.

The answer lay in the CFM56, the first of a new breed of small fans in the 20,000-lb (89-kN) thrust class.

Engine experiments

The CFM56 was first used in 1979, when the CFM56-2 was picked to re-engine the DC-8-60 and this gave Boeing the confidence to begin work on the new 737 in early 1980. The resulting 737-300 retained about 70 per cent commonality with the Series 200, with minor wing improvements such as extended wingtips. The most radical feature was the lengthening of the fuselage by the addition of two plugs forward and aft of the wing. This allowed the new model to take advantage of the increase in power to provide additional passenger and baggage capacity. To cater for longitudinal stability problems, a dorsal fin fillet was added.

The first CFM56-3 engines caused something of a problem when installed on the prototype 737-300. There was insufficient ground clearance for the engines to be attached without modification. The problem was solved by moving all the engine accessories from underneath the engine to the sides, so that the nacelle need to be only as deep as the compressor blade. This solution gives a characteristic squashed shape to the nacelle.

On 24 February 1984, the first 737-300 flew. Certification was achieved on 14 November and by the 28th of the month, the first delivery was being made to USAir. Southwest Airlines flew the type's first revenue-earning service on 7 December. By 31 March 1990 orders covered 948 aircraft, of which 602 had been delivered. Many 737-200 operators, and not a few new ones, came to Boeing for the new aircraft. Douglas could only offer updated versions of the JT8D-powered MD-80 until the new-technology fan-powered MD-90 became available. Many of the US majors bought the 737-300 in huge quantities,

The Series 500 is of similar length to the original Series 200. The aircraft is particularly suited to lower-density, longer-distance services.

Left: Piedmont Airlines took delivery of the first 737-400 in September 1988. The airline's aircraft were configured to carry 146 passengers.

Below left: The 737 has competed for sales with Airbus' A320 series. The Series 400 has the largest capacity and was a direct rival of the lengthened version of the A320, the A321.

while across the globe influential majors, charter carriers and small national airlines alike adopted the type.

Modern cockpit

The two-person crew had the latest in avionics and systems to aid them. INS and Omega navigation was optional, and newer aircraft had a full electronic flight instrumentation system (EFIS). Another welcome option was Boeing's windshear detection and guidance system. Digital autothrottle was fitted as standard. With regulatory permission, the 737-300 can undertake extended-range operations over water or undeveloped land, being able to travel further than the statutory one-hour's flying time to the nearest airport.

With the 737-300 proving to be a great success, Boeing produced a family of variants offering different range/load capabilities. The first variant to be developed was the 737-400, a lengthened version offering greater capacity but with negligible reduction in range. The first details of this type were announced in June 1986; the first aircraft made its maiden flight on 19 February 1988.

The 737-400 is considerably longer than the Series 300, having

Right: Nowhere have second-generation 737s been more widely appreciated than in the inclusive tour charter section. Germania was attracted by the aircraft's unrivalled economy over medium-haul sectors.

Right: Formed in the late 1980s, South Korea's Asiana Airlines chose the Series 300 and 400 versions of the 737 to operate its domestic and regional short/medium-haul services.

a 6-ft (1.83-m) plug forward of the wing and a 4-ft (1.22-m) plug aft. To maintain performance, uprated CFM56-3B-2 (22,000-lb/97.86-kN thrust) or CFM56-3C (23,500-lb/104.5-kN thrust) engines are fitted. To cope with a raised maximum take-off weight the undercarriage and outer wings were beefed up and a tail bumper was fitted as standard. Internally, the 737-400 offers a typical mixed-class accommodation for 146 passengers, although high-density charter operators regularly carry 170. The FAA certification awarded on 2 September 1988 covers the aircraft for up to 188 passengers.

Piedmont Airlines was the launch customer, and it received its first aircraft on 15 September

1988. The airline was subsequently absorbed into the huge USAir concern, itself an early customer for the 737-400 and now part of US Airways. Sales were brisk, particularly among charter operators, which found the increased capacity ideal for their type of work. By 31 March 1990, orders stood at 224, but doubts were cast over the new aircraft and its engines after a CFM56-3C-engined 737-400 of British Midland crashed while attempting an emergency landing at East Midlands Airport in England, but despite a brief grounding, the aircraft were soon plying their trade again.

Further development of the Series 400 resulted in an

increased-weight version, with revised avionics, increased fuel capacity and local strengthening. Power came from further uprated CFM56-3C-1 engines of 25,000-lb (111.2-kN) thrust.

To complete its new-technology family of 737s, Boeing needed an aircraft of the same capacity as the original Series 200. Originally known as the 737-1000, this was announced on 20 May 1987 as the 737-500. Combining the features of the 737-300 and -400, the -500 has a reduced length of 101 ft 9 in (31 m), comparing with that of the 737-200 of 100 ft 2 in (30.53 m). Accommodation is for 108-132 passengers.

Power comes from the CFM56-3B-1 of 20,000-lb (88.97-kN) thrust, or the same engine derated to 18,500-lb (82.29-kN) thrust, depending on customer preference. With auxiliary fuel tanks, a 737-500 with 108 passengers has a still-air range of 3,450 miles (5552 km), making it easily the longest-legged of the family.

With the development of its Next Generation 737s, Boeing closed what now became 737 Classic production in 2000.

Second generation today

VARIG of Brazil has a large fleet of Boeing 737s, including 25 Series 300s. The reliability and economy of the second-generation 737 persuaded the airline to purchase Next-Generation Series 800s.

The only replacement for the 737 turned out to be another 737. The trio of 737-300, 737-400 and 737-500 dominated the market throughout the 1980s and well into the 1990s. As their place has been taken by the Next-Generation 737s, so Boeing has come to call the -300, -400 and -500 the '737 Classics'.

Virgin launched its Express subsidiary to link its North American passengers with European destinations. It operated 737-300s for a number of years in the 1990s before relaunching its short-haul routes as holiday airline Virgin Sun.

In an era of US airline deregulation, Boeing was faced with rising customer demand for an improved small airliner to take the place of older 737s and the 727. Both types were becoming less economical to operate and faced tougher international noise and environmental regulations. There was also the threat of Europe's Airbus A320, which promised a quantum leap in technology. Thus a new generation of 737 was developed. The 737-300 programme was launched in March 1981, with orders for 10 each from Southwest Airlines and USAir. The 737-300 also borrowed the 757-200's interior design, which included large enclosed overhead bins, galleys and lavatories located fore and aft, and a wider cabin.

First deliveries of the new 737 went to USAir, followed by aircraft for Southwest Airlines. Southwest was the first to put its new 737-300s into revenue service, on services from Dallas and Houston. The UK CAA awarded type certification on 29 January 1985, the same day that Orion Airways became the first non-US operator. During 1981 and 1982 orders for the 737-300 were almost non-existent, but they accelerated rapidly in 1983 and 1984. A total of 1,061 737-300s was delivered from 1981 to 1999., the last in December 1999.

Boeing 737-400

In December 1985 Boeing decided to offer a 737 with a fuselage stretch that would add three more seat rows. The 737-400 was formally launched in June 1986, with an order for 25 (with 30 options) from Piedmont Airlines. A total of 486 737-400s was ordered over the type's 12-year production period from 1986 to 1998. The last 737-400 was delivered in February 2000.

Boeing 737-500

The Boeing 737-500 was launched on 20 May 1987 with an order for 38 aircraft from Southwest Airlines. The 737-500 was designed as a replacement for the 737-200, that incorporated the newer technologies of the 737-300 and -400. The aircraft seats between 108 and 138

The Series 400 has the largest 737 Classic capacity. LOT has six examples, which are configured to carry 147 passengers in a two-class layout.

The second-generation Model 737s have proved popular with leasing companies. One such organisation, Sailplane Leasing, provided the Russian carrier Aeroflot with 10 Bermudan-registered 737-4MOs, which were used on European routes.

passengers depending on seating layout.

Advanced technology

Significant technology developed for the 757 and 767 was incorporated into the 737-500. This included the wing leading-edge design for aerodynamic efficiency; lightweight advanced composites on flight control surfaces, aerodynamic fairings and engine cowlings; and weight-saving aluminium alloy wing skins. A fully integrated flight management system (FMS) provides automatic control and guidance of the aircraft. With optional equipment, the FMS makes Category IIIA automatic landings possible. The same EFIS cockpit is fitted to the -500 as is found on the -300 and -400, allowing a common crew type rating across all three versions.

The 737-500 also introduced Boeing's windshear detection system. Windshear is caused by a violent downburst of air that changes speed and direction as it strikes the ground. The system alerts flight crews to windshear and provides flight-path guidance.

The first 737-500 rolled out of the Renton plant on 3 June 1989; the maiden flight came on 30 June 1989. The 737-500 received its FAA certification on 12 February 1990 and the first delivery was made to Southwest on 2 March 1990. On 15 February 1991 a 737-500 for Lufthansa became the 2,000th 737 to be delivered and it was also Lufthansa's 100th 737. By June 1999 all 389 737-500s ordered had been delivered.

The largest operator of the 737-300 is Southwest Airlines – a company that has built its phenomenal success entirely around the Boeing 737. Southwest currently has a fleet of 194 737-300s, plus 25 737-500s (and 210 737-700s). Indeed, Southwest was the launch customer for the Next-Generation 737. USAir (which, renamed as US Airways after it absorbed Piedmont, became the 737-300 launch customer alongside Southwest) is another substantial 737 operator, with a fleet of 67 737-300s and 45 737-400s. United Airlines is yet another important customer, with a mix of 35 737-500s and 76 737-300s. Delta also has a small fleet of 737-300s (although it still has a sizeable fleet of active 737-200s). The Classic 737 family fitted admirably into the US hub-and-spoke concept of airline operations. The range of different aircraft sizes, all with a common crew type rating and

Left: British Airways has long been a staunch supporter of Boeing designs and has operated -200, -300, -400 and -500 (illustrated) versions of the 737.

essentially the same technical specification, allowed operators to mix and match aircraft to routes, depending on load and frequency.

European Classics

The Classic 737s also sold well to existing 737 operators in Europe, with airlines like Lufthansa, Aer Lingus, Air France and British Airways placing the family into service. The 737-400, in particular, found a valuable niche market in Europe as its mix of long range and high capacity appealed to IT holiday charter airlines. Europe was also an important market for the 'baby' 737-500. The launch customer for the 737-500 was Norway's Braathens SAFE, even though the first actual deliveries went to Southwest. In 1990, when it took delivery of its first 737-500, Ireland's Aer Lingus was the first airline in the world to have all three variants in service at the same time. Europe also saw the end of the Classics when, on 28 February 2000, the last two 737-400s were delivered to CSA Czech Airlines. These aircraft were the last of the Classic 737s to roll off the Renton production line. In all, a grand total of 1,936 examples of the Classic 737-300, -400 and -500 aircraft were built.

Left: Configured to carry 121 passengers, Luxair's two 737-5C9s are named after famous chateaux in Luxembourg. This model of 737 allows the airline to operate to destinations which would be inaccessible to the Series 400 without refuelling.

Boeing's new generation of 737s has continued the unprecedented success of the world's favourite airliner. This example is a 737-600, originally known as the 737-500X, which is the smallest of the family.

Boeing
737-600/700/800/900

New generation

Faced with increasing competition from Europe's A320 family, Boeing took a long, hard look at its Classic 737. Instead of launching a whole new type, Boeing overhauled the basic design, making it more efficient and 'operator friendly'. The result was the Next-Generation 737, which looks a lot like its predecessors, but hides many changes inside.

Equivalent to the Classic 737-300, the Boeing 737-700 was the first of the new generation to be launched, and had attracted 1,030 orders by August 2005.

Keeping the basic fuselage sizes the same, in 1993 Boeing launched the 737-X programme. Three versions were initially on offer: the 737-500X, the 737-300X, and the 737-400X (a stretched version of the 146-seat 737-400). To further emphasise the difference between the Classic and Next-Generation 737s, or 737NGs, the new aircraft were all soon redesignated. The 737-500X became the 737-600, the 737-300X the 737-700 and the 737-400X the 737-800. In 1997 a fourth model, the 737-900, was added. This version is a further-stretched 737-800. The 737-600 – slightly larger than the 737-500 – is the smallest member of the family and can carry 110 to 132 passengers. The 737-700 can accommodate between 126 and 149 seats. The 737-800 can carry between 162 and 189 passengers. Finally, the 737-900 is capable of carrying 177 to 189 passengers. Though the 737-900 is longer than the -800, its seating capacity is limited by the number of emergency exits.

Boeing had several key aims for its 737NGs. The new aircraft had to have greater range, higher cruise speed, a (41,000 ft/ 12496 m) cruise capability, lower fuel burn, decreased emissions and noise, and reduced maintenance costs. In addition, the new models would offer flight deck commonality with earlier 737s and allow flight crews to maintain the same type ratings.

To achieve this, the 737NGs called for improved engines, with a new wing and several other aerodynamic refinements. They also needed a redesigned cabin and a modernised flight deck. They are powered by derivatives of the FADEC-equipped CFM56-7 turbofan. The CFM56-7 has a 10 per cent higher thrust capability than the CFM56-3C and to take additional advantage of the engine's increased thrust, the 737NG's vertical fin and horizontal stabiliser are larger.

The 737NGs incorporate a new, advanced-technology wing design with increased chord and span. This boosts fuel capacity and efficiency, which in turn extends range. Overall, the range of the Next-Generation 737s is approximately 3,300 nm (3,795 miles; 6111 km), giving a 737NG true US transcontinental reach. The design of the new 737s incorporates important

Tunisair is unusual in currently operating all three generations of Boeing's 'Babyjet'. The airline has already seven 737-600s (illustrated) and one 737-700 in service.

Below: A staunch supporter of Boeing designs, Air China selected the 737-800 thanks to its ability to carry almost 200 passengers combined with the economy of the CFM56-7B engine.

Above: Transavia Airlines is a low-cost Dutch operator, offering scheduled and charter services to leisure destinations. The airline currently has 18 737-800s in service.

interior improvements pioneered on the 777.

Baseline version

The 737-700 is the baseline 737NG and was the first of the family to be launched, on 19 January 1994, when Southwest Airlines signed an order for 63 aircraft. The first 737-700 was rolled out on 8 December 1996 and flew on 9 February 1997. FAA type approval was awarded on 7 November 1997. However, JAA approval was delayed until 19 February 1998. Southwest is the leading customer for the 737-700, with a total of 249 ordered. Other important 737-700 customers include Alaska Airlines, Continental Airlines, easyJet and Germania, alongside lessors ILFC, GE Capital and Bouillioun Aviation Services. A special version of the 737-700 (the 737-700IGW QC) has been developed for the US Navy as the C-40A Clipper. Fitted with a side cargo door and a combi interior, the C-40 is replacing the C-9 fleet. Eight have been delivered, with a ninth on order, and the USN has a requirement for up to 30 aircraft.

On 5 September 1994 the 737-800 was launched. The first 737-800 customer to identify itself was Hapag-Lloyd, which ordered an initial batch of 16. The first 737-800 made its maiden flight on 31 July 1997 and received its FAA type certification on 13 March 1998. JAA certification followed on 9 April. To date, the largest order for 737-800s has been placed by Ryanair, which has signed for 230. Other important customers include Air Algerie, Air Berlin, American Airlines, Continental Airlines, Delta, KLM, Olympic Airways, Transavia, THY plus GE Capital and ILFC. In addition, the 737-800 is the basis for the US Navy's 108 P-8A Multi-Mission Maritime Aircraft for service from 2013.

Scandinavian Airlines became the launch customer for the 737-600 on 15 March 1995, when it ordered 35 aircraft. The first 737-600 made its maiden flight on 22 January 1998 and SAS took delivery of its first example on 18 September. On 10 November 1997, Alaska Airlines became the launch customer for the Next-Generation 737-900, with an order for 10. Boeing has been toying with the launch of a higher-capacity 737-900X for sometime and a 30 June 2005 Lion Air order for 30 such aircraft, plus 30 options, will probably see the model developed.

Sales figures

Since programme launch, Boeing claims that the 737NG family has outsold all other aircraft in its market segment. The 737NGs have proved popular, but not universally so. Sales of the 737-600 have been disappointing, but discontinuation of the Boeing 717 may ease the problem. Current 737-600 orders stand at 73. The 737-900 has also been slow to win orders, with just 55 on order. By August 2005 total 737NG orders stood at 2,726.

Deliveries of the 737-900 began to launch customer Alaska Airlines in May 2001. The lengthened and strengthened fuselage can accommodate 177 passengers in a two-class layout.

Boeing Business Jet (BBJ)

The BBJ is an innovative offshoot of the 737NG with which Boeing has developed a new market niche. Together with engine supplier General Electric, Boeing launched the BBJ in July 1997 as a dedicated, large-capacity business jet with a 6,000-nm (6,900-mile; 11104-km) range. The 737-700BBJ (illustrated) combines the fuselage of the 737-700 with the strengthened wing and landing gear of the larger, heavier 737-800. Large blended winglets to further boost performance are available as a customer option. The BBJ can carry up to 68 passengers and is available in a wide range of interior fittings to suit the needs of all customers. The first aircraft was rolled out in September 1998, with GE as the launch customer. Boeing has also added a larger 737-800BBJ to its line up. Announced BBJ orders currently stand at 95.

Boeing 747

Introduction

One of the most familiar sights in modern civil aviation, the 'Jumbo Jet' helped to create a new era of mass-market long-distance air travel.

No sooner had the first long-range jets entered service in the early 1960s, than a boom in traffic and forecasts for continuing growth indicated a need for larger aircraft. The fact that airports and airspace were already congested suggested that increased flight frequency and better aircraft utilisation were no longer enough to meet future demand. While Douglas was able to stretch its DC-8 series, Boeing's 707 did not lend itself to a similar exercise. At the same time, both US manufacturers were competing with Lockheed to fulfil a USAF requirement for a large logistic transport, made possible by the availability of new high bypass-ratio turbofan engines.

In the event, both lost out to Lockheed's C-5A Galaxy in September 1965, and

Above: Pan Am and Boeing had already caused a stir by their bold decision to go ahead with the revolutionary 707, and the pair teamed up again to launch the 747. The airline received its first aircraft in 1969 and the 'Jumbo' was soon creating an impressive spectacle at airports around the world.

Top: With its eye-catching colour scheme, the CP Air-owned Empress of India (C-FCRA) stands out against the white of the Rockies. The aircraft is typical of the early 747s in that it displayed remarkable longevity and remained in service into the late 1990s.

Boeing never created a prototype 747. Instead, the original aircraft, a demonstrator, was rolled out on 30 September 1968 at Paine Field, Everett. The aircraft first flew the following February and has since remained Boeing-owned. The logo of each airline to have shown an interest in the 747 is displayed on the forward fuselage – a hint at the global success that was to come.

immediately switched to the commercial market in order to salvage something from the considerable design effort. While Douglas eventually produced the medium-capacity DC-10, Boeing decided to make a great leap into the unknown, taking its biggest step to date in the airliner market. It did, however, have the support of Pan Am, which had always been bolder than its contemporaries in setting the pace of airliner development. But early designs for a double-deck aircraft not

Below: This ANA 747-400D, with its unique paint scheme, is called Marine Jumbo. The scheme was designed by a 12 year-old Japanese girl who won a contest to commemorate ANA's carriage of its 500 millionth passenger. The -400D was developed to replace the high density 747SRs used on Japanese domestic routes.

Above: British Airways operates a large fleet of 747-400s, its 100 and 200B (illustrated) series aircraft having been retired. The 747 has proved immensely successful on the carrier's long-haul routes, which it now alongside the airline's twin-engined Boeing 777s.

much wider than the 707 found little favour with Pan Am and other potential customers; neither did a mid-wing, wide-body design with upper and lower cabin areas. The airlines felt that such an aircraft would pose serious problems for emergency evacuation, and was virtually impossible to use as a convertible passenger/freighter.

The final design

After experimenting with some 50 double-deck design concepts, Boeing ceded to the airlines' concerns and came up with a new low-wing design with four wing-mounted engines, and based on a single deck. It provided seating (nine to 10 abreast) for up to 380 passengers. Below the cabin floor, there was plenty of room for cargo, and the main cabin could be converted to an all-

The latest production version of the Boeing 747, the -400 is a greatly improved development of the -300, with reduced operating costs, increased range and significant weight reductions. The Series 400 also introduces an all-glass, two-crew cockpit.

freighter configuration, with a hinged nose option for ease of loading. Boeing, however, kept an upper storey for the cockpit, and a lounge reached via a spiral staircase. This parabolic frontal section was faired down gradually to the circular cross-section, streamlining the unique appearance of the big Boeing. Pratt & Whitney was tasked to produce a powerplant for the 747, capable of generating a thrust of more than 40,000 lb (178 kN). The result was the JTD9 high bypass-ratio turbofan, then the most powerful jet engine in the world.

Armed with this new design, Boeing went back to the airlines in January 1966. This time, the reception was much more

favourable and, on 13 April 1966, Pan Am placed an order for 25 aircraft, including two all-cargo machines. Although Boeing had pointed out to Pan Am that it would need further orders from other airlines before firmly committing itself to the programme, its confidence in the market potential of the 'Jumbo Jet', as it was soon dubbed, was growing by the minute. It immediately began construction of an entirely new factory at Everett, and production proceeded at a bewildering pace, breaking all previous records. Boeing's commitment was soon translated into more orders and, within a year, around 20 major airlines had signed for more than one hundred 747s.

The modern 747

Since then, the 747 has gone from strength to strength. It now flies with airlines all over the world and carries thousands of passengers every day. The aircraft comes in many different civil versions which vary from the Combi to the extra long-range LR series, used by Japan Air Lines. The 747 has also attracted the attention of the military and there are several further variants, such as the E-4 series, which operate in the communications, transport and refuelling roles. A 747-400, armed with an anti-missile laser and designated YAL-1A, is also being developed in the US. An even more radical use for the 747 is NASA's ferry aircraft which carries the Space Shuttle Orbiter.

Accompanied by Boeing's F-86 Sabre chaseplane, which adds a useful sense of scale, the first 747-100 embarks on the type's maiden flight. The undercarriage remained extended throughout.

'Jumbo' shapes up

Showing great courage and foresight, Boeing forged ahead with probably the most radical jetliner in history, creating the first of the wide-bodies and revolutionising air transport in the process.

Boeing finalised its 747 design with a flight deck placed above the ceiling of the passenger deck, forming a slight blister above the nose and extended to the rear in an upper deck for, typically, 32 passengers. The main deck could seat up to 500 passengers in high-density, 10-abreast seating (3+4+3), but 350 was judged a more likely number, with an ultra-luxurious first-class section (seating passengers in pairs along the sides of the nose) extending right up to the radar filling the tip of the nose.

Boeing went for a high cruising speed, with the Model 747 adopting an advanced design of wing with the exceptional sweepback angle of 37° at 25 per cent chord. The leading edge was given an ambitious high-lift system, with three sections of Krüger flap hinged down from the undersurface of the wing inboard of the inner

engines, five sections of novel variable-camber flap between the engines, and five more sections between the outer engines and the tip on each side. The variable-camber flaps resembled traditional slats, but comprised flexible skins carried on pivoted links in such a way that, as they were hydraulically extended ahead of and below the leading edge, they arched into a curve to give maximum control of the airflow at high angles. On the trailing edge were placed enormous triple-slotted flaps, with each section running on steel tracks with prominent fairings projecting behind the trailing edge. Above the wing on each side were added six sections of aluminium honeycomb spoiler, four outboard for control in flight (augmenting the roll power of the conventional trailing-edge low-speed ailerons) and two ground spoilers inboard to

destroy lift after landing and thus increase braking power. High-speed ailerons were added at the trailing edge behind the inboard engines where the flaps could not be used.

Unprecedented scale

Although the engine installation looked conventional, being arranged on four widely separated wing pylons, it was on a scale never before seen except

on the military C-5A. In fact, Boeing picked the losing engine supplier in the C-5A engine competition, Pratt & Whitney, whose JT9D was offered as a robust and reliable turbofan of the new high-bypass-ratio type with a thrust of 41,000 lb (182 kN). Extremely difficult engineering problems had to be solved in hanging the engines, in arranging a fan-duct reverse and hot-stream spoiler, and in reducing drag.

Another tough engineering problem was the landing gear, eventually solved by using four four-wheel main-gear bogies, two of them on tall inward-retracting legs pivoted to the wings and the other pair on

Boeing's 747 manufacturing facility was built at Everett, just north of Seattle. Building work on the forested site began in spring 1966 and the first 747 was rolled out in September 1968.

Both the JT9D and CF6 (illustrated) turbofans were tested beneath the wing of a B-52. The problems later encountered when the JT9D was installed on the 747 failed to show up, however.

Even on its first flight, the 'Jumbo', appropriately registered N7470, was proudly displaying the symbols of the 28 airlines which had signed up for the 747.

forward-retracting units pivoted to the fuselage, the four retracted bogies lying together in a large bay amidships under the floor. All flight controls were hydraulically powered, the rudder and elevators being divided into equal-size halves, no tabs being used anywhere. The APU (auxiliary power unit) for ground air-conditioning and electric power was placed in the extreme tail of the fuselage.

Not only did Boeing have to build the 747, it also had to build a factory for this purpose, and the new plant at Everett, swiftly created in a 780-acre (316-ha) clearing in a forest, is the largest building (in cubic capacity) in the world. Together with many other programmes, Boeing's commitments were awesome, and employment in 1968 peaked at 105,000, compared with 60,000 in World War II. The risk on the Model 747 easily topped one billion dollars but, thankfully, orders kept rolling in, and when the first aircraft off the production line (Ship RA001) emerged from the new plant on 30 September 1968, a total of 158 orders had been gained from 26 airlines.

Engine snags

With so new and complex an aircraft it would have been surprising if there had been no snags, but in fact the difficulties, mainly centred on the engines, were prolonged. In crosswinds, the engines were difficult to start and ran roughly, and distortion (so-called ovalisation) of the casings caused blades to rub in a way that had not been apparent in more

than two years of ground testing and flight development using a B-52 Stratofortress. Pratt & Whitney had to devise a Y-shaped frame to hang the engine differently, and eventually produced a new version of the JT9D that avoided the problem, although the first flight was delayed until 9 February 1969. This aircraft was retained by Boeing for many development purposes. The first to be delivered was handed over to Pan American on 12 December 1969. It was this airline that, after an unprecedented amount of engineering and training effort, investment in new ground facilities and a last-minute engine problem, finally entered the Model 747 into service on the New York-London route on 22 January 1970.

Popularly called the 'Jumbo Jet', the Model 747 hit the headlines as well as the pockets of its customers and the world's airport authorities. For a while it appeared almost to be premature, because traffic did not grow as expected and load factor (proportion of seats filled) was often low. With great courage, Boeing continued production at maximum rate, and both the orders and the variants continued to grow. From the outset, Boeing had organised a vast manufacturing programme with major sections of airframe made by subcontractors: Northrop made the main fuselage sections, for example, and Fairchild Republic built the flaps, ailerons, slats and spoilers. With such large structures, exceptional precision was needed if there

were not to be problems when the parts all came together at Everett. One unusual assembly technique was to mount aircraft on air-cushion pads so that they could be easily moved in any direction across a smooth concrete floor.

Multiple variants

The initial model was the 747-100, which had achieved a total of 167 orders before Boeing introduced the much improved 747-200. The new variant offered greater fuel capacity and increased weights, with a succession of improved and more

powerful variants of the JT9D, along with General Electric CF6 and Rolls-Royce RB.211-524 turbofans being offered as customer options. Several models of the basic 747-200 were made available, including the 747-200B passenger aircraft, the -200B Combi with provision for the carriage of passengers and main deck cargo simultaneously, the -200C Convertible, for use in either the passenger or cargo role, and the -200F pure freighter.

Subsequently, in addition to further subvariants of the -200, Boeing produced the 747-300 with an extended upper passenger deck, and the short-fuselage, ultra-long range 747SP, before taking the 747 into the 1990s and beyond with the high-technology 747-400, which remains in production.

Inside the Everett assembly hall during the early 1980s, three 747-200s and a single SP are visible. As seen from their rudder colours, two of the -200s are destined for Alitalia and Air France, while the SP is for Qantas.

Boeing 747
Operational history

Remarkably, it was not until the mid-1990s that any challenge was offered to the 747's monopoly and, even then, Boeing responded with new winning designs.

Lufthansa was the earliest European operator of the 747, acquiring the first of its airliners and freighters in 1970. With the purchase of 747-400s, its fleet has now been considerably upgraded, with none of the original aircraft left in service.

The beginning of the spacious age – this is how launch customer Pan American Airways described the Boeing 747 on 22 January 1970. It was truly a momentous day in the annals of commercial air transport. Although minor engine problems had delayed service introduction by several weeks, and overheating had caused a further hold-up when the aircraft was readied for take-off, the 747-100, christened *Clipper Young America* by President

Nixon's wife Pat, left New York at 1.52 am and arrived at London's Heathrow Airport later that day. Pan Am took delivery of all its 25 aircraft (later orders brought the fleet to 60) during that year, and introduced the type on other transatlantic routes, as well as on trans-Pacific services. American Airlines followed suit in March 1970, and the first foreign operator was Lufthansa, putting the type on the Frankfurt-New York run in April. By the end of the year, 747s were also flying

with Air France, Alitalia, Continental, Delta, Japan Air Lines, National, Northwest Airlines and United.

The 747 quickly established itself on the world's long-haul routes, but the early years were anything but trouble-free, two aircraft being destroyed. The first accident with loss of life occurred on 20 November 1974, when a Lufthansa 747 crashed at Nairobi. Worse was to come on 27 March 1977, when 583 people died as 747s belonging to KLM and Pan Am collided on the ground at Tenerife in the Canary Islands.

Another problem was that the bottom had fallen out of the air transport market as a result of the oil crisis in 1973, forcing many airlines to cut back services

and put some 747s into storage. These misfortunes proved to be only a temporary hiccup, however, and had no lasting effect on the career of the 747.

747 upgrades

As early as June 1968, Boeing had announced the availability of a heavier model with improved payload and range which, as the 747-200B, entered passenger service with KLM in February 1971. More powerful Pratt & Whitney engines brought higher take-off weights, and CF6-50 and RB.211 engines also became available. KLM took delivery of the first GE-powered 747 Combi in October 1975, while British Airways ordered the Rolls-Royce powerplant for its 747-200Bs. The

Left: Northwest Airlines was the first airline to receive the 747-400 series. The airline was a natural recipient of the new aircraft, as much of its business is conducted across the Pacific, where the additional range of the -400 is useful.

Below: Pan Am and Boeing collaborated on a number of projects and the 747 represents their greatest success. Pan Am was the first airline to order the 747 and, even by that stage, had been intrinsically involved in the design.

KLM has retired its earlier 747s, like the -200 seen here, but still owns over twenty 747-400s.

The future

With Airbus penetrating the high-capacity market with the A340-600 and A380, Boeing began considering new 747 derivatives. Through various proposals which included fuselage stretches and producing a 747-400LRX with the wing and strengthened undercarriage of the -400 freighter for extra range, these matured as the extended-range 747-400ER and 747-400ERF. In summer 2005, however, it was becoming increasingly likely that Boeing would launch a stretched 747-400 Advanced. This new machine would offer increased range and feature the engines of the all-new 787 Dreamliner.

latter airframe/engine combination set a world record on 1 November 1976, when taking off at a weight of 840,500 lb (381250 kg)

Pan Am also persuaded Boeing to produce a variant which could carry a full payload non-stop on its longest route between New York and Tokyo, as the 747SP. Boeing continued to look towards increasing the 747's passenger load and, in June 1980, revealed the 747SUD (stretched upper deck). This was essentially a Model 200 with the upper deck extended by 23 ft (7 m), providing economy seating for up to 69 passengers. It was redesignated 747-300 by the time of its maiden flight on 5 October 1982, and entered service with launch customer, Swissair. Later, the latest materials and technology made the 747-400 a much more advanced aircraft, with a new wing, a two-crew glass cockpit and considerably enhanced performance. Externally, it is similar to the -300, apart from its large winglets. Even before the first roll-out on 26 January 1988, 18 operators had placed orders for 118 aircraft. Northwest Airlines was the launch customer with an order for 10 aircraft placed on 22 October 1985. Japan Airlines operates the 747-400D (Domestic), fitted out for 546 passengers in a two-class arrangement. From May 1990, 747-400 derivatives became the only 747s on offer.

Boeing 747-200B

Among the most gaudy and brightly-coloured of the 747s to have flown so far were the two aircraft operated by Braniff on the 'Big Orange' service between Dallas and London-Gatwick, until the airline went bankrupt in 1982. A new Braniff emerged as a domestic operator and the 747s (including one 747SP) were sold. This aircraft was a Series 200, powered by Pratt & Whitney JT9D-3 engines.

Records
On 12 November 1970, a test 747-200B set a new heavyweight record by taking off at a gross weight of 820,700 lb (372261 kg). An even more remarkable fact is that the cabin of the 747 is longer than the distance covered by the first flight of the Wright brothers, a sign of how far aviation progressed in the 20th century.

Accommodation
The 747-200B has a cabin length of 187 ft (57 m) and a width of 20 ft 1½ in (6.13 m). The basic layout of the aircraft provides seating for 48 first-class and 337 economy-class passengers (including a 16-passenger upper deck lounge). Alternatively, 447 passengers can sit nine-abreast in single-class conditions, or 500 passengers can sit ten abreast, with 32 on the upper deck. The aircraft is flown by a flight crew of three.

747-200 variants
The 747-200 was produced in a number of variants. These included the -200B, a Combi version, and the -200C, a factory-built, fully convertible variant that can be configured for all-passenger, all-freight or a combination load. A special freighter version of the 747 was the -200F, with straight-in loading of bulk cargo through a hinged nose (called a visor by Boeing). The -200M designation is applied to -200Bs that have been modified to incorporate side cargo doors.

Powerplant
Depending on customer choice, the 747-200 was delivered with Pratt & Whitney JT9D-7R4G2 turbofans rated at 54,750 lb (243.5 kN) thrust, General Electric CF6-50E2 turbofans rated at 52,500 lb (233.5 kN) thrust or Rolls Royce RB.211-524D4-B turbofans rated at 53,110 lb (236.2 kN) thrust.

A 747 operator since 1970 (as BOAC), British Airways ordered 57 examples, the last of which was delivered in 1999. The airline's controversial 'World Images' colour scheme, with themed tailfin designs, was applied to a number of 747s, including 747-436 G-BNLR which displays the Far Eastern-inspired 'Rendezvous' design.

Fuselage and accommodation

The Series 400 has the same extended upper deck as introduced in the 747-300. Not only does this provide extra seating, but it improves aerodynamic flow around the forward fuselage, reducing drag and allowing a slight increase in normal cruise Mach number. BA's aircraft are operated in a number of seating configurations, providing accommodation for up to 351 passengers, the exact configuration used depending upon the route on which the aircraft is expected to operate. The most capacious 747-400s are the 747-400Ds used by Japanese airlines on domestic routes. These can carry as many as 566 passengers in a high-density, two-class layout.

Wing structure

While retaining the same wing structure as earlier models, the 747-400 employs new materials (advanced alloys in the main) in its construction to achieve a considerable weight saving. The Series 400's wing, despite a 17-ft (5.18-m) span increase, to 211 ft 5 in (64.44 m) overall, is actually lighter than that of the 747-300. With its fuel tanks full the aircraft's wing bends downward slightly, causing the tips of the winglets to swing out and increase span to 213 ft 64.92 m) overall.

Boeing 747-400 variants

Apart from the basic 747-400 passenger variant, three other versions based on the standard -400 have entered service:

747-400 Combi: mixed passenger/freight version. Identical to the all-passenger version, but with a 120-in x 134-in (305-cm x 340-cm) side cargo door (SCD) in the port rear fuselage, aft of the wing. Two end zones of the cabin have a strengthened floor with cargo handling gear (including a roller floor)

747-400F: All-cargo, full freighter version. This version is structurally identical to the 747-400, but has the original short upper deck of the 747-100/200, to save weight. Uses the same SCD as the Combi aircraft, but also features a 136 in x 98-in (345-cm x 249-cm) nose door. The -400F has a maximum take-off weight of 870,000 lb (394632 kg) and can carry a typical 44,000-lb (19958-kg) payload over 5,000 nm (9253 km, 5,750 miles)

747-400D (Domestic): This special version, announced in October 1989, is intended for high-density domestic routes in Japan (where airlines like JAL and ANA already operated the 747-200SR). The 747-400D is configured for 5a maximum 66 passengers in a two-class layout. As the 747-400D fleet can expect to accrue a much higher number of cycles compared to the rest of the worldwide 747 population these aircraft have a strengthened structure, no horizontal fin fuel tank and use de-rated engines.

747-400ER (Extended Range): Increased maximum take-off weight of 910,000 lb (412770 kg) for a range of 7,670 nm (8,827 miles; 14205 km). Boeing Signature cabin, using 777 interior design.

747-400ERF: Freighter version of 747-400ER.

Boeing 747-436

G-BNLE *City of Newcastle* was the fifth 747-436 delivered to British Airways (and the 753rd 747 completed by the Boeing Airplane Company) and was delivered in late 1989. Most of the airline's 747-400 fleet was named after British cities, though the aircraft later lost their names as they were repainted in the 'World Images' and current 'Union Flag' colour schemes.

Powerplant

The 747-400 is offered with Pratt & Whitney PW4056, General Electric CF6-80C2 or Rolls-Royce RB.211-524G/-524H engines generally rated at between 56,000 and 58,000 lb st (249.2 and 258 kN), though variants of both the P&W and GE engines are available for the 747-400 rated at up to 62,000 lb st (276 kN). Most Series 400 operators have chosen the GE engine, but British Airways followed Cathay Pacific Airways' lead in specifying RB.211s for its aircraft and was later joined by Air New Zealand, Cargolux, QANTAS and South African Airways in choosing the Rolls-Royce engine for some or all of their 747-400s. A feature of the RB.211 is the use of wide-chord fan blades at the front of the engine, these being lighter and less vulnerable to bird strike damage.

Compared to the 747-200F, the 747-400 Freighter can carry 20 per cent more payload over ranges more than 1,000 nm (1,152 miles; 1853 km) longer. HL7419 is operated by South Korea's Asiana Airlines which also flies Series 400 airliners.

Winglets

The main identifying features of the 747-400, compared to the otherwise similar 747-300, are the former's 6-ft (1.83-m) high graphite composite winglets, fitted to reduce drag caused by spanwise migration of boundary layer air. The drag-inducing vortices which would otherwise result are caused by the difference in air pressure between the upper and lower surfaces of the wing.

Fuel

The bulk of the 747's fuel is housed between the spars of the wing, in four huge internal tanks. In addition there is a centre-wing tank and reserve tanks in the outer wings. The 747-400 also has an optional tailplane fuel tank, with a capacity of 2,748 Imp gal (12492 litres), feeding directly into the centre-wing tank and giving the aircraft another 340 nautical miles (650 km, 404 miles) of range at normal cruise altitude. Total useable fuel capacity with the tailplane tank installed is increased to 47,700 Imp gal (216,846 litres), weighing over 386,000 lb (175086 kg), or about 45 per cent of the maximum take-off weight of a 747-400. Design range with 420 passengers aboard an aircraft operating at the highest optional take-off weight is 7,135 nautical miles (8,211 miles;13214 km) with fuel reserves; ferry range is around 9,675 miles (15570 km).

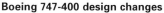

G-BNLE

Boeing 747-400 design changes

The basic 747-400 fuselage length is no different to all the other 747s that have gone before it. Boeing has never stretched the 747, though plans for such a move are now being considered as part of Boeing's answer to the challenge from the A380. Several other aspects of the 747's design were changed on the -400, however, and these include:

- wingspan extended by 6 ft (1.83 m), with additional composite wingtips measuring a further 6 ft (1.83 m) in length
- additional fuel tank installed inside the tail fin, adding 3,300 US gal (12492 litres)
- carbon fibre brakes, saving 1,800 lb (816 kg) in weight
- PW901A auxiliary power unit, reduces APU fuel-burn by 40 per cent
- increased maximum take-off weight, up to 870,000 lb (394632 kg)
- higher thrust General Electric CF6-80C2, Pratt & Whitney PW4056 or Rolls-Royce RB.211-524G/H turbofans
- six-screen EFIS cockpit fit for two crew operation
- re-styled cabin, with typical three-class seating for 412 passengers
- up to 7,200-nm (13325-km; 8,280-mile) range, with 400 passengers and baggage

Among the world's first all-jet airlines, Air India sold its last propeller-driven aircraft (a Constellation) in June 1962 and has been operating 747s since March 1971. Its first 747-400 (pictured) was delivered in 1993 and is one of 11 in the Indian flag-carrier's fleet.

Boeing 747SP
Mini 'Jumbo'

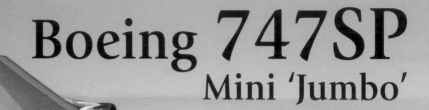

Delivered in March 1976, this aircraft (ZS-SPA) was the first of six Boeing 747SPs delivered to South African Airways. On its delivery flight the aircraft set a new world non-stop distance record, emphasising the type's long-range capabilities.

As the original ultra-long range airliner, the Boeing 747SP was not the prettiest aircraft ever built, nor did it break any sales records – but breaking performance records was another matter. Seattle's 'special performer' flew higher, further and faster than any of its contemporaries and set many speed and distance records during its career.

Soon after the launch of the 747-100, it became clear that many customers needed a similar aircraft capable of covering great distances. Douglas and Lockheed were eating into this market with the DC-10 and the TriStar, but Boeing felt it had the edge with its existing four-engined design. Boeing took the basic 747-100 and chopped out 48 ft (14.60 m) of fuselage, losing about 100. Everything else was left untouched, so the new smaller, lighter aircraft would have the same engines – and all the power – of a 747-100 with reduced fuel consumption and increased range. The uninspiring in-house design name of 747SB (short body) was dropped in favour of the attention-getting title 747SP (Special Performance), and the project received its official go-ahead on 23 August 1973.

This new version boasted increased rate of climb, cruising altitude and cruising speed and a range in excess of 6,904 miles (11112 km). The aircraft's centresection was redesigned to retain the 747's trademark upper deck, along with the rear fuselage

Right: The first 747SP made its maiden flight on 4 July. The SP's shorter fuselage and larger tail fin were highlighted when parked adjacent to a standard Model 747.

Below: Braniff International's distinctive orange colour scheme adorned three 747SPs in the early 1980s. This example was returned to Boeing in 1981 before being sold to the Omani government in July 1984.

that was radically 'pinched in' to fit the tail unit. The reduction in length necessitated an extension of the fin by 5 ft (1.52 m). The fin chord was also extended by 5 ft and a distinctive double-hinged rudder was fitted. The tailplanes were lengthened by 10 ft (3 m). The standard engine was the 46,950-lb (209-kN) JT9D-7A. Alternatively, 51,600-lb (229.6-kN) RB.211-524 turbofans were

available. Thirty-nine of the 45 SPs built were powered by JT9Ds.

The launch order came from Pan American, which ordered 10 in September 1973, with 15 options. Boeing sales executives predicted a 20-year production run and planned at least six distinct versions (such as an SP Combi). The first SP, the 265th production 747, was rolled out on 19 May 1975 and the maiden

CAAC ordered the 747SP in 1980. When the organisation was dismantled in 1988, the aircraft were transferred to Air China.

flight took place on 4 July. The maiden flight was described as one of the most ambitious first flights in Boeing's history and included a full stall and speeds up to Mach 0.92. On 4 February 1976 the 747SP received its type certification from the FAA.

Pan Am accepted its first aircraft on 5 March 1976 and the type entered service on the Los Angeles-Tokyo route on 25 April. On 3 November 1975 the fourth SP undertook a month-long international sales trip, equivalent to three times around the world. Several unofficial non-stop distance and speed records were set during this tour. A South African Airways (SAA) aircraft later set a new non-stop distance record of 10,290 miles (16560 km) from Everett to Cape Town on its delivery flight during 23/24 March 1976 and still had

two hours and 27 minutes of fuel on board. Over 1-3 May 1976 Pan Am's *Clipper Liberty Bell* set a new round-the-world record of 46 hours 26 minutes over a distance of 23,137 miles (37234 km). On 2 August 1977 Pan Am's *Clipper New Horizons* (*Liberty Bell* renamed) set a round-the-world record via the poles of 54 hours and 7 minutes for a distance of 26,230 miles (42212 km), plus six additional FAI records. Finally, United Airlines' *Friendship One* set a new round-the-world record of 35 hours 54 minutes over a distance of 23,125 miles (37216 km) on 29/30 January 1988.

In the end, the 747SP failed to be a success for several reasons. It was too expensive – at roughly $28 million it was dearer than all its competitors. Its market was limited – although Boeing made

serious proposals to 40 other potential customers, not one signed up. Finally, the performance of the 747-200 largely caught up with that of the SP, while still retaining its original passenger and cargo capacities.

A total of 45 747SPs was built for customers such as Braniff, CAAC, China Airlines, Iran Air, Korean Air Lines, Pan Am, QANTAS, SAA, Syrian Arab Airlines and TWA, with the last

delivery coming in 1989. This was, in fact, a specially-ordered VIP aircraft, and the last true airline delivery occurred in 1982. The largest operators were Pan Am and United, the latter obtaining Pan Am's 10 aircraft when it took over its Pacific routes during the late 1980s. United began to retire its fleet from 1995 onwards. One ex-United aircraft was been modified to serve as NASA's Stratospheric Observatory For Infra-red Astronomy. Today, a little over half the SPs built are still in service and Iran Air is the largest operator, with four examples.

VIP flagship

The 747SP has proved to be a popular VIP aircraft. Boeing attempted to sell it to the US government as a replacement for the then AIR FORCE ONE, a VC 137. Attempts were also made to sell an SP to the Shah of Iran. The first VIP sale was made to King Khaled of Saudia Arabia. This aircraft (HZ-HM1, later re-registered as HZ-HM1B when replaced by a 747-300) was outfitted with a fully equipped hospital and a luxuriously appointed interior. Other VIP SPs with government/royal owners have included three in the UAE (Abu Dhabi and Dubai); two in Qatar, Saudi Arabia and Bahrain; and one in Oman. The Omanii aircraft (A40-SP) and one UAE aircraft (A6-ZSN, seen immediately below) were fitted with a satellite communications dome behind the main 'hump'. Another of the UAE aircraft (A6-SMR) was fitted with a 'glass' EFIS cockpit and is thus unique among SPs. A VIP 747SP (YI-ALM) was also delivered to the government of Iraq, though it wore basic Iraqi Airways colours.

Above: Pan Am was the launch customer for the 747SP, having ordered 10 examples in September 1973. N533PA Clipper Freedom was the third built and the first to be delivered in March 1976.

Below: The longest continuous operator of the type is Syrian Arab Airlines. Its two Boeing 747SP-94s were delivered in May and July 1976 and remain in service three decades later.

Above: One of the more recent operators of the 747SP in Asia was Mandarin Airlines of Taiwan. The airline has leased this example from China Airlines since August 1992.

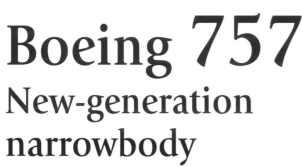

Boeing 757
New-generation narrowbody

Designed to replace the prolific Boeing 727 on the production line, the Model 757 had little in common with its predecessor. New, efficient engines and a modern cockpit made the aircraft a cost-efficient option for a number of the world's larger carriers.

Above: The Boeing Model 757 and 767 projects were launched in a blaze of publicity in the late 1970s. It would, however, be a number of years before the 757 order book began to fill.

Top: Delta was the first operator to select the Pratt & Whitney PW2037 engine. It operated its 757s alongside Boeing 767s and Lockheed TriStars on US domestic routes.

Until the 727, no airliner had notched up 1,000 sales. The 727 sold 1,832, the last thousand being gained despite the existence of the Airbus A300B which offered greater comfort, far better fuel efficiency and much less noise. Even though no airlines in the early 1970s seemed to want to buy the quiet widebody, Boeing could see that it would have to improve the 727, and its first idea was the stretched 727-300 with fuel-efficient engines. By 1976 this had become the 7N7, with just two engines hung under a wing more like that of the A300B.

Increasingly, attention focused on the biggest 7N7 versions, and Rolls-Royce came into the picture with the new RB.211-535 engine of an initial 32,000-lb (144-kN) thrust. It was obvious that, instead of trying to sell engines for European A300B and A310 aircraft, Rolls-Royce was eager to get aboard the new Boeing, and it was backed to the hilt by British Airways. Indeed, in 1976-78, great efforts were made by Boeing, British Airways and Rolls-Royce to get the British aircraft industry to build 757 wings instead of joining Airbus Industrie.

In 1979 the decision was taken to drop the T-tail and mount the horizontal tail on the fuselage. A little later, the old 727 'cab' – giving commonality with the 707, 727 and 737 – was discarded in favour of the wider nose and flight deck of the 767. By this time Boeing was already in full development, the go-ahead being announced in early 1978 and British Airways and Eastern placing launch orders on 31 August 1978.

Slow sales

Initially, Boeing was very disappointed in sales of the 757. Thanks to its narrow body, it had been planned to offer the lowest fuel burn per passenger-kilometre of any jetliner, yet no new customers appeared until, in April 1980, three were signed for by Transbrasil and three by Aloha. Both selected the CF6-32 engine, in which General Electric proposed to collaborate with Volvo Flygmotor of Sweden. Still there were no sales until at last, in November 1980, came the breakthrough Boeing had been waiting for – 60 for Delta. The giant US line deferred its choice of engine, and when, in December 1980, it announced its decision, it was for yet a third engine, the Pratt & Whitney PW2037. Pratt & Whitney marketed the engine as the most efficient in the world and the attraction of this proposed performance encouraged American Airlines, at the end of

Despite a strong home lobby canvassing for the national airline to buy Airbus, British Airways signed up as the launch customer for the 757, its first aircraft entering service in February 1983.

Eastern was the first airline to place the Model 757 into service, this occurring on 1 January 1983. The airline eventually received 25 examples, delivered from 1983 to 1986.

Air Europe, owned by the International Leisure Group, was one of a number of European operators which found the aircraft an economical choice for charter flights.

1980, to announce selection of the PW2037 for its 757s, before it had even announced it would buy the Boeing aircraft! In January 1981 GE announced that it would no longer compete in this market, and ended CF6-32 development. Aloha and Transbrasil subsequently picked the PW2037, though this meant delayed delivery.

The first 757 was rolled out at Renton on 13 January 1982, to make its first flight on 19 February. It was the first time that a major US airliner had been launched with a foreign engine, but development of the 535C had progressed so much more efficiently than predicted that everyone (except P&W) was delighted. Scheduled services began with Eastern on 1 January 1983, and with British Airways on 9 February. By this time, Boeing had thought better of its original plan to offer various sub-types of 757, and early sales were of the 757-200 type, with a fuselage length of 154 ft 10 in (46.96 m), customers merely having two choices of engine and a choice of regular or long-range fuel capacity.

Although the nose and cockpit section are similar to those of the appreciably wider 767, the main tube section of the fuselage is almost identical to that of the 707, 727 and 737. Boeing offered nine interior arrangements for 178 to 239 passengers, seated basically in a 3 + 3 arrangement with a central aisle. Customers could have three doors each side plus four overwing emergency exits or four doors each side. In most configurations there is a galley at the front on the right and another at the rear on the left, and toilets at the front on the left and two or three either amidships or at the rear.

Technically, the 757 is extremely conventional. The wing has a quarterchord sweep of 25°. The leading edge is fitted with full-span powered slats, though these have a gap at the engine pylon, there being a single large slat inboard and four sections outboard. On the trailing edge are inboard and outboard flaps mounted on faired tracks. All are double-slotted, except the outer portion of each inboard flap which is single-slotted to avoid interference with the jet wake. Outboard are powered all-speed ailerons of quite long span. Ahead of the flaps are two inboard and four outboard spoilers on each wing, the innermost being a ground lift-dumper only. The other ten spoilers are opened together as speed brakes or differentially for roll, augmenting the ailerons. The horizontal tail is pivoted to serve as the longitudinal trim control, carrying the graphite-composite elevators. Likewise, the fixed vertical tail carries a graphite rudder.

New systems

In its systems the 757 did break some new ground, notably in the use of laser-light gyros in the navigation IRS (inertial reference system). It was also, as it had to be, one of the new breed of all-digital aircraft. There was simply no way that Boeing could have launched a jetliner in the late 1970s with the analogue-type avionics of the 707, 727 and Classic 737s and 747s. The flight deck, very like that of the 767, is a mix of old and new, the new parts including basic EFIS displays and an EICAS (engine indication and crew-alerting system). The overall flight management was a generation earlier than that of the A320, but it did offer automatic trajectory guidance, terminal navigation, thrust management and an optional feature offering some protection against windshear. A Garrett APU is mounted in the tailcone, the ECS (environmental control system) packs are under the floor in the centre section, and there are two ram-air turbines to provide emergency electrical and hydraulic power in flight. Each main gear is a four-wheel bogie retracting inward, with Dunlop wheels, tyres and carbon brakes. The steerable twin-wheel nose gear retracts forwards, all gear doors being of Kevlar.

From the start of service the 757 did all that was asked of it, and the 535C did more. It was soon clear that this was the most trouble-free engine in history, almost never suffering an inflight shutdown. Over the first four years of service the engine-caused removal rate was only 0.051 per thousand flight hours, described as 'many times better than the previously claimed industry best'. In October 1984 the advanced E4 entered service, and quickly established not only a reputation for reliability which is, if anything, even greater, but also a reduction in fuel burn of over 10 per cent. The rival PW2037 followed it into service on 1 December 1984, and – though Pratt & Whitney continued to claim the 'lowest fuel consumption' – the unequalled combination of economy, reliability and low cost of ownership resulted in the British engine being selected by every one of the next 11 customers for the 757. Two further advantages for the 535E4 were that the 757 powered by this engine was officially measured as 'the quietest jet with over 100 seats and that it was the only version FAA-approved for EROPS (extended- range operations) such as over the North Atlantic. Many airlines, including several UK charter operators, began operating E4-powered 757s on services to North America.

An important customer to have picked the Pratt & Whitney engine (in the uprated PW2040 version) was United Parcel Service, which ordered the 757-200PF (Package Freighter). This is a dedicated freighter, with a windowless fuselage and a large cargo door in the port side. It can carry 15 standard containers on its main deck.

757 today

The 757 is the backbone of many major airline fleets, particularly in the USA. Adept at handling both transcontinental and short-range shuttle routes, the 757 has matured into an efficient specialised freighter, a head-of-state transport and now the high-capacity, stretched 757-300.

US domestic airlines were always the 757's principal market, with operators such as American Airlines operating large fleets. America West is one of many smaller carriers, operating 13 examples on shuttle services between West Coast towns and cities.

Typical of the many European charter airlines which operate the 757, Monarch Airlines has a fleet of seven examples, which fly the popular Mediterranean, USA and Caribbean holiday routes.

Europe and America are the centres of 757 operations, though significant sales have been won in the Far East. Furthermore, European airlines were behind the development of the final member of the 757 family, the stretched 757-300, which was designed to appeal to IT (inclusive tour) charter airlines.

The US remains the 757's stronghold. Many airlines there chose the bigger, twin-engined Boeing to replace their 727s. Leading that pack was Delta Airlines which ordered a total of 116 757-200s between 1980 and 1999. American Airlines was also a major US customer, signing up for 103 aircraft between 1988 and 1996. Other North American 757 operators include United Airlines, Northwest Airlines, Continental

Airlines, US Airways, TWA and American TransAir. Away from the regular airline world, UPS is the primary operator of the 757-200PF freighter version – indeed, the Package Freighter variant was developed specifically to a 1985 UPS order and the first example was delivered on 16 September 1987.

In Europe the 757 is popular among holiday charter airlines, where operators have included Air 2000, Air Europe, Airtours International, Condor, JMC, LTU, Monarch Airlines, Thomas Cook and Transavia. China has proved to be an important market since Boeing sold its first 757 to CAAC in 1987. Operators have included China Southern, China Southwest, China Xinjing Airlines, Shanghai Airlines and

Xiamen Airlines. Among the most significant 757 customers have been the international aircraft leasing companies, which were early adopters of the type. Several lessors have 757s on their books, the most important of which include ILFC, Ansett Worldwide Aviation and GPA Ltd.

Boeing took the 757 into a new realm in August 1996 when it won an order for four aircraft from the US Air Force. Designated C-32A, these 757-200s are used for VVIP

transport tasks in the hands of the 89th AW, where they replaced VC-137s. In addition to the USAF examples, other air arms have also acquired the 757 and the type has also attracted orders from civil VIP and business jet operators.

Boeing sold a total of 1,049 757s, with the majority remaining in service. It is difficult to place the 757 into a particular market slot, however, since airlines use it to fly both transatlantic services and high-frequency shuttle routes. One concern that operators did have, particularly in Europe, was that the 757 did not have enough seating capacity to benefit fully from its long legs. This was the driving force behind the development of the 757-300.

The USAF's four C-32As are powered by Pratt & Whitney PW2040 turbofans and were delivered between May and November 1998.

Above: Flying Colours began operations in 1997 and in March 2000 it was integrated with Caledonian, forming JMC Airlines, which was later renamed as Thomas Cook Airlines. The latter has a current fleet of 17 757-200s.

Royal Brunei Airlines operated two smartly painted 757-2M6s, powered by Rolls-Royce RB.211-535E4 turbofans. The aircraft were delivered in 1986 and served into 2004.

Concerned that Airbus was eating into its potential market with longer-range derivatives of the A321, Boeing revived earlier plans for a scaled-up 757. Boeing considered two versions, the higher gross weight 757-200X and a larger aircraft altogether, the 757-300X. It chose the second option and launched the 757-300 at the 1996 Farnborough Air Show. The new 757 could carry 20 per cent more passengers, and increased the available cargo volume by nearly 50 per cent. Designed to carry 243 passengers in a typical mixed-class configuration, the 757-300 can accommodate up to 289 in charter service, putting its capacity between that of the 757-200 and the 767-300.

Maximum take-off weight has increased to 272,500 lb (123600 kg) to preserve the passenger/cargo load capability.

Launched in 1996, the 757-300 entered service in 1999 with Condor Flugdienst. Seat-mile costs have been reduced by around 10 per cent compared to the airline's 757-200s.

The wing, landing gear and portions of the fuselage were strengthened and new wheels, tyres and brakes added to handle the extra weight. Because the 757-300 is longer, Boeing made several modifications to protect against possible damage from tail strikes during take-off and landing. A retractable tail skid, similar to that on the 777-300, was added.

The two-crew flight deck of the 757-300 is similar to that of the 757-200, and the two are cross-crew qualified. Latterly, flight deck improvements were made to the 757. These included the addition of the Pegasus flight management computer (FMC) and an enhanced engine indication and crew alerting system (EICAS). With the Pegasus FMC, operators could choose optional software providing the ability to use the global positioning system and satellite communications.

The EICAS upgrade replaces existing computers with enhanced devices that are software driven. The new EICAS has improved built-in test equipment functions that allow for improved self-diagnosis of faults in a more readable format. Other improvements to the 757 have included an enhanced ground proximity warning system (EGPWS), a new software-loadable flight control computer (FCC) and an enhanced windshear warning system. The 757-300 also incorporated the latest technology air data/inertial reference system (ADIRS).

Although parts of the 757-300 were manufactured at Boeing facilities in Wichita, Kansas, and by external suppliers at many locations (including major sub-contractor Northrop Grumman), major assembly was undertaken in Renton. The 757-300 was launched with an order for 12 aircraft from Germany's Condor Flugdienst on 2 September 1996. The next customer was Icelandair, which announced an order for two at the 1997 Paris Air Show. The first aircraft was rolled out on 31 May 1998 and made its maiden flight on 2 August. By that time, additional orders had been received from Condor and Arkia Israeli. FAA certification was awarded on 22 January 1999, with JAA approval following on 25 January. The first 757-300 was handed over to Condor on 10 March 1999 and entered service nine days later. Arkia Israeli Airlines took delivery of its two 757-300s in January/February 2000. The first of an eventual four 757-300s ordered by Icelandair was delivered in March 2002. Despite Boeing's high hopes, sales of the 757-300 remained slow. When 757 production ended late in 2004, just 55 orders had been placed for the -300.

The 757-300 was the longest single-aisle twinjet ever produced. The aircraft's cabin interior is the same as that used in the company's next-generation 737 family, giving a more open, spacious feel.

Boeing 767 Twin-jet widebody

In the late 1970s, Boeing launched the wide-bodied Model 767 airliner project in response to Airbus' success with its A300. Offering excellent range performance, the aircraft was soon ordered by major airlines around the world.

Boeing eventually dominated the jet airliner club with the Model 707, an epoch-making airliner that successfully married swept-wing technology with lightweight, powerful turbojets. At this juncture, Lockheed dropped from the competition, leaving Douglas as the only rival to Boeing's meteoric rise in the market. The 707 initiated a memorable sequence of aircraft designations, each of which proved to be as successful and as revolutionary in its own way. The 717 designation was used by the KC-135 tanker series, built in huge numbers for the USAF, and was later reapplied to the MD-95 when Boeing inherited the twinjet from McDonnell Douglas. The 727 was a revolutionary trijet that brought jet power to the smaller fields and short-haul routes, a tradition continued with the twinjet 737.

Then came the 747, ushering in a new era of wide-body transports powered by high bypass ratio turbofans.

European competition

Flying nearly three years after the 747 had first been delivered, the European Airbus A300 offered a different kind of competition to Boeing's dominance. It entered an area where rival products were nothing more than paper projects, and consequently established itself rapidly as a world-leader. Technological excellence was at the heart of the Airbus' success, which was continued with the A310. Both Boeing and McDonnell Douglas were caught out, neither having any aircraft with which to compete in this twin-engine, medium-haul, high-density market.

Boeing's answer lay in the 7X7 programme. This project was under discussion and study for 10 years, and during a long gestation had several different configurations, including the use of a T-tail, overwing engines and many other features. In July 1978, the company eventually announced the launch of the aircraft as the 767, in the same month as Airbus announced the go-ahead of its A310. Also proceeding roughly in parallel with the 7X7 was the 7N7, a narrowbody airliner intended to replace the 727, but sharing many of its larger brother's features. Despite its redesignation as the 757, this aircraft actually followed the 767 into service.

Boeing eventually settled on a conventional configuration for the 767, and although this mirrored

Above: Following its roll-out, the prototype 767 was towed across the highway from assembly plant to active apron in preparation for its maiden flight from Everett, Washington, in September 1981.

*Top: The first European 767 operator was Britannia Airways, which received eight examples, mainly for its Mediterranean destinations. This example operated with the airline from 1984 to 1995 and was named **The Lord Mountbatten of Burma**.*

United Airlines was the launch customer for the Model 767. Built as a 767-222, N605UA was the sixth example to be delivered to United and was later converted to ER standard.

Boeing relied on the loyalty of US carriers such as Delta to home-produced designs for initial 767 orders. The sixth aircraft built, N101DA, was used for proving flights before entering service in March 1983.

that of the much smaller 737, it also looked remarkably like the Airbus with which it was in direct competition. Critics, especially in Europe, were quick to point out this fact, but to be fair Boeing had pioneered the configuration nearly 20 years earlier! Also, it must be remembered that there is every chance that two superb design teams will arrive at the same answer if it happens to be the right one.

Where the Boeing design differed was that it had a smaller fuselage and bigger wing. The latter was designed to provide higher-altitude cruise performance, and also, not surprisingly, higher gross weights for future enlarged versions. What was surprising was the fuselage, for although the narrow diameter of the 767 (compared to the A300 and A310) produced less drag and consequently greater range, it could not accept standard cargo/baggage containers, and the standard eight-abreast seating was rather cramped. In broad terms, the Airbus products were better in load-carrying performance, but inferior in terms of range and altitude.

Despite the shortcomings of the design, the 767 was virtually assured of a large market at home, where the giant domestic carriers were crying out for a suitable type to transfer large numbers of passengers between US cities at economic rates. Nevertheless, this market provided the 767 with fewer sales than might once have

been expected, for the Airbus products had made small yet notable in-roads into the xenophobic US domestic market. Eastern and Pan Am were important Airbus customers, and these have been joined in recent years by many more, particularly since the smaller A320 family has been available.

Notwithstanding this European competition, the 767 at once began to pile up the orders. An order of 30 from United Airlines had sparked the final go-ahead for the airliner on 14 July 1978. Other giants such as American Airlines, Delta Air Lines, Trans World Airlines and USAir also acquired the type, although the latter's aircraft were picked up when the carrier absorbed Piedmont.

Powerplant variety

Construction of the prototype began on 6 July 1979. From the outset, the 767 was designed with two different engines in mind, according to customer preference. These were the products of Pratt & Whitney (JT9D) and General Electric (CF6). The first aircraft (N767BA) flew on 26 September 1981, with Pratt & Whitney power. The next three aircraft from the line also featured this powerplant. General Electric engines powered the fifth aircraft, and this flew for the first time on 19 February 1982.

After an intensive flight trial period, FAA certification for the 48,000-lb (213.5-kN) thrust Pratt & Whitney JT9D-7R4D-powered aircraft was received on 30 July

Piedmont Airlines was an early operator of the 767-200ER, using the aircraft on ETOPS services across the North Atlantic. The airline was absorbed by USAir in 1989 and the aircraft were repainted in their new owner's colours.

1982, allowing the first delivery to be made to United Airlines on 19 August. The General Electric powered aircraft, with CF6-80A engines of the same power, received its certification on 30 September, 22 days after United had begun revenue-earning services. Delta received the first CF6-powered 767 on 25 October, with services beginning on 15 December.

These 767-200s, with the others that rapidly followed, were soon showing excellent economy over medium-haul routes, Delta's aircraft being configured with 18 passengers in first-class and 186 in economy, while United opted for a 24/180 split. Both operators would join the ranks of 757 operators, flying the smaller aircraft alongside the 767 from major hub centres.

As recounted earlier, the large wing of the Boeing 767 made the basic Series 200 a natural step for considerable development. Aimed particularly at overseas customers, the 767-200ER was introduced, this offering a higher gross weight (345,000 lb; 156490 kg) and

increased fuel capacity for a considerable range increase. Two further increases in weight and fuel capacity were also developed under the 767ER designation, the heaviest weighing in at 387,000 lb (175540 kg). Design range was extended from under 3,730 miles (6000 km) for the basic versions, to 7,836 miles (12611 km) in the heaviest ER variant.

The -200ER version proved popular overseas, especially with small operators seeking new jet equipment, but without the requirement for the capacity of a Boeing 747. Those in geographic isolation have found the incredible range performance of the 767ER perfect for covering the longest sectors, Air Mauritius and QANTAS being good examples. Indeed, during a delivery flight on 17 April 1988, one of the Air Mauritius machines covered the 8,727 miles (14044 km) between Halifax, Nova Scotia, and its new home non-stop, in a flight lasting 16 hours 27 minutes. This set a world distance record for a twin-engined commercial aircraft. In contrast, and in answer to some of the 767's early critics, the longest-ranged A310 could only manage approximately 5,700 miles (9175 km).

Although United and Delta were the initial customers for the 767, other US majors followed them in adopting the type. American Airlines currently operates a total of 86 Model 200s, 200ERs and 300ERs.

Left: Asiana Airlines has operated 767-300, -300ER and -300F aircraft. This 767-38E was the first to be delivered to the airline and began services in October 1990.

Below: Seen over Mount St Helens, which erupted in 1981, the first test 767-300 flies in Boeing's house colours. After trials, the aircraft was delivered to JAL in December 1986.

Beyond the 200

The range of the original 767-200 was increased in the 767-200ER, but to answer calls for yet more capacity and increased range, Boeing developed the 767-300 and 767-300ER. These workhorses have now been joined by the radically redesigned 767-400, which raises the capabilities of the 767 family to a whole new level.

The 767 was Boeing's first wide-bodied twin and one of the pioneers of transatlantic and trans-Pacific ETOPS.

When the 767-200 entered service, with United Airlines in September 1982, it faced competition from the Airbus A300 and A310 families, in particular the long-range A300-600R and the A310-300. Boeing developed the 767-200ER to offer more range, but to provide more seats, the 767 had to be stretched. Boeing announced the 767-300 stretch in February 1983 and hoped that the new aircraft would be ready for delivery in early 1986. However, it was not

until September 1983 that the first firm order, from JAL, was placed.

The first 767-300 flew on 30 January 1986 and was certified in September. The first customer delivery was made to JAL on 25 September. The -300 incorporated a 253-in (6.42-m) fuselage extension, in the form of two plugs, forward and aft of the wing. In a typical two-class seating layout, the 767-300 can accommodate 261 passengers (about 20 per cent more than the -200), or 210 in a three-class layout. However, maximum seating capacity is dictated largely by emergency exit capacity and since 1989 the -300 has been permitted to

operate with up to 360 passengers.

The 767-300 boasted a maximum take-off weight (MTOW) of 350,000 lb (158760 kg) and a range, with 261 passengers, of 4,150 nm (4,772 miles; 7680 km).The initial engine options for the 767-300 were the 50,000-lb (222.5-kN) General Electric CF6-80A2 or the Pratt & Whitney JT9D-7R4D. In the years that followed, a wide range of variations was developed, tailored almost to the needs of individual customers. Pratt & Whitney later introduced its 56,750-lb (252-kN) to 60,000-lb (267-kN) PW4000 family, and Rolls Royce its 60,600-lb (270-kN) RB.211-524H. Launch customer Japanese Airlines chose the basic CF6 engines, while the JT9D made its debut on a Delta Air Lines aircraft, in November 1986.

Longer reach

The decision to launch the extended-range 767-300ER, in 1984, came soon after the launch of the basic -300. The development aircraft first flew on 9 November 1986, but Boeing had no orders for the ER until American Airlines ordered 15, in March 1987. The -300ER incorporated more fuel and thus had a much increased MTOW. When Boeing first unveiled the -300ER it set the MTOW at 380,000 lb (172368 kg) but, by 1986, the design had been revised several times to allow an MTOW of up to 407,000 lb (184615 kg). By 1993 this had grown to some 412,000 lb (186883 kg). Engine choices included the CF6-80C2B2 and the PW4000. Austria's Lauda Air became the launch customer for the Pratt & Whitney engine in April 1987. More powerful Rolls-Royce RB.211-524G/H engines were certified in December 1989 and British Airways was the launch customer for this combination.

The 767-300/-300ER not only proved popular with existing 767

customers, but also helped to fill the gap in Boeing's product range below the 747, before the arrival of the 777. A total of seven airlines opted for the -300, while another 36 placed the -300ER into service. By 10 August 2005, orders (and deliveries) for the 767-300 stood at 104 (104) along with 520 (505) for the 767-300ER.

Next generation

By the late 1990s, the 767 was facing increasingly stiff competition from the Airbus A330 and even the A340. In answer to

this, Boeing took the 767-300 airframe and stretched it yet again to hold more fuel and more passengers. The new aircraft became the Boeing 767-400ER and it was formally launched in January 1997. Soon afterwards, Delta became the launch customer with an order for 21, in March 1997. In October a second order, for 26 aircraft, was placed by Continental (although later reduced to 16). The -400ER is intended to fit between the 767-300ER and the 777-200 in Boeing's line-up. It is aimed at replacing ageing TriStars, DC-10s

All Nippon Airways has been one of the 767's most important export customers. The airline's 58 examples are a mixture of 767-200, -300, -300ER and -300F variants and are all powered by CF6-80 engines.

and A300s and is targeted at potential A330-200 customers.

The 767-400ER adds another 253-in (6.42-m) fuselage stretch, again in a plug on either side of the wing. Passenger capacity is raised to 303 in a standard two-class layout, or 245 in a three-class layout. MTOW is increased to 449,735 lb (204000 kg) and the -400ER has a design range of 6,500 miles (10460 km).

More power

Higher-thrust versions of the standard engines, the CF6-80C2 and PW4060, have been developed, all rated in the 60,000-lb st to 62,000-lb st (267-kN to 276-kN) class.

Boeing initially included winglets in the 767-400ER

design, but these have been replaced by a pair of swept-back wingtip extensions. These raked wingtips are a less complex aerodynamic feature than conventional winglets, but offer similar improvements in wing performance. The new wing has an overall span of 170 ft 4 in (51.82 m), compared to the 156-ft (47.45-m) wingspan of the 767-300. The 767-400ER features the advanced six-screen EFIS cockpit of the 777 (which is also cross-compatible with the 737NG family and the 747-400) and a 777-style passenger cabin interior. The first 767-400ER made its maiden flight in August 1999 and the type entered service in 2000. Orders currently stand at 38, from a total of three customers.

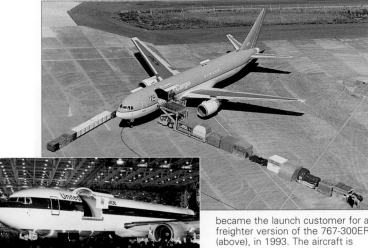

became the launch customer for a freighter version of the 767-300ER (above), in 1993. The aircraft is also known as the 767-300 General Market Freighter and differs from the UPS version in having mechanical freight-handling on the main and lower decks, air conditioning for animals and perishables on the main and forward lower decks and more elaborate crew facilities. The first aircraft flew in June 1996 and was delivered to Asiana on 23 August of the same year.

Freighter versions

In January 1993 UPS placed an order for the dedicated 767-300F freighter (inset above). A mock-up was completed in early 1994 and the first example flew on 20 June 1995. UPS has ordered a total of 32 -300Fs. South Korea's Asiana

The 767-400 is marketed as the 767-400ER and features sharply swept-back wing extensions which reduce take-off distance, increase climb rate and improve fuel consumption. The two major customers, as of August 2005, are Continental Airlines with 16 and Delta Air Lines with 21.

Boeing 777 Introduction

British Airways has remained faithful to Boeing, by purchasing the 777 in the face of stiff competition from Airbus. The American manufacturer has produced one of the most capable airliners on the market, allowing it to compete head on with both the twin-engined Airbus A330 and the four-engined A340.

New design and manufacturing initiatives to support Boeing's commitment to deliver a 'service ready' product have propelled aircraft manufacture into the computer age.

Back in the winter of 1986, Boeing discarded plans to build a larger 767 in favour of an entirely new twin-turbofan airliner to fit between the 767-300 and 747-400. In doing so it accepted that to meet the increasing competition from Airbus it had to harness new technology and take a pioneering leap in the development process. This decision was spurred on by the knowledge that by the time the new aircraft would enter service in 1995, the market would already be occupied by three competing types, the three-engined McDonnell Douglas MD-11 and, more significantly, the four-engined Airbus A340 and its twin-engined A330 stablemate. Then, still referred to as the 767-X, the new aircraft was presented to airlines on 8 December 1989, and launched into production, as the 777, on 29 October 1990, following a launch order for 34 firm aircraft plus 34 options from United Airlines.

Digital design

Making full use of new digital design and definition techniques, the 777 took shape with virtually no paper drawings. It became the first airliner to be 100 per cent digitally defined and pre-assembled, using the Dassault/IBM-developed CATIA CAD/CAM (computer-aided design/computer-aided manufacturing) software system. This powerful tool allows parts and systems to be viewed in three-dimensions, with misalignments and errors easily corrected on a computer screen, ensuring enhanced accuracy and fewer production changes. It also eliminated the need for costly full-scale mock-ups to be built.

Boeing also tackled the 777 programme from a multi-disciplinary perspective, establishing 238 design/build

Below: Boeing's T-38 Talon chase-plane lends some scale to the first 777 prototype (N7771). The unique nature of the 777 programme extended to flight testing, which utilised nine airframes, each assigned to a different aspect of the test schedule. Such an intensive and rapid test period gave airlines confidence in the new aircraft, Boeing receiving several advance orders from carriers convinced that they would suffer a minimum number of teething problems.

Left: United Airlines began revenue-earning services with the 777 on 7 June 1995, having received its first aircraft on 15 May 1995. United was a crucial partner during 777 development, keeping Boeing design teams in touch with the real world of day-to-day airline flying. With United's guidance, Boeing was able to optimise such features as overhead baggage bins, cabin entertainment systems and even interior decor. Here, one of the airline's 777s poses with a Boeing airliner of a much earlier period, the Model 247. The 247 is often described as the first airliner of truly modern design.

Cathay Pacific was the first airline to choose the Rolls-Royce Trent 800 turbofan for its 777s. The British engine had been flown on a Boeing 747-100 test bed in March 1995, before its first flight on a Boeing-owned 777 on 26 May 1995. Two Cathay aircraft were subsequently used in certification and service readiness trials.

teams which, via access to a common database, were able to work concurrently from concept to completion. But Boeing took this process a step further by making suppliers and airline customers an integral part of the design teams, giving both unprecedented access to the design process from an early stage. This 'working together' concept considerably reduced post-engineering changes and provided fewer 'in-service' surprises and enhanced reliability. It also ensured that customer airlines were receiving exactly the aircraft they required.

Testing and validation of aircraft systems installation was undertaken in a purpose-built Flight Controls Test Rig and Systems Integration Laboratory (SIL), identifying any potentially expensive problems.

The 777 stands out not only through its innovative design and manufacturing concepts, but also through its incorporation of leading-edge technologies, which keeps Boeing in the vanguard alongside Airbus.

The 777 features a new aerodynamically efficient, large-area swept wing, with increased thickness and long span. These features optimise the wing for improved payload/range characteristics, enhanced climb performance, and a Mach 0.83 cruise, at higher altitudes than previous airliners. A folding wingtip option was made available, allowing operations from gates and taxiways used by other wide-bodied aircraft, but has not been taken up.

Undercarriage advances

Another area where the 777 differs from other heavy aircraft is its use of a two-leg main undercarriage, with six-wheel bogies, and the use of 'clever' brakes, which reduce wear through alternate application of brakes during taxiing. The 777 was Boeing's first fly-by-wire (FBW) airliner and the world's first to achieve 180-minute ETOPS (extended-range twin operations) clearance from the outset.

The first 'Triple Seven' was unveiled to the world during a roll-out celebration at Everett on 9 April 1994 and took off on its three-hour 48-minute maiden flight on 12 June.

'Triple Seven' testing

Nine aircraft were used in the flight test programme; five powered by Pratt & Whitney PW4000 engines, two by General Electric GE90s and two by Rolls-Royce Trent turbofans. Simultaneous Federal Aviation Administration and Joint Airworthiness Authorities certification was awarded on 19 April 1995 and service entry with United Airlines on the Chicago-London route occurred on 7 June 1995. The initial model was the 777-200, with a higher gross weight and longer range 777-200IGW (Increased Gross Weight) variant entering service with British Airways on 9 February 1997. Boeing planned several future variants and these have matured into the 777-200F, 777-200LR, 777-300 and 777-300ER. The 777-200IGW is now designated as the 777-200ER.

At the time of the 777's first flight, Boeing had firm orders for 147 aircraft but, by June 1997, the order book had grown to 323 from 25 customers, including re-orders from impressed customers. Although late on the market, the early success of this 'paperless' aircraft would appear to vindicate Boeing's leap of faith and by August 2005, total 777 orders stood at 702, with 525 aircraft delivered.

Despite the continued growth of its 777 fleet, All Nippon Airways operated A340s for a time. ANA received its first 777 in December 1996, initial construction work on this, Boeing's 50th 777, having been started in the preceding May. By early 1996, the rate of 777 production had risen from three and a half per month to five.

Technical details

Subcontracting component manufacture to other companies is common in the airliner business, but Boeing went one stage further with its 777.

Aerospace manufacturing companies in Japan have been associated with Boeing products since the 1970s. This was particularly true of the 767, with Mitsubishi, Kawasaki and Fuji taking a 15 per cent workshare in the 767-200/-300. These three companies, represented by the Japan Aircraft Development Corporation (JADC), were therefore an obvious choice for the 777.

A final agreement between Boeing and JADC, signed on 21 May 1991, made the Japanese companies risk-sharing partners for 20 per cent of the entire 777 programme. This unprecedented move, along with sizeable subcontracts which were issued to companies around the world, allowed Boeing to use the very best manufacturers.

Representatives of JADC's constituent companies and two important Japanese subcontractors, Japan Aircraft Manufacturing Co. Limited and ShinMaywa, were soon based in Seattle.

Other subcontractors play a less major, but nonetheless important role in 777 manufacture.

Boeing carries out all 777 final assembly and flight testing. The barrel sections of the airliner's mid- and rear-fuselage are built by JADC in Japan. A hoist holds the Boeing-built wings, which are united with the Japanese-built centre section.

Structural breakdown

Boeing sources 777 structural components from companies in the US and from abroad. US subcontractors include Kaman, Northrop Grumman and Rockwell, while international suppliers include Aerospace Technologies, Alenia, EMBRAER, Boeing Australia, Korean Air, Shorts and Singapore Aerospace.

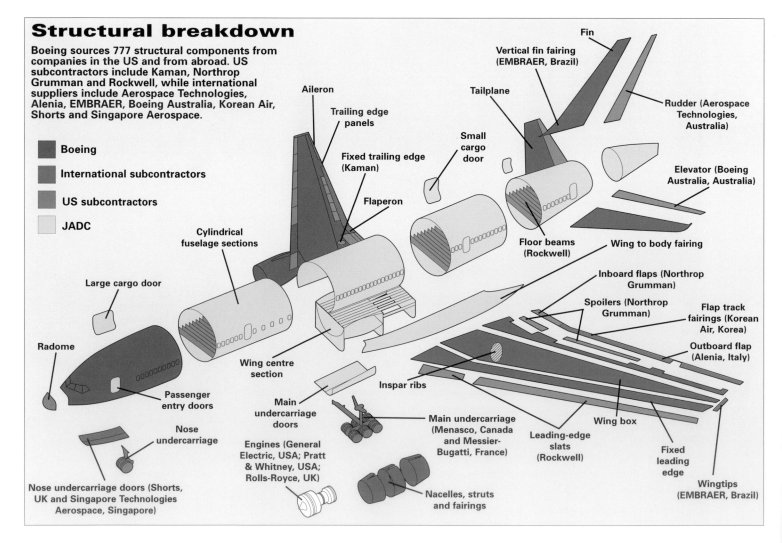

■ Boeing
■ International subcontractors
■ US subcontractors
□ JADC

Fin
Vertical fin fairing (EMBRAER, Brazil)
Tailplane
Rudder (Aerospace Technologies, Australia)
Aileron
Trailing edge panels
Small cargo door
Elevator (Boeing Australia, Australia)
Fixed trailing edge (Kaman)
Flaperon
Floor beams (Rockwell)
Wing to body fairing
Cylindrical fuselage sections
Inboard flaps (Northrop Grumman)
Spoilers (Northrop Grumman)
Flap track fairings (Korean Air, Korea)
Large cargo door
Outboard flap (Alenia, Italy)
Radome
Wing centre section
Inspar ribs
Passenger entry doors
Main undercarriage doors
Main undercarriage (Menasco, Canada and Messier-Bugatti, France)
Wing box
Nose undercarriage
Leading-edge slats (Rockwell)
Fixed leading edge
Engines (General Electric, USA; Pratt & Whitney, USA; Rolls-Royce, UK)
Wingtips (EMBRAER, Brazil)
Nose undercarriage doors (Shorts, UK and Singapore Technologies Aerospace, Singapore)
Nacelles, struts and fairings

777-200

As lead customer for the 777-200, United Airlines flew its first revenue-earning service with the type between London and Washington, DC, on 7 June 1995. United was initially unhappy with its 777s, leading to much public animosity between the airline and Boeing. These problems were resolved, however, with United ordering a total of 60 777-200 and -200ER aircraft.

Australian input
Australian aerospace companies provide many of the components for the tail section of the 777. The all-composite rudder is made by Aerospace Technologies, while the elevators are fabricated by Boeing Australia.

Fly-by-wire
Airbus had flown its first fly-by-wire airliner, the A320, as early as 1987, giving it a considerable lead over Boeing. The 777 emerged with a highly advanced system, however, with Britain's GEC-Marconi Avionics taking responsibility for the primary flight control computers.

Fuel capacity
A single integral tank in each wing, combined with a centre-section tank, gives the 777-200 a fuel capacity of 13,905 Imp gal (63216 litres). Both the 777-200ER and -300ER extended-range models, have a second centre-section tank, allowing an extra 6,195 Imp gal (28163 litres) of fuel to be carried, for a total capacity of 20,100 Imp gal (91379 litres).

Fuselage cross-section
During the early- to mid-1980s, Boeing perceived a need for an aircraft with a capacity between that of the 767-300 and 747-400. In order to provide such a machine, the company opted for a fuselage cross-section of 20 ft 4 in (6.20 m), which compares with 16 ft 6 in (5.03 m) for the 767 and 21 ft 3½ in (6.49 m) for the 747. According to customer requirements, seats may be arranged in the 777 up to a maximum of ten abreast.

Folding wingtips
A reduction in span to 155 ft 3 in (47.32 m) is possible with the provision of optional folding wingtips. This would allow the 777 to use airport facilities designed for older wide-bodied airliners such as the A300. No airline has taken the wing-fold option.

Cabin Layout
Boeing achieved maximum flexibility with the 777 cabin. The 777-200 offers maximum seating for 440 passengers. Internal fittings such as galleys and toilets are easily re-positioned throughout the cabin thanks to plumbing and electrical connections being available across wide areas.

Unique undercarriage
Menasco/Messier-Bugatti designed the six-wheeled main undercarriage units. Using a multi-bogie arrangement allowed weight to be distributed more evenly onto the runway surface, avoiding the need for a third, auxiliary main unit, mounted on the fuselage centreline.

Cockpit systems
In keeping with modern airline practice, the 777 is flown by a crew of two. Cockpit instrumentation is based around an advanced five-screen electronic flight instrumentation system, which uses Honeywell colour liquid crystal display screens in place of conventional analogue instruments.

A family of airliners
As lead customer, United began operations with the basic 777-200. Like British Airways, United has since opted for the 777-200ER which allows a maximum range of 8,441 miles (13584 km) with 305 passengers. Having flown late in 1997, the stretched 777-300 provides a 5,700-mile (10556-km) range with 368 passengers.

General Electric's 92,000-lb st (409.30-kN) GE90-92B entered service on the 777-200IGW with British Airways in November 1995.

Powerplant

The high technology 777 is propelled by the most powerful engines yet developed for application to a commercial aircraft. Further developments of these engines have seen thrust ratings up to 115,300 lb (513 kN) being achieved in order to power heavier versions of Boeing's twin jet.

Customers have a choice of three big high bypass-ratio turbofan engines, specifically aimed at the 777. The only all-new engine is the General Electric GE90 which, at a diameter of 10 ft 2½ in (3.12-m) has the biggest fan among the competing engines. It uses solid composite wide-chord fan blades, single-crystal blades in the high-pressure turbine to withstand the high temperatures, and a double-annular combustor to reduce noxious emissions. The GE90 has been certificated up to 115,300 lb st (513 kN) in its most powerful GE90-115B form for the 777-300ER.

Pratt & Whitney's derivative PW4000 was the launch engine for the 777, entering service with United in June 1995. It has a 9-ft 3¾-in (2.84-m) diameter fan with shroudless hollow titanium blades, single-crystal high-pressure turbine blades and an

A technician lends scale to the fan and nacelle of a Trent 800 on a Singapore Airlines 777. Note the distinctive shape of the fan blades and the exceptionally broad nacelle.

advanced combustor to reduce emissions. Certification has been received for thrusts up to 98,000 lb st (436 kN) in the PW4098 version.

The Rolls-Royce Trent 800 is derived from the highly-successful RB.211 family of three-shaft engines and entered 777 service with Thai International in April 1996. It has a diffusion bonded/ superplastically-formed wide-chord fan with a diameter of 9 ft 1¾ in (2.79 m) and also uses single-crystal high-pressure turbine blades. The Trent's maximum certificated thrust is 93,400 lb st (415 kN) in the Trent 895 on the 777-200ER, but it is capable of producing up to 95,000 lb st (422 kN).

Boeing and Rolls-Royce have tested this unusual nacelle and exhaust nozzle configuration on a Trent 800. The test aircraft is a 777-200ER and take-off noise levels have been reduced by some 4 dB.

ETOPS and undercarriage

Keen to avoid the extra weight and structural compromise represented by an underbelly main undercarriage leg, Boeing opted to fit the 777 with six-wheel main undercarriage bogies. The aircraft has also been certified to the highest possible degree for ETOPS operations.

The 777 was the first commercial aircraft to achieve 180-minute ETOPS certification at the time of its service entry. To achieve this industry first, the reliability of each engine type was evaluated in 3,000-cycle accelerated stress and endurance tests, and one aircraft with each different engine combination was dedicated to a 1,000-cycle flight test programme to simulate airline service. In addition, the Honeywell GTCP331-500 APU, now a flight-critical part

of the aircraft's operation, also had to undergo a 3,000-cycle test series to validate satisfactory operation in extreme hot and cold weather conditions. The P&W-powered 777 obtained ETOPS clearance on 30 May 1995.

Undercarriage

The retractable tricycle landing gear was the largest on any commercial aircraft. It differs from that of other heavy aircraft in having six-wheel bogies on each leg, eliminating the need for a

third, centreline main leg and simplifying the braking system. Steering rear axles are automatically engaged by the nose gear steering angle. As carbon brake wear is determined by the number of applications, rather than pressure, the Bendix Carbenix 4000 carbon brake system is programmed to apply brakes to alternate sets of three

*The 777's **ETOPS** qualifications are founded on the proven reliability of its engines and systems, as well as its comprehensive avionics fit.*

wheels only, when initial toe-pedal pressure is used during taxiing. Full toe-pedal pressure activates all six brakes on landing or during an aborted take-off.

Above: In order to spread its weight over the maximum possible area on the ground, the 777 uses unusual triple pairs of mainwheels. It has no centreline main gear leg.

Left: Twin wheels are used on the nose gear, with all wheels having Honeywell Carbenix 4000 carbon brakes. The main gear retracts inward, while the nose gear retracts forwards.

N7771 was the second 777 to fly, making its maiden flight on 12 June 1994. The aircraft has remained with Boeing and has been used extensively on flight test and promotional duties.

Boeing 777 variants

Boeing has successfully used the 777-200 airframe as the basis for incremental, and important, improvements and the larger 777-300 has moved the big Boeing twin-jet firmly into 747 territory. On 15 February 2005, Boeing unveiled its super long-range 777-200LR Worldliner, following this in May with the derived 777F freighter.

The 777 was designed to fill the gap between the 767 and 747, but Boeing initially drew up plans for a range of variants based solely on the -200 airframe. The first 'A-Market' aircraft was aimed at US domestic operators, and had an outline gross weight of between 505,000 lb and 515,000 lb (229068 kg and 233604 kg). This later rose to a maximum take-off weight of 545,000 lb (247210-kg), which is now standard for the 777-200. Carrying a load of 349 passengers, the 'A-Market' 777-200 could cover about 4,830 miles (7773 km). The increased-range 'B-Market' 777 that followed had a similar passenger capacity but with transatlantic range. It introduced a substantially higher gross weight of between 580,000 lb and 590,000 lb (263088 kg and 267624 kg). Plans were also drawn up, but later dropped, for a transpacific 'C Market' 777. Boeing simplified the designations by referring to the variants as the 777-200A and 777-200B, respectively, but this approach was later changed – ostensibly to fall in line with Boeing's established practice of not differentiating between similar aircraft with different operating weights. The 777-200A then became simply the 777-200 and the 777-200B became the 777-200(IGW) – Increased Gross Weight.

The IGW variant offered an impressive maximum range of up to 7,590 miles (12215 km), but in 1992 Boeing began to study ways in which even more performance could be squeezed out of the existing 777-200

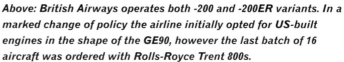

Above: British Airways operates both -200 and -200ER variants. In a marked change of policy the airline initially opted for US-built engines in the shape of the GE90, however the last batch of 16 aircraft was ordered with Rolls-Royce Trent 800s.

Below: Many of the early purchasers of the 777-200 (seen here) later opted to acquire the improved and extended range -200ER. United has some 53 777s in service.

Above: Two of Cathay Pacific's four 777-200s were used for certification and service readiness trials for the Trent-powered version before certification was granted in April 1996.

The majority of 777s in service in 2005 are 777-200ERs, which offer the same passenger carrying ability as the initial -200, combined with an increase in range of over 2,000 miles (3218 km). Egyptair operates three examples powered by PW4000 engines.

airframe. By accommodating yet more fuel, and upping the maximum take-off weight to 632,500 lb (286902 kg), Boeing could extend the 777's range to around 8,510 miles (13695 km). This version was initially known as the 777-200B+, but later (briefly) became the 777-200HGW (Higher Gross Weight). The weight was increased again, to 656,000 lb (297824 kg) for the definitive production-standard variant which boasted a maximum range of 8,861 miles (14260 km). This is now the standard production version and, in yet another name change, the model is now known as the 777-200ER (Extended Range).

777-300

The 777-300 is stretched by 33 ft (10 m) from the 777-200. As a result, capacity is increased to between 368 and 386 passengers in a typical three-class configuration. In an

all-economy layout, the 777-300 can accommodate as many as 550 seats. The 777-300 can serve routes up to 6,710 miles (10,805 km) with almost the same passenger capacity and range capability as the 747-100/-200 models, but burning one-third less fuel and with 40 per cent lower maintenance costs. Baseline maximum take-off weight is now 660,000 lb (299375 kg). Formal authorisation for the programme followed announcements at the 1995 Paris Air Show that ANA, Cathay Pacific, Korean Airlines and Thai Airways intended to order 31 aircraft. The first 777-300 was delivered to Cathay in June 1998.

Since 1997 Boeing had been studying improved performance versions of both the 777-200 and 777-300, as the 777X (777-200X and 777-300X). A 'shrink' version, the 777-100X, was under consideration in the mid-1990s but was eventually shelved. The importance of the

777X programme increased as Airbus pressed ahead with the A340-500 and A340-600. Despite their four-engined configuration, the new A340s are aimed squarely at the 777 market, while also seeking to take sales from the 747-400. Throughout the late 1990s a 777X launch was expected 'imminently', but never came, as Boeing fought a tough behind-the-scenes battle to convince airlines that it could meet its projected performance levels. In February 2000 the 777X was formally launched, as the awkwardly-named 777 Longer-Ranged Derivative (LRD). In July 2000 the first commitments were received from lessors GECAS, during the Farnborough air show. The deal for 10 777 LRDs, with another 10 options, was confirmed in October 2000. Also that month, Air France announced its intention to acquire 777 LRDs as part of a larger 777 order.

LRD to ER and LR

The 777-200 LRD and 777-300 LRD were to use the same basic airframe as their predecessors, mated with new engines and increased fuel loads, for their new 'long-range' capability. The 777-200 LRD was intended to achieve a range of 8,860 nm (10,194 miles, 16,405 km) – making it (according to Boeing) the longest-ranged airliner in the world. The 777-300 LRD would offer 747-class passenger capacity over 747-400 ranges, with 777 operating costs. Power would be supplied by the General Electric GE90-115B and a derated version, the GE90-110B1, would power the 777-200 Longer-Range Derivative. In the event, the 777-300 LRD evolved into the 777-300ER with a 775,000 lb (351534 kg) maximum weight and 115,300-lb (513-kN) -115B engines for a range of 7,880 nm (9,069 miles; 14,594 km). The -200 LRD emerged as the 777-200LR Worldliner (Longer Range), with a 766,000 lb (347452 kg) maximum weight, 110,100-lb (489 kN) thrust GE90-110B1 engines and a maximum range of 9,420 nm (10,841 miles; 17,446 km). The -300ER is already in service, while the -200LR is scheduled for service entry with Pakistan International Airlines in January 2006. An all-freight 777F derivative of the -200LR should enter service late in 2008.

The 777-300 can provide a similar seating layout to the 747 combined with the economy of a twin-engined layout.

Right: Emirates is unusual in operating 777-200, -200ER, -300 and -300ER variants. This 777-300 was the first of four to be leased by the airline and was delivered in November 1999. All of Emirates 777s are Trent-powered.

Boeing 777 operators

Air France, Alitalia, British Airways, KLM and Lauda Air have all ordered 777s for operations out of Europe. Air France has ordered 777-200ERs (illustrated), -300ERs and 777Fs.

Placed into service by United Airlines in the summer of 1995, Boeing's 777 has fulfiled the manufacturer's expectations with more than 700 ordered. The availability of three different powerplants for the three 777 variants allows airlines to acquire an aircraft tailor-made to meet their specific requirements.

United Airlines became the launch customer for the Boeing 777, when the US airline giant signed an initial contract for 34 aircraft, plus 34 options, in October 1990. United's 777 order was part of an even bigger deal that also included 30 747-400s and 30 options – at the time one of the largest single commercial aircraft orders ever placed. United's order was for the baseline Pratt & Whitney PW4077-powered 777-200 (then known as the 'A-Market') version. When Boeing launched the longer-range 'B-Market' version (which became the 777-200IGW and then the

777-200ER) the French charter airline Euralair actually became the first announced customer, in June 1991, with an order for two aircraft. However, this order was cancelled in 1996 and the honour of becoming the 777-200ER launch customer passed to British Airways.

BA order

In August 1991 BA ordered 15 777s, plus 15 options. The first five of these would be 777-200s, with the remainder selected as longer-range 777-200ERs, although the carrier's earliest long-range 777s were delivered as IGWs, not to the definitive

Carrying markings to celebrate Cathay Pacific's 50th anniversary in 1996, VR-HNA was the first of four 777-200s delivered to the airline. Since Hong Kong's handover to Chinese rule the VR- prefix has been replaced by China's B- designator.

-200ER standard. This first order for the 777-200ER also launched the all-new General Electric GE90 engine. The GE90-77B was adopted in preference to the Rolls-Royce Trent 877 – the first

time in nearly 30 years that BA had not chosen a Rolls-Royce engine option where one existed. Unfortunately, British Airways' experience with the GE90 was not entirely a happy

Below: Thai Airways International was the first airline to receive the Rolls-Royce Trent-powered 777-200, in April 1996. A follow-up order for six similarly-powered 777-300s was placed in 1995.

Below: United Airlines was the launch customer for the 777 placing its initial order for the 777-200 in October 1990. The first aircraft was delivered in May 1995.

Below: Asia has been an important region for the 777, with sales outstripping those to European carriers. China Southern Airlines operates four 777-200s and six 777-200ERs.

Above: Powered by General Electric GE90 engines, Saudi Arabian Airlines' 23 Boeing 777-200ERs are configured to carry 244 passengers in a three-class layout. They were delivered between 1997 and 2001.

one, and the engine suffered embarrassing teething troubles in its early days. The GE90 also proved to have a higher fuel burn than expected and suffered excessive gearbox wear that saw it taken off North Atlantic services in 1997. These difficulties are perhaps reflected in British Airways' surprise adoption of the Trent 800 for its latest batch of 777 orders, placed in August 1998.

The launch order for the Trent 877 came with a deal for an initial six 777s by Thai International in June 1991. The next customer to take delivery of a Rolls-Royce-powered 777 would be Cathay Pacific, which ordered 11 aircraft (777-200s and -300s) in May 1992. In November 1995 another 777 'mega-deal' was made by Singapore Airlines, and its associated leasing company SALE, when they placed a huge order for Trent-powered 777s.

The second 777 to fly, on 15 July 1994, was the first aircraft for United Airlines. The first GE90-powered aircraft, for British Airways, flew on 2 February 1995. Meanwhile, the first Trent-powered aircraft, destined for Cathay Pacific, flew on 26 May that same year. Following the award of the 777's FAA and JAA type certification on 19 April 1995, United Airlines took delivery of its first aircraft on 17 May. Approval for 180-minute ETOPS (Extended-range Twin-engined OPerationS) was issued for the 777 on 30 May 1995. The

first 777 revenue flight (UAL921) was made by United on 7 June 1995, from London-Heathrow to Washington-Dulles. The next airline to take delivery of a PW4000-powered 777 was All Nippon Airways, in October 1995.

The GE90 suffered several problems in its flight test programme and this set back 777 deliveries to British Airways. Certification was finally awarded on 9 November 1995 with the first deliveries following three days later. BA had planned to launch 777 operations in October, but in the event the first service was flown on the London-Dubai-Muscat route, on 17 November 1995. After British Airways, China Southern was the next airline to take delivery of a GE90-powered 777-200, in December 1996.

The first Trent-powered 777 was delivered to Thai Airways on 31 March 1996, with the first aircraft for Cathay Pacific following on 9 May. The next Trent 777 operator was Emirates Airlines, which took delivery of its first aircraft in June 1996.

1997 saw the first deliveries of the 777-200IGW (777-200ER) with aircraft going to three operators in quick succession. British Airways (GE90-94B) took delivery of its first example on 6 February 1997, followed by China Southern (GE90-94B) on 28 February and United Airlines (PW4090) on 7 March. The first operator of a Trent 895-powered 767-200ER was Malaysian

Airlines, which took delivery of its first aircraft on 23 April.

'Stretched' sales

When Cathay Pacific placed its initial 1992 order for 11 777s, with 11 options, it specified that some of these aircraft could be converted to the new stretched 777 then under development. In June 1995 this aircraft was officially launched as the 777-300, with orders from Cathay Pacific, All Nippon, Korean Air Lines and Thai International. All were existing 777 customers, and some – like Cathay – were switching existing 777-200 options to the new -300. While Cathay expected to be the first 777-300 customer, the first delivery was actually made to JAL on 15 May 1998. The first Cathay aircraft arrived on 22 May 1998.

Japan Airlines launched the long-range development of the

777-300, initially the Long-Range Derivative and later the 777-300ER, when it ordered eight 777-300 LRDs on 31 March 2000. Taiwan's Eva Air followed suit on 27 June with an order for three 777-200 LRDs, the type which finally surfaced as the 777-200LR, and four 777-300 LRDs. A further eight -300ERs was ordered in 2002. In July 2000 more commitments came from lessors GECAS, with a deal for 10 777-300ERs, followed by an order for four more in 2003. In October 2000, Air France announced its intention to acquire ten 777-300ERs as part of a larger 777 order and added a further four similar machines in February 2005.

The latest 777 variants, the -200LR and 777F, are subject to orders from EVA Air and PIA, and Air France, respectively, with other carriers showing strong interest in both derivatives.

Emirates has four 777-300ERs on order and will eventually lease a further 15 similar aircraft, to fly alongside a fleet of 23 leased 777-300s. The aircraft are configured in either a 364-seat three-class, or 434-seat two-class layout.

Bombardier CRJ

Canada's commuter

The Bombardier CRJ is a ground-breaking aircraft. It was the first of the new breed of regional jets that swept the airline marketplace during the 1990s. Based on the proven Challenger business jet family, the CRJ has given birth to a whole new family of its own, with a range of versions in production.

Canadair was already a well-established firm when it was acquired by Bombardier in 1986. Canadair's main product was the wide-bodied Challenger business jet and this twin-engined, T-tailed design became the basis for a whole new class of aircraft – backed by substantial funding from Bombardier. Using a stretched Challenger airframe, Canadair launched its Regional Jet – a type of aircraft which conventional wisdom had always decreed could not exist. The argument, until then, had always been that only turboprops could operate on routes of less than 500 miles (805 km), with relatively small passenger loads (40/50 seats). The counter argument ran that

the latest developments in small turbofan engines could make the figures work and that passengers would always choose jet-powered aircraft in any case – once one airline introduced jets on its regional routes, the others would be forced to follow.

Design finalisation

By June 1988 Canadair had decided on the fundamental design features of its Regional Jet. The aircraft was, indeed, a scaled-up Challenger 601, stretched to accommodate 50 passengers and powered by two General Electric CF34-3A turbofans. The Regional Jet was launched on 31 March 1989 with 56 commitments, but only one identified firm customer –

Capable of non-stop services over 2,265 miles (3646 km), the CRJ100LR was the longest-range version of the original 100 Series. Lauda Air was the launch customer and received eight examples between 1994 and 1996.

Lufthansa subsidiary DLT, which had signed for six firm aircraft, and six options. In June 1989 Bombardier bought the Northern Ireland-based firm Short Brothers, which became the chief provider of sub-assemblies for the Regional Jet programme. This also had the useful side-effect of eliminating Shorts' competing FJX design. At the same time, however, EMBRAER announced

its own EMB-145 proposal, which would become the Canadair Regional Jet's main rival.

During 1989 the Regional Jet's order book expanded to 126 commitments from nine customers. On 15 May 1990 DLT signed the first firm contract for a Regional Jet, ordering 13 aircraft and securing 12 options. Final assembly of the first aircraft began in late 1990 and, at that

Above: The CRJ200 cockpit display includes an integrated all-digital suite with dual primary flight displays and dual multifunction displays. A ground-proximity warning system (GPWS) and a windshear detection system are fitted as standard.

Left: Lufthansa CityLine remains one of the most significant CRJ operator outside the US. The airline has 43 CRJ100LR/200LRs and 20 of the larger CRJ700 in service.

Left: Skywest is one of a number of airlines which operate the CRJ200 and CRJ700 on connection flights for the major carriers. Skywest's 134 CRJ200s are flown in Delta Connection (left) and United Express colours.

Below: Air Nostrum operates under a franchise agreement with Iberia of Spain, its aircraft flying in Iberia Regional colours. The airline has, so far, received 32 of 56 CRJ200ERs ordered.

year's Farnborough Air Show (in September), Canadair announced a growth version of the original Regional Jet 100, the Regional Jet 100ER. This version had a higher maximum take-off weight, with an additional centre fuel tank to extend range.

The first Regional Jet was rolled out on 6 May 1991 and made its maiden flight on 10 May. Following a 1,400-hour, 14-month test programme, the RJ was awarded its Canadian Type Approval on 31 July 1992, although US and European certification was delayed by several months.

The aircraft's name has changed several times over the intervening years, abbreviated first to RJ and then expanded to CRJ, in the late 1990s, to differentiate it from the competing 'RJs' that have sprung up. The first RJ100 was delivered to Lufthansa CityLine (into which DLT had been merged) on 19 October 1992. Full JAA certification was awarded on 14 January 1993, by which time CityLine had three aircraft in service. The US RJ launch operator, Comair, took delivery of its first aircraft on 29 April 1993, and put the type into service on 1 June.

The Xerox Corporation placed a new development of the RJ into service in January 1994, when it took delivery of the first Corporate Regional Jet. An extended-range corporate version, the Special Edition, was launched in 1995.

In February 1994 Canadair announced the introduction of the RJ100LR (Long Range), along with a series of improvements to the RJ100 and RJ100ER.

The RJ100 was replaced by the CRJ200 as the standard production version in 1996 and the first delivery was made to Tyrolean Airways on 15 January. The CRJ200 is powered by improved CF34-3B1 engines and so can cruise higher, further and faster than the RJ100, with a 50-passenger load. CRJ200ER and CRJ200LR versions, with higher operating weights and increased range, are also available. The latter has a maximum range of 2,307 miles (3713 km). Three equivalent hot-and-high versions – the CRJ200B, CRJ200BER and CRJ200BLR – have modified CF34-3B1 engines.

Fuselage stretch

On 27 May 1999 the prototype of the 70-seat CRJ700 made its maiden flight. The CRJ700 (previously the CRJ-X) was launched in 1997 and Brit Air received the first aircraft in February 2001. The stretched CRJ700 is powered by the CF34-8. The standard CRJ700 Series 701 seats between 64 and 70 passengers, while the Series 705 seats 75.

In October 1999 Bombardier announced the 90-seat CRJ900 which is based on the CRJ700 with two additional fuselage plugs, taking the overall length to 118 ft 9 in (36.19 m). The basic aircraft has an 86 to 90-passenger interior with two-by-two seating at 31-in (78.70-cm) pitch. Other new features include five per cent higher-thrust CF34-8C5 engines, strengthened landing gear, increased underfloor baggage capacity with an additional underfloor baggage door and two additional overwing emergency exits. Like the CRJ700, it is available in ER and LR versions.

Above: As well as commuter and regional airlines, the CRJ100/200 has been purchased in small numbers by major corporations attracted by the aircraft's economy and low noise signature.

Below: First flying in May 1999, the CRJ700 is a 70-seat derivative of the CRJ200. Orders currently stand at 295, with entry into service, with Brit Air, occurring in February 2001.

Bombardier

By the late 1980s the Dash 8 had established itself, along with the ATR 42, as a market leader for the 40-passenger commuter aircraft market. Domestic operators in this role included Canadian Airlines (seen here) and Air Canada.

Dash 8 Q Series

Canadian commuter

Previously renowned for its rugged bushplanes, de Havilland Canada placed its faith in a new market – commuterliners. The Dash 8 introduced a new level of sophistication and remains in production by Bombardier in a number of distinct variants today.

During the 1970s de Havilland Canada began studying the prospects for an aircraft to fill the gap between the DHC-6 Twin Otter, typically seating 20, and the Dash 7 seating around 50. By 1979 these studies had crystallised into the Dash-X project, disclosed at that year's Paris Air Show. On 2 April 1980 it accepted an order from NorOntair for two, designated as DHC-8s, or Dash 8s, showing that the design was going ahead. The first of four flight prototypes

made its maiden flight on 20 June 1983. Orders came in a healthy stream, reaching 137 by mid-1987 and topping 150 by 1988.

In planning the Dash 8, careful note was taken of changing requirements. There was never any doubt that the aircraft should have a high wing, two turboprops, a pressurised cabin and good STOL qualities. At the same time, it was clear that almost all sectors would be flown from reasonable airports, and the field length was pitched at the 3,280-ft (1000-m)

level, appreciably longer than for all previous DHC aircraft. This fitted in well with the modest size of wing needed for cruising faster than the Dash 7, in order to get close to jet schedules on short sectors within the USA. At an early date, 36 seats was decided upon as the optimum size, and this has continued to be a popular size, though – like almost all its rivals – the Dash 8 has since been developed into a number of stretched versions.

With the wholly conventional wing design more or less decided, attention turned to powerplant

choice. After carefully looking at the General Electric CT7, de Havilland Canada's choice of engine predictably fell on the home product, the Pratt & Whitney Canada PW120A turboprop, rated at 1,800 shp (1432 kW). The aircraft's original 13-ft (3.96-m) diameter propellers were Hamilton Standard products, each with four glass-fibre blades.

The fuselage is of almost circular section, with a maximum diameter of 8 ft 10 in (2.69 m). Again, the structure is conventional, with adhesively bonded stringers and cut-out reinforcement. Almost the only striking feature is the nose, which is a long pointed cone

Dutch airline Schreiner Airways operated Dash 8 Series 300s on behalf of SABENA of Belgium. The aircraft had a single-class configuration for 48 passengers.

Below: Austrian carrier Tyrolean has been a staunch supporter of the type since receiving its first Series 100 aircraft in May 1985. The airline has since acquired the Series 300 and Series 400.

The increased capacity of the Series 300 appealed to airlines such as Lufthansa CityLine, helping to decrease the seat cost/mile ratio.

Below: Great China Airlines (now Uni Air) was the launch customer for the Series 400 (illustrated), ordering six with six options. It now operates Q200s, Dash 8-300s and Q300s.

angled downward so that its upper line almost follows the angle of the pilots' windscreens. The latter are flat, while the large side windows are curved and bear structural loads in flight. There is a passenger/crew door forward on the port side, with integral airstairs, and a baggage/cargo door on the same side behind the wing. The 30-ft (9.20-m) long passenger cabin of the original aircraft normally has nine rows of 2+2 seats, each row being opposite a window. The rear compartment area is 300 cu ft (8.5 m³) and can accept a spare engine or 2,000 lb (907 kg) of cargo (depending on the amount of baggage). There is normally a toilet and small buffet. A movable rear bulkhead enables mixed passenger/cargo operations to be flown, and the Dash 8 can be operated in the all-cargo mode, in which case the payload is 9,409 lb (4268 kg). Normal fuel capacity is some 695 Imp gal (3160 litres), in integral tanks outboard of the engines. Auxiliary long-range tanks can be provided. The Dash 8 can fly four 115-mile (185-km) sectors with full payload on internal fuel, or a single sector of 1,025 miles (1650 km).

New versions

Early in the 1980s de Havilland Canada (DHC) planned a Dash 8 Series 200, with 2,200-shp (1614-kW) PW122 engines, and displayed a model of a proposed 200M in anti-submarine warfare configuration, but this subsequently gave way to the more developed Triton maritime patrol version of the Series 300. The latter was announced in 1985 and first flown (by stretching the first prototype Dash 8) on 15 May 1987. This had 2,380-shp (1775-kW) PW123 engines and fuselage plugs ahead of and behind the wings, which extend the fuselage by 11 ft 3 in (3.43 m) to provide standard seating for 50 passengers. Wingtip extensions increased the span from 85 ft (25.91 m) to 90 ft (27.43 m). Other changes include dual ECS air-conditioning packs, a Turbomach T-40 APU, a rear service door on the starboard side and more space for toilets and coat-hanging. Maximum weight is increased from 32,402 lb (14968 kg) to 41,000 lb (18642 kg). Cruising speed is increased to a maximum of 326 mph (526 km/h), but there is little change in other aspects of

performance. Deliveries of the Series 300 began in February 1989, immediately following certification.

In June 1987 DHC, by now a subsidiary of Boeing, disclosed its interest in a further stretched version – the Series 400. This had additional plugs added to the front and rear fuselage, extending the length by a further 22 ft 5 in (6.83 m) to 107 ft 9 in (32.84 m), allowing the aircraft to seat up to 78 passengers.

In 1990 the improved Series 100A was introduced, with a restyled interior and PW120A engines. However, at this time Boeing announced its intention to sell DHC and in January 1992 the company was absorbed by Bombardier Inc. of Canada. Bombardier's stewardship has seen the progressive introduction of new models, including the Series 100B with PW121 engines allowing enhanced airfield and climb performance, the Series 200A which is an increased payload/performance version of the 100A with PW123C engines, the 200B with PW123D engines for full

power at high ambient temperatures, the Series 300A/B/C which have, respectively, increased payload/range, airfield performance and hot-and-high performance and the Series 400.

Q Series

In 1996 Bombardier redesignated the production versions Dash 8 Q100, Q200, Q300 and Q400 in recognition of a redesigned interior and noise and vibration suppression system (NVS) which reduced cabin noise levels by 12 dB. It uses the slogan 'The Quiet One' to promote the series.

Today, all four variants remain in production, with the first Q400s having been delivered in 1999. Total orders for the Dash 8 series have exceeded 780 and, although the introduction of the new generation of regional jets has undoubtedly affected sales, Bombardier is confident that the aircraft will remain in production for many more years. Indeed, it currently has an order backlog of two Q200s, 23 Q300s and 50 Q400s.

Military operators

The only non-standard aircraft of the original Series 100s were six for the Canadian Department of National Defence. Two of these were CC-142 transports and were fitted with rough-field landing gear, strong cargo floors, long-range tanks and special avionics. The other four were CT-142 navigation trainers, distinguished by their extended noses. Even more remarkable aircraft are the two E-9As (left) completed by Sierra Research of Buffalo for the USAF. These are flying datalinks operating up to 230 miles (370 km) off the Florida coast, performing radar surveillance and sending back voice and telemetry data during test, training and drone operations. Equipment includes a large, electronically-steerable, phased-array radar in a fairing on the right side of the fuselage, an APS-128D sea surveillance radar in a ventral radome and extensive internal avionics. The only other military operator is Kenya, which operates three Series 103s in the transport role.

de Havilland Canada DHC-6 Twin Otter

Canada's STOL liner

Excellent STOL performance, good load-carrying capability and the ability to land on virtually any surface made the Twin Otter the world's standard 'go anywhere' light transport.

De Havilland Canada, with a long history of manufacturing successful utility and bush aircraft behind it, began detail design work in November 1963 on a twin-engined development of the DHC-3 Otter. An experimental Otter powered by two Pratt & Whitney Canada PT6 turboprops had earlier shown great promise, and this engine was selected for the new design, which was designated DHC-6.

DHC's design philosophy was to create an aircraft which could operate unsupported in the most inhospitable environment, from land, water, ice or snow. It was to offer good short take-off and landing characteristics, have low operating costs and simple maintenance requirements, and employ as many components and as much of the production tooling of its single-engined forebear as possible.

The Twin Otter retained the Otter's wing section (although with increased span), its fuselage cross-section and many other components. The resulting design was a conventional strut-braced high-wing monoplane of all-metal construction with double-slotted trailing-edge flaps

Above: Between 1979 and 1985 the Civil Aviation Administration of China purchased 11 Twin Otter Series 300s for operations in less accessible areas of the country.

Top: The Twin Otter had global appeal, operating on every continent, and sold to both civil and military customers. This example is one of two purchased by Air Mali in 1973.

and drooping ailerons to enhance STOL performance, cruciform tail surfaces with a slightly swept fin and fixed tricycle undercarriage with float or ski options.

Work began on the prototype in July 1964 and the first flight occurred on 20 May 1965. In July 1966 the first production-standard Series 100 went into service with launch customer Trans-Australia Airlines, followed shortly by the Ontario Department of Lakes and Forests.

Commuter liner

Although designed primarily with the needs of bush operators in mind, the Twin Otter quickly attracted great interest from airlines operating feeder and commuter services.

After 115 Series 100s had been completed, production was

Developed as a bushplane, the Twin Otter is very rugged, with exceptional performance. Series 100s (seen here) are identified by their shorter, more rounded nose.

switched to the Series 200 introduced in April 1968. This featured an extended nose housing a larger baggage compartment, and an expanded rear baggage area.

From the spring of 1969 DHC began delivering the definitive production Twin Otter – the Series 300. Improvements included a large two-part passenger/cargo door on the port side, an additional passenger door to starboard, separate crew doors, increased fuel capacity, optional wingtip tanks, an increase in maximum take-off weight and the powerplant upgraded to the PT6A-27s. The floatplane version of the Series 300 differed in having the shorter nose of the Series 100 fitted.

Special versions of the Series 300 have included the 300S, with upper wing spoilers, high-capacity brakes and an 11-seat cabin. This was developed for operations on the STOLport service, run by Air Canada subsidiary, Air Transit Canada, between Ottawa and Montreal. A maritime patrol variant was developed in 1977 for Greenlandair Charter to operate on ice patrol and surveillance duties. It incorporated a Litton

LASR-2 search radar in a chin radome, Omega navigation system, four observers' stations with bubble windows, additional fuel capacity, and 'finlets' on the tailplane similar to those installed on floatplane variants.

Optional equipment developed for the Twin Otter included a ventral baggage pannier, a cabin-mounted chemical retardant tank for firefighting missions and oversize low pressure 'tundra' tyres for soft field operations.

Survey version

Among the most extensively modified examples were two Series 300s delivered to China and Kenya for geophysical survey work. These aircraft were equipped with a Scintrex Tridem airborne electromagnetic system housed in two wingtip pods. They also carried a long noseboom housing a proton magnetometer, a VLF electromagnetic system, a radiometric spectrometer sensor in the rear cabin and a strip camera and sophisticated Doppler navigation system for accurate positioning during survey runs.

The ruggedness and reliability of the Twin Otter has also resulted in the aircraft being chosen for a number of particularly demanding roles. One Series 300 was flown in support of the British Trans-globe Expedition operating from remote strips. Other Series 300s have been used for many years by the British Antarctic Survey. Able to operate in the harshest of climates, the aircraft supports the British survey team throughout the Antarctic summer and is one of the few aircraft types to have been based on this continent. In the winter the aircraft returns to the UK for much needed maintenance.

Throughout the 1970s and 1980s the Twin Otter was in widespread service around the world with both commuter airlines and specialist operators. Since the last of the 844 Twin Otters left DHC's Downsview factory in 1988, the numbers in service (particularly in airline use due to the advent of newer and more efficient types) have steadily declined. However, the Twin Otter's great ability to operate from any terrain in remote areas has ensured its popularity with smaller operators and it is likely to continue its important but little recognised work well into the 21st century.

Twin Otter Series 300

In the 1980s, a fleet of Twin Otters and DHC-8 Dash 8s was operated on behalf of NorOntair (based at North Bay) by other airlines such as Labrador Airways, Air Dale and Bearskin Lake. This Series 300 is painted in the company's standard bright colour scheme which also served as a conspicuity aid during the winter, where aircraft might have had to force-land in the snow. The bird motif represents the loon, a well-known bird of eastern Canada.

High-lift wing
Along with a high power/weight ratio, the Twin Otter's high-lift wing gives the aircraft its excellent STOL performance. Rectangular in form, the high-mounted mainplanes have a single bracing strut and very effective NACA-type double-slotted flaps along the entire length of their trailing edges. The outer halves act differentially as ailerons for roll control. Wing loading is moderate, allowing good manoeuvrability and a low stalling speed.

Powerplant
Series 200 Twin Otters are powered by two Pratt & Whitney PT6A-20 engines developing 579 shp (432 kW). The Series 300 is fitted with the 620-shp (462-kW) PT6A-27. The three-bladed Hartzell propellers are fully-feathering.

Flight crew
The Twin Otter is usually operated by a crew of two, although single-pilot operation is possible. The control column, located on the aircraft's centreline, has 'Y' arms at the top, carrying the pilot's and co-pilot's control wheels.

Reshaped nose
The popularity of the Twin Otter with commuter airlines prompted DHC to fit the Series 200 and 300 with a lengthened nose, containing an additional baggage hold.

CF-TVP

norOntair

De Havilland Canada DHC-7 Dash 7

Civilian STOL

Renowned for its family of rugged 'bush' aircraft and STOL freighters, de Havilland Canada made a bold step into the 'third level' airline market with its outstanding DHC-7 Dash 7.

Many of the 'third level' airlines emerging in the 1960s had a requirement for an aircraft seating 15-20 passengers. DHC's solution to this was the DHC-6 Twin Otter, a high-wing STOL machine, powered by two PT6A-20 turboprops. As the airlines matured and looked for larger aircraft, they had little choice but to consider machines such as Fokker's F27, and DHC realised that there was a strong market opportunity for a new 48-seat aircraft with good field performance which would appeal especially to existing Twin Otter users. Thus the new DHC-7 was conceived and given the obvious but effective name, Dash 7.

Design work began in 1972, and the first prototype made its maiden flight on 27 March 1975.

US certification

DHC pressed on urgently with the test-flying and soon brought a second prototype into the programme to speed up the certification process.

The Canadian Department of Transport awarded a Canadian-type approval certificate on 19 April 1977, which was followed immediately by FAA type certification. By now, the basic model in standard

Above: The high wing of the Dash 7 is an integral part of its STOL design. An additional benefit of such a configuration is ease of passenger access, since the cabin doors are close to the ground.

Top: The first prototype de Havilland Canada Dash 7 is seen flying over Toronto. With its impressive STOL capabilities, the Dash 7 was a worthy successor to the DHC-6 Twin Otter.

passenger configuration had been given the designation Dash 7 Series 100 and DHC was ready to begin deliveries.

Sound design concept

The DHC-7 was designed specifically for short-haul routes of around one hour's duration. DHC gave special consideration to environmental factors because of the need for many operators to fly from smaller airports, which were often located close to city centres. As a result, the Dash-7 has demonstrated particularly low

Both of Inex-Adria Aviopromet's Dash-7 Series 102s are seen outside DHC's factory in October 1982.

Operated by Transport Canada, C-GCFR is a Series 150 modified to Dash 7IR (Ice Reconnaissance) standard. Equipment includes a SLAR in a port fuselage fairing, and an observation cupola.

noise levels and, in testing of the aircraft for approval under the American FAR Part 36 noise regulations, the Dash 7 was flown into Chicago's Meigs Field Airport at noise levels which were virtually inaudible against a background of normal Chicago road traffic.

DHC aimed to give the Dash 7 excellent short-field performance and it has a FAR Part 25 take-off field length of 2,260 ft (689 m) and a landing distance of 1,950 ft (594 m) at maximum take-off gross weight, at sea level under standard conditions. The high-aspect ratio wing is fitted with

double-slotted large-chord flaps which extend across 80 per cent of the wingspan. In addition, the four turboprops are positioned well apart, augmenting the airflow across the wings and flaps with maximum propeller thrust. As a consequence, considerable safety advantages accrue to the Dash 7 in critical 'go-around' situations arising from an aborted landing.

Short-field landings are particularly effective with the combined use of spoilers, propeller pitch control and standard wheel braking. Normal practice is to move the propellers into ground fine pitch control as soon as the main wheels touch the ground. This neutralises up to 90 per cent of the wing lift immediately. At the same time, the inboard spoilers are deployed. When the

nosewheels touch down, the pilot deploys the outboard spoilers and completes the landing run with the anti-skid mainwheel braking system. This ability, along with the DHC-7's low level of noise emissions, helped to promote fledgling airline services to city airports, including London's now extremely successful Docklands airport.

Powerplant
All versions of the Dash 7 were powered by four 1,120-shp (835-kW) Pratt & Whitney Canada PT6A-50 turboprops fitted with four-bladed Hamilton Standard 24 PF constant-speed propellers.

Dash 7 variants
Two basic main variants were developed: the Series 100 (and its Series 101 all-cargo sub-variant); and the Series 150 (and its Series 151 all-cargo sub-variant) with increased weights and extra fuel capacity.

Passenger load
Standard seating is provided for 50 passengers in a four-abreast arrangement with a centre aisle. Alternatively, 56 passengers may be accommodated in a high-density layout.

DHC-7 Dash 7 Series 110

Dash 7 Series 110 G-BRYA, the 62nd aircraft produced, was delivered to Brymon Airways in October 1981 and named *Ville de Paris.* **The name was appropriate because it was, at times, operated on behalf of Air France. When Brymon became a subsidiary of British Airways in 1993, the name was changed to** *Aberdeenshire/Siorrachd Obar Dheathain.*

High-set tailplane
The high-mounted tailplane of the Dash 7 is kept well clear of the considerable wash from the aircraft's four propellers. Such a configuration must be carefully designed, however, since the tailplane must be mounted high enough to avoid it being aerodynamically blanked by the wing at high angles of attack. Such blanking can result in a deep stall and catastrophic loss of control.

Turnaround
With its ability to use short runway lengths and to make steep landing approaches, the Dash 7 is able to fit into otherwise crowded airport traffic patterns. This effectively increases airport capacity, while the DHC-7's ability to disembark and re-embark passengers quickly increases the cost-effectiveness of the aircraft.

Fuel capacity
Each wing contains two integral fuel tanks giving the Series 100 a total capacity of 1,243 Imp gal (5652 litres). Refuelling is accomplished via a single pressure refuelling point on the underside of the rear fuselage.

Dash 7 into service

Pelita Air Services' fourth Dash 7 was the hundredth aircraft built. Pelita's Dash 7 fleet numbers six aircraft.

The Dash 7, by helping to pioneer the use of STOLports, has assured itself a place in the history books. Almost two decades after the first flight of the last machine built, it is still proving useful with more than 70 remaining in service.

The first DHC-7 operator was Rocky Mountain Airways of Denver, Colorado, which placed its initial aircraft in service at the end of 1977 on routes to the local mountain ski resorts. A pair of Dash 7s also reached Greenlandair to supplement and expand the operations carried on for some time by Twin Otters. The airline, now Air Greenland, flies its Dash 7s in the most extreme winter conditions, performing operations from very demanding airfields which are almost permanently covered in snow and ice. The Dash 7s fly from Godthaab, the main base of Air Greenland and service Narsarsuaq and Kulusuk among other destinations. In many cases, these airfields are surrounded by mountains and the ability of the Dash 7 to make a very steep approach is critical. In fact, the backbone of Greenlandair's fleet before the arrival of the Dash 7 was the Sikorsky S-61 helicopter, which provided the only practical and safe method of operation to and from many of the airline's destinations. The company also used the Dash 7s to provide support for the USAF strategic radar base at Thule.

Alyemda of Yemen was an early customer for the Dash 7, its rugged construction and STOL ability being ideal for the conditions in the country.

STOL effectiveness

Several of the commuter airlines that have bought the Dash 7 have made use of the 'Separate Access Landing System' concept which had been promoted by DHC. This involves the use of either limited, or stub, sections of runway which are available only because of the aircraft's unique ability to manoeuvre onto such sections outside the general flow of the airport's traffic. This system has been operated successfully by Ransome Airlines at New York and Washington National, and by Golden West Airways which has used it at San Francisco. In Europe, Maersk Air has used the same techniques at Copenhagen. In Canada, the Dash 7 was able to develop services into downtown airports at Toronto and Montreal. City Express Airlines had four

De Havilland Canada proposed many military roles for the Dash 7, including those of freighter and maritime patrol, but almost all of the 114 built entered civil service. Only Canada and Venezuela bought new aircraft for military service, while the US Army acquired used machines. CC-132 132001 was one of two Canadian Armed Forces Dash 7s operated as CC-132s, for passenger and freight transport between various locations in Europe in support of the Canadian NATO detachment. 132001 was in service between 1979 and 1987.

The proposal for a new airport right in the heart of London, at Canary Wharf, hinged on the short-field performance and low noise levels of the Dash 7. Brymon Airways was quick to take advantage of the new facility, as was Eurocity Express. Eurocity Express was founded in 1986, becoming London City Airways and merging into British Midland in September 1990. Eurocity Express was based at London City Airport and used Dash 7s on routes to conventional airports.

Dash 7s which it used to link these two cities with the capital, Ottawa, on a very-high-frequency schedule, and the quick turnaround of the aircraft was vital to the feasibility and success of this service.

STOLport operations

In the UK, the principal operator to adopt the Dash 7 was Brymon Airways. Again, Brymon was a large Twin Otter user and purchased five Dash 7s to meet its requirement for greater-capacity aircraft. The Dash 7 was a key factor in the joint venture between Brymon and the John Mowlem construction group to develop a STOLport in London's Docklands. Approval for the 2,600-ft (792-m) runway to serve the City of London was given in May 1985, the short-field performance and low noise levels of the Dash 7 being the basis on which the government sanctioned construction of the airstrip. Brymon operated routes from the STOLport to Brussels, Amsterdam, Paris, Rotterdam and Frankfurt, with substantial time savings for business travellers from central London.

The Dash 7 has also gained a few military orders. The first of these was for two aircraft for the

The Dash 7s of Air Greenland (formerly Grønlandsfly, or Greenlandair) feature a large forward freight door on the port side has proved useful when carrying equipment for the oil industry.

Canadian Armed Forces (CAF), which needed them to transport high-ranking passengers and freight around Europe. These aircraft received the CAF designation CC-132 and were delivered to No. 412 Squadron at Lahr, West Germany. One of the machines was fitted with a 22-seat rear cabin, a central galley area and a forward VIP section for 10 senior passengers. The other aircraft was built to Series 101 standard with a cargo door, and was used on the weekly scheduled service operated by the Canadians between the Squadron's base at Lahr and Gatwick (where it collected passengers from the transatlantic CAF Boeing 707 service). On the return flight, the Dash 7 dropped off passengers at Chievres and Maastricht before returning to its home base. These aircraft were later replaced by Dash 8s. A single Dash 7 has been operated by the Venezuelan navy since 1982.

A more recent military user is the US Army, which has at least

Atlantic Southeast Airlines' Dash 7 Series 102 N502GG has flown with at least three other airlines during its lifetime. The demand for second-hand Dash 7s remains high.

eight second-hand Dash 7s in use for the Airborne Reconnaissance Low programme. After modification by California Microwave and ESL Inc, the Dash 7s are operated as sophisticated electronic reconnaissance aircraft, in quasi-civilian colour schemes.

In 1986, with the Dash 7 reaching the end of its 114-aircraft production run, DHC had been seriously considering the possibility of building a stretched version known as the

Series 300. In market surveys carried out during 1982, there was a strong indication of interest in such a development, but it was decided that the Dash 8 (a twin-engined aircraft without STOL capability) should receive priority. When Boeing acquired DHC, all work on the Dash 7 ceased, leaving the Dash 8 as the company's main product. Even so, it is typical of the rugged DHC-7 that more than 70 per cent of Dash 7s continue to fly in revenue-earning service.

Long-lived Douglas DC-8

Although its passenger-carrying days are over, the DC-8 remains a hard-working freighter that is still in service, albeit in dwindling numbers, around the world. Most surviving aircraft are late-production Series 60s or the re-engined, CFM56-powered Series 70, introduced during the 1980s. As a result of several overhaul and upgrade programmes, the worldwide DC-8 fleet still has many active years ahead of it.

Above: Venice-based Aeronavali became the world authority on DC-8 passenger-cargo conversions. The large forward freight door is open on this aircraft.

Top: Not all of the passenger DC-8s saw out their days with airlines. A40-HMQ served with the Oman Royal Flight. It was built as a DC-8-63CF and converted to -73CF standard (illustrated) in 1982.

Douglas built six basic versions of the DC-8, in three fuselage lengths. By the time production ended in 1972 the final DC-8-60 versions – launched as the 'Super Sixty Series' – were over 36 ft (10.97 m) longer than the basic aircraft, accommodating up to 250 passengers. It was this ability to stretch the DC-8, a feature which had been built into its design from day one, that contributed to its longevity. The DC-8 will probably outlive its great rival, the Boeing 707, because it has proved to be so adaptable. Today, however, apart from a handful of military and VIP aircraft, there are no DC-8s in (regular) passenger service. Instead, the DC-8 family has carved an important niche for itself as a freighter, and many operators have spent a lot of money on upgrading and improving their ageing aircraft.

In all, McDonnell Douglas built

a total of 556 DC-8s. The first major changes to the standard aircraft were driven by the arrival of new noise and environmental regulations, which took force in the early 1980s. McDonnell Douglas looked at re-engining options for the DC-8, which included fitting the Pratt & Whitney JT8D-209 engines of the MD-80, or completely new CFM56 turbofans. In March 1979 United Airlines launched the first DC-8 re-engining programme, opting to fit the CFM56 to its fleet of 30 DC-8-60s, at a cost of $400 million. In fact, the CFM56 became the only new engine option and McDonnell Douglas announced that the modified aircraft would be known as the Series 70. Only Series 60 DC-8s were selected for conversion, and so re-engined DC-8-61s became DC-8-71s, -62s became -72s and -63s became -73s.

A new joint venture company called Cammacorp was established by McDonnell Douglas, CFM International and Grumman (Grumman built the new engine nacelles), charged with gaining a new FAA Supplemental Type Certificate (STC) for the DC-8-70 Series and began work on its first conversion, a DC-8-61. This aircraft was redelivered to United Airlines, as a DC-8-71, on 10 May 1981 and made its first revenue flight on 16 May.

A number of conversions (44) was handled at the Douglas facility, in Tulsa. Three customers

– Delta, UTA and Air Canada – opted to undertake the work themselves, under agreement with Cammacorp.

The 22,000-lb st (98.12-kN) CFM56-2 engines brought the DC-8 into full compliance not only with the Stage 2/Chapter 2 noise regulations of the mid-1980s, but also with the far more stringent Stage 3/Chapter 3 standards, that were brought into full effect in mid-2000. Hand-in-hand with this came a substantial increase in performance and a 25 per cent reduction in overall fuel burn. Over a 3,000-nm (3,450-mile,

Preparations for the the 1991 Gulf War saw the US Civil Reserve Air Fleet mobilised, with the result that a number of DC-8 cargo conversions saw active service as strategic airlifters. This aircraft is a Hawaiian Airlines DC-8-62F.

Emery Worldwide Airlines maintained a large fleet of DC-8 freighters. This included examples of the DC-8-54F, -62F, -63F, -71F and -73F (illustrated).

5552-km) sector, McDonnell Douglas claimed that a DC-8-71 burned 17,000 lb (7711 kg) less fuel than a DC-8-61. More power and greater economy pushed the range of a Series 70 to a maximum of 6,300 miles (10138 km), or about 25 per cent more than a Series 60. The CFM56-2 turbofan provided 17 per cent more power than a JT3D-7 engine and 22 per cent more power than a JT3D-3B. The new engines also reduced take-off roll by about 10 per cent and improved climb performance by 16 per cent.

The last of 110 Series 70 conversions was a DC-8-72, delivered to NASA in April 1986. Major customers included United Airlines, Delta Air Lines, Flying Tiger, UPS, Air Canada and UTA.

To these airlines the DC-8-70 Series offered low acquisition and running costs, coupled with the ability to fly into noise-sensitive airports around the clock thanks to the Stage 3/Chapter 3 compliance. Furthermore, for those aircraft that were not already configured as freighters, the cargo conversion process was straightforward and several companies began to offer DC-8 freighter modifications.

Freighters and hush-kits

McDonnell Douglas developed its own freighter conversion in

For the long-range transport of passengers and cargo, the French air force flies three Airbus A310s and two DC-8-72s.

the mid 1970s. This involved the removal of all seating and passenger facilities, fitting a strengthened cargo floor, with rollers, and adding an 85- x 140-in (2.15- x 3.55-m) main cargo door in the forward port fuselage. All windows were removed and replaced with blank plugs. The US firm later sold its design to Italy's Aeronavali (now part of Alenia). Aeronavali's Venice facility became the main centre for cargo conversions, which included a major contract for 25, placed by lessors GPA in the early 1990s. A handful of other cargo conversions was carried out by firms such as Zantop, PSA and Stambaugh Aviation.

For DC-8 operators who cannot meet the cost of

re-engining their aircraft, but who still need to meet today's noise rules, several hush-kit options have been developed for the JT3D engine. These include the 'SilentKnight' hush-kit designed by the Aeronautical Development Corp., plus Stage 3/Chapter 3 solutions developed by the Burbank Aeronautical Corp. and Quiet Technology Venture (previously Quiet Nacelle Corp.). In 1990 US charter operator MGM Grand Air became the launch customer for the BAC hush-kit, while the QTV hush-kit was first fitted to Fine Air DC-8s in 1997.

Another engine-related modification was conducted by Page AvJet for Airborne Express, in the USA. In 1991 Airborne Express started to have the long-duct engine pylons and nacelles of the DC-8-62/63 refitted to all its DC-8-61 freighters, allowing them to accommodate the BAC

Stage 3 hush kit.

Today, the largest DC-8 operator is United Parcel Service (UPS), which has a fleet of 47 DC-8-70 freighters. UPS launched an ambitious upgrade for all its DC-8s and Boeing 727s, adding a four-screen EFIS cockpit, INS, colour weather radar, autopilot and complete electrical re-wiring. By 1995, work on all its DC-8s had been completed, bringing what had previously been 14 different levels of equipment up to a common standard.

Other major DC-8 operators include ATI-Air Transport International (six DC-8-60s and 13 DC-8-70s), ABX Air (23 DC-8-60s), Arrow Air (seven DC-8-60s) and Astar Air Cargo (nine DC-8-70s). All of these airlines are pure cargo-carriers. By summer 2005, the worldwide DC-8 population was approximately 200 aircraft.

As one of the world's leading parcel movement companies, UPS uses the DC-8 to fill the gap in its cargo capacity between the smaller Boeing 727 and 757, and the larger A300, MD-11, 767 and 747.

Douglas DC-9

Series 10, 15 and 30

If the capacity for development is the mark of a great design, the DC-9/MD-80/MD-90 family deserves a place in that small and exclusive category.

Over a 15-year period, Douglas had based an entire line of transports on the DC-4, before it moved into the jet age with the DC-8, which entered service in 1959.

The first jets to appear on long-distance services contrasted sharply with the older aircraft used on shorter flights, particularly in the USA, but there was no basic agreement on the best way to replace the latter. Some argued that fast turboprop aircraft would not be much slower than the jets on the shorter routes, and would be more economical. Others felt that the travelling public would regard the jet as standard, and would identify any propeller-driven aircraft as old-fashioned. The correct size for such a new aircraft was also a matter of controversy and, as a result, the market for new short-haul aircraft became a fierce and confusing battlefield. Lockheed and Vickers were pushing advanced turboprop aircraft. France already had the Caravelle short-haul jet in production. Neither Boeing nor Douglas had any firm programme to offer, but each believed that jets were the solution. Both started out by looking at scaled-down versions of their big jets, and by 1959 Douglas had made serious presentation of the first

DC-9, with four Pratt & Whitney JT10 turbojets, to United Airlines and other major carriers. But at the end of 1960, United and Eastern (the two biggest US domestic carriers) placed orders for the advanced Boeing 727.

Douglas immediately saw that there was room for a smaller aircraft. Of its two US rivals, Boeing was preoccupied with the 727 and Lockheed was still salvaging the Electra programme. The competition would most probably from the Caravelle. United had ordered 20 Caravelles in 1959, and the US airframers were worried that lower European labour rates would give the type a competitive edge.

Following the launch of the 727, Douglas, Sud-Aviation and General Electric began to hold serious discussions about the joint development of an improved and Americanised Caravelle, powered by General Electric's CJ805-23 aft-fan engine. But the Caravelle was already eight years old and, from

Above: Rolled out from Douglas's production line at Long Beach, California in February 1965, the DC-9 Series 10 was the shortest variant developed. The T-tail and rear-mounted engines can clearly be seen in this view.

Top: Regional American airline Republic operated a fleet of DC-9-50s throughout the early 1980s. The airline was later taken over by Piedmont which, in turn, was later absorbed by US Air.

Below: Wearing the colours of launch customer Delta Air Lines, this DC-9-14 illustrates the original short fuselage, which offered a maximum passenger capacity of 90.

Wearing the colours of the now defunct US regional airline Best, this DC-9-15 operated throughout the late 1970s and early 1980s.

Right: SAS inspired the production of the DC-9 Series 20 and Series 40. The carrier also flew -30s, as here.

the systems viewpoint, it was a first-generation turbine airliner. With General Electric engines, it would also be close in capacity to the 727. Then, in May 1961, the British Aircraft Corporation announced the go-ahead for its BAC One-Eleven, a smaller, but completely new aircraft.

In 1962, Douglas salesman began to show airlines a completely new design, the D-2086. Like the Caravelle, One-Eleven and 727, it had rear-mounted engines, a clean wing and a short landing gear, the last being particularly important because the new jet was designed to operate in the absence of complex ground-handling facilities. Like the 727, the D-2086 would have to use shorter runways than those used by the big jets. The development of airports in the USA had lagged behind the expansion of the airlines, and the new jet would have to use the same runways as slower piston-engined types.

The wing design philosophy, however, was closer to that of the Caravelle than the advanced wing of the 727; Douglas selected a relatively large and moderately swept wing, with double-slotted trailing-edge flaps. The powerplant was to be a pair of Pratt & Whitney JT8Ds – the very promising turbofan engines under development for the 727. The JT8D was a little more powerful than necessary, but it provided room for growth and would be common to the airlines' 727 fleets.

This was the DC-9, launched with a 15-aircraft order from Delta Air Lines in April 1963, with an option for a further 15 examples. By this time, the One-Eleven was only a month away from its first flight, and had secured major US orders from American and

Mohawk Airlines; speed would be vital if the DC-9 was to catch up. The flight-test programme was intensive. The first aircraft flew on 25 February 1965, and five were flying by June. The initial production version – the DC-9-10 – was certified in November.

Modified version

By the time Delta started operations with the new type, Douglas was well advanced with the development of a new and considerably modified version, designed primarily for operations on the east coast of the US and in Europe, where runways in the 10,000 ft (3050 m) bracket were generally available, and where the 727's near-transcontinental range was not needed. The new version was to be stretched by 15 ft (4.57 m), raising passenger

capacity from 80 to 105. The wing was slightly increased in span, and fitted with full-span leading-edge slats, and the JT8Ds were used at their full design rating. The first order for this new version, the DC-9-30, was received from Eastern Airlines in February 1965. The higher-rated engines were also made available on the basic aircraft, as the DC-9 Series 15 or DC-9-15.

The DC-9-30 was substantially bigger than any One-Eleven, and was more economical, but it faced competition from the new Boeing 737, launched just two months later. Douglas held one decisive advantage; the DC-9-30 would enter service in early 1967, before the first 737 flew, and the airline industry was growing so rapidly that airlines were racing to be the first to bring jets into competitive markets.

To take advantage of its lead, Douglas decided to build up production as fast as possible, so that the maximum number of airlines could receive DC-9s before Boeing could start delivery of 737s.

The DC-9F (Series 30) was fitted with an upward-hinging door on the port fuselage, forward of the wing. This example was operated by Alitalia, which received its first aircraft on 13 May 1968.

Right: Through the 1970s, the majority of DC-9s sold were -30s. Toa Domestic Airways (TDA) was the only customer for the DC-9-40, apart from SAS. TDA had an extensive fleet, including 22 DC-9s.

DC-9

Series 20, 40 and 50

Delivered to Hawaiian Airlines in July 1978, this DC-9-51 was one of a total of 96 Series 50s built between 1974 and 1981. The majority of these remains in service today.

Left: The prototype DC-9 Series 40 (seen here overflying **Queen Mary***) first flew in November 1967. The 71 production aircraft were delivered to* **SAS** *and* **TDA**.

The success of the DC-9 Series 30 enabled Douglas to develop new versions, tailored to meet customers' needs. However, spiralling costs and increased competition led to the company's demise and subsequent takeover by the McDonnell organisation.

With Boeing preparing to launch its 737 competitor to the DC-9, Douglas responded in the mid-1960s by offering to meet any configurations the customer might express. It even developed two versions of the DC-9 specifically for Scandinavian Airlines System. These were the DC-9-40, stretched by two seat rows compared with the -30 to match the seating capacity of the 737-200, and the DC-9-20, a 'hotrod' version with the original short fuselage, the high-lift wing of the -30 and the same high-thrust engines as the -40. Douglas offered customers a huge variety of other options: different fuel capacities, different engine models and different weights, as well as a wide choice of finishes and internal fits.

The sales strategy was phenomenally successful. The DC-9 sold as no airliner had sold

before, and Douglas had orders for more than 400 aircraft by the end of 1966. Douglas was also going broke, and doing so very quickly. It was still spending money on DC-9 development, in all its versions, and new versions of the DC-8 were also on the point of certification. Moreover, Douglas was losing money on every DC-9 that it delivered; the company had sold many aircraft at low 'introductory' prices, but they were proving more expensive to build than had been predicted. Because production had been built up so fast, a great many

DC-9s were being produced 'off the top of the learning curve'; assembly procedures were still being refined, and the workers were still learning their jobs, so that each aircraft was taking more man-hours to build than would be the case later in the programme. This particular problem was compounded because Vietnam War production had already used up all of southern California's pool of trained aerospace workers, and because there were some 20 different airline configurations on the production line within a few months of the first deliveries. War production was also causing delays in the supply of components. The crisis came to a head when deliveries began to slip behind schedule, and some of the airline customers launched

massive lawsuits to recover their estimated losses. Facing bankruptcy, Douglas was taken over by the McDonnell company at the end of April 1967.

The new management brought DC-9 deliveries back on schedule, and the aircraft retained its hard-won status as the world's best-selling twinjet airliner through the early 1970s. The type was selected by a number of large European carriers, outselling the 727 and 737 in that market. The aircraft also went on to equip affiliated charter airlines. Delta and Eastern were major US operators; outside the trunk airlines, too, the DC-9 proved popular with the US regional airlines.

Nearly all the DC-9s sold in this period were DC-9-30s; TDA was the only customer for the DC-9-40 apart from SAS, and demand for the short-runway performance of the DC-9-10 diminished as airport development proceeded

Designed specifically for SAS for operations from shorter regional airport runways, only ten DC-9-20s were built.

Right; Essentially a Series 30 with a 6-ft 4-in (1.87-m) fuselage stretch, the DC-9-40 was ordered by TDA for its high-capacity short-range domestic routes.

worldwide. The DC-9-20 remained an SAS special. An all-cargo version, the DC-9-30F, was delivered to Alitalia in 1968; a main-deck cargo door was also fitted to the DC-9-30CF (convertible) and DC-9-30RC (rapid-change convertible) variants, both of which were delivered in some numbers. In the course of the 1970s, the -30 was made available with more powerful JT8Ds, higher weights and auxiliary fuel tanks in the lower fuselage, the latter option proving attractive to European charter airlines, which needed an aircraft to fly non-stop from northern Europe to the Canaries.

Competition in the twin-jet market grew more intense in the early 1970s, as Boeing introduced its new Advanced 737 series. The DC-9, though, was an inherently easier aircraft to stretch than the Model 737; McDonnell Douglas took advantage of this attribute of the design in mid-1973 by launching the 139-seat DC-9-50. The second major stretch of the

DC-9, the -50 compared with the -30 as the latter had compared with the -10. The fuselage of the new version was 14 ft 3 in (4.34 m) longer than that of the basic DC-9-30; higher-thrust engines, also to be offered on the -30, were standard, but the wing was externally unchanged and the maximum take-off weights were only slightly increased. The -50 was not intended as a replacement for the DC-9-30, but as a complement to it. It had better economics, but was less flexible in terms of range and runway performance.

Quiet powerplant

Swissair was the first customer for the -50, and started operations in August 1975. The aircraft performed as advertised, but was, inevitably, noisier than the -30s to which the people around Swissair's base airports were accustomed. The community reaction caused Swissair to cut back its planned purchases of DC-9-50s, and the airline, a loyal

Douglas customer, started to press for a new and quieter large-capacity DC-9.

In the early 1970s, the US government had launched a number of programmes aimed at reducing aircraft noise. One of these was the development of a modified JT8D with a larger-diameter fan and other changes, specifically intended to make future versions of the 727, 737 and DC-9 significantly quieter.

Meanwhile, McDonnell Douglas was engaged in a long drawn-out sales effort in Japan, where a number of airlines, of which TDA was the largest, were operating turboprop-powered aircraft out of 4,000-ft (1200-m) airfields, and where local opposition to extending runways was uncompromising. In early 1975, McDonnell Douglas proposed a DC-9-QSF (quiet, short-field) to the Japanese airlines, a -40-sized version with refanned engines and a highly modified wing. The main change was a new, wider centresection, to which the existing outer wings were attached. Adding extra span in the middle, rather than at the tips, meant that the extra strength required could be built into the new centresection, avoiding some redesign and retooling; the centresection could also be made deeper to hold more fuel.

While the Japanese market never opened up, the new wing and engines formed the basis for a new DC-9 variant to supersede the -50. With a new wing, much increased weights and refanned engines, the revised aircraft would have better economics than the DC-9-50, the operating flexibility of the -30, and lower noise. First discussed in 1976, the type was initially known as the DC-9-RSS (refan, super-stretch) and then as the DC-9-55. It became clear that it would be the biggest redesign in the history of the DC-9. Its fuselage would be another 14 ft 3 in (4.34 m) longer than that of the -50. The bigger wing would mean new flaps and changes to the control system. The new centresection would house a heavier landing gear, and the entire central structure would have to be beefed up to handle higher weights. The greater weight and wing area meant a larger tailplane which, in turn, would require modifications to the fin. To make the aircraft more attractive in the 1980s, the systems and electronics would also be thoroughly overhauled. The new version would take slightly longer to develop, from go-ahead to certification, than the original, brand-new DC-9-10 and was later designated as the DC-9 Super 80.

Above: BWIA began DC-9-51 operations in 1977. A 'new look' interior gave the cabin a more spacious and modern appearance, appealing to passengers accustomed to widebody comforts.

Right: Europe proved to be an excellent market for the DC-9. The DC-9-50 was popular with airlines such as Inex-Adria, which used the aircraft on holiday routes as well as on scheduled flights connecting European cities.

Left: In 1981 Finnair received the last DC-9 Series 50 to be built. The type was used on regional scheduled services.

DC-9 variants

A major competitor to Boeing's 737 throughout its production life, the DC-9 was sold in a number of major variants culminating in the Series 50. The aircraft also formed the basis of the MD-80 family.

Ozark Airlines was one of the initial DC-9 operators, ordering six Series 10s, the first of which was delivered in May 1966.

DC-9 Series 10

The initial DC-9 production version was the DC-9 Series 11. The DC-9-11 did not have its centre fuel tank activated, keeping the maximum take-off weight below 80,000 lb (36287 kg), allowing two-crew operations in line with US regulations. For export customers the tank was activated and the DC-9 was offered in the form of the DC-9-12 with Pratt & Whitney JT8D-1 or JT8D-7 engines and the DC-9-14 with JT8D-1s, -5s or -7s. In the event, the US regulations were relaxed in 1965 to a 90,000-lb (40823-kg) limit, allowing the Series 14 to be offered to US airlines as well. Bonanza Air Lines was the only carrier to adopt the initial Series 11 in service, taking delivery of three examples (above right). No customers were found for the Series 12 and production centred on the Model 14, of which Texas International, Delta Air Lines, Air Canada, TWA, Eastern Air Lines, West Coast Airlines, Continental (right) and AVENSA of Venezuela all purchased examples. The extra fuel carried by the Series 14 increased the aircraft's range to over 1,000 miles (1609 km) with a standard payload. A total of three Series 11s and 54 Series 14s was produced.

DC-9 Series 15

The ultimate version of the initial variants was the Series 15, which featured 14,000-lb st (63-kN) JT8D-1 or JT8D-7 engines. This version carried the standard passenger load of 79. Major operators of the DC-9-15 included KLM (above) and TWA, and a total of 55 entered airline service around the world. Two convertible passenger/cargo versions of the Series 15, designated DC-9-15MC (multiple change) and DC-9-15RC (rapid change), were produced for Trans-Texas Airways (five) and Continental Airlines (19) respectively. These aircraft featured reinforced cabin floors and and an upward-hinged cargo door on the port side.

DC-9 Series 20

The DC-9 Series 20 was developed specifically for operations from short runways. The driving force for the variant was SAS's requirement for a Convair CV-440 replacement. To meet performance criteria, Douglas married the Series 10 fuselage to the longer-span Series 30 wing and integrated upgraded JT8D-11 engines, each producing 15,000 lb (67.50 kN) of thrust. This allowed the aircraft to operate from 4,500-ft (1372-m) runways at 84°F (29°C) ambient temperature, permitting operations on all but one of SAS's domestic routes. The first of ten DC-9-21s, for the sole operator SAS, entered service in January 1969.

DC-9 Series 40

The Series 40 was created by lengthening the existing plugs ahead and aft of the wing on the standard Series 30 by 38 in (96.5 cm) each, allowing two extra seat rows to be added and passenger capacity to rise to 115. Like the Series 20, the aircraft met the needs of SAS which required a high-capacity short-range aircraft. The DC-9-40's limited range was not appealing to most carriers and the only other customer was TOA Domestic of Japan which received 22 examples. SAS, however, did place a significant order for 49 examples (right).

DC-9 Series 40

The breakthrough in DC-9 sales was triggered by the decision of the FAA in April 1965 to abolish a weight limit for airliners with two-man crews. Douglas moved quickly to offer a new model with an increased maximum take-off weight. The basic model was stretched by 15 ft (4.57 m), allowing an extra five rows of seats and increasing maximum capacity to 119. However, a more typical all-coach arrangement consisted of 105 seats at a 34-in (86-cm) seat pitch. The first of the Series 30s was the DC-9-31 (right, top) which was priced at $3.4 million and was powered by 14,000-lb st (68-kN) JT8D-1 or -7 engines and had a maximum take-off weight of 98,000 lb (44444 kg). The fuselage extension was achieved by adding a 114-in (290-cm) plug forward of the wing and a 65-in (165-cm) plug aft. The baggage and cargo volume was also increased by some 50 per cent. To prevent an inhibitory take-off run, the wingspan was increased by 4 ft (1.22 m) at the tips and full-span leading-edge slats were fitted. Unofficially known as the 'king-size' DC-9, the first sale of the DC-9-31 was announced on 28 April 1965 when Allegheny Airlines ordered four examples. The DC-9-32 (right) again increased the power, with JT8D-9/-11 or -15 engines and its maximum take-off weight increased to 108,000 lb (48988 kg). The final variant of the Series 30 was the DC-9-34 which featured 16,000-lb st (72-kN) JT8D-17 engines and had a maximum take-off weight of 121,000 lb (54885 kg). The three standard Series 30 versions, along with the DC-9-33 (powered by JT8D-9 engines), were offered in rapid-change, convertible freighter or all-freighter versions. The all-freight versions were allocated the 'F' suffix (below right; DC-9-33F). The other variants followed the suffix system established for the Series 15, with convertible freighters receiving the suffix 'CF' (right; DC-9-32CF and below left; DC-9-34CF), and the rapid-change versions receiving the suffix 'RC'. In all, 589 standard Series 30s were produced, with the largest customers being Allegheny Airlines (61), Delta Airlines (63) and Eastern Airlines (72). The biggest export order came from Air Canada, which received a total of 44. In addition, 27 DC-9-30CF/RC combis were delivered along with five DC-9-30Fs. The sole military customer for the Series 30 Combi was the Kuwaiti air force, which received two DC-9-32CFs.

DC-9 Series 50

The DC-9 Series 50 introduced yet another stretch to the airframe, increasing the overall length to 133 ft 7 in (40.71 m), allowing a maximum of 139 passengers to be carried. The wing was identical to that fitted to the Series 30, but installed thrust was increased to 32,000 lb (144 kN) by incorporating the JT8D-17 engine. The production versions were designated DC-9-51 and a total of 96 was delivered. Major customers included Republic (28), Finnair (left; 12), Swissair (12) and Hawaiian (10).

C-9 variants

During the Vietnam War, the DC-9-30 was seen as the ideal basis for a dedicated aeromedical transport aircraft. Modifications included the provision of a special-care compartment, galleys, and toilets fore and aft, and the addition of a third access door, 11 ft 4 in (3.45 m) wide, in the front fuselage with an inbuilt hydraulic ramp to facilitate the loading of litters. Accommodation was provided for up to 40 litters or more than 40 ambulatory patients, two nurses and three aeromedical attendants. This version was designated C-9A Nightingale (below) and entered service in

1968. A total of 21 C-9As was delivered to the USA. In addition, three C-9C executive transports were operated by the 89th Airlift Wing. A subsequent version of the DC-9 was developed as the C-9B Skytrain II (below), ordered by the US Navy as a fleet logistic transport. Combining features of both the Series 30 and 40, a total of 19 aircraft was manufactured for use by US Navy logistic support squadrons in the USA, while two were delivered to the US Marine Corps' Station Operations and Engineering Squadron. The US Navy subsequently purchased 10 similar DC-9-30s.

EMBRAER
EMB-120 Brasilia

Brazilian commuter

When EMBRAER introduced its Brasilia twin-turboprop feederliner, it was seen as another progressive design from the company that had built the successful EMB-110 Bandeirante. The EMB-120 went on to become a popular small airliner throughout the Americas, and gave EMBRAER the confidence to launch a new family of regional jets that have helped revolutionised the world airline market.

Above: The prototype Brasilia made its first flight in July 1983 and is seen here undergoing wet runway trials. A large nose-mounted instrumentation probe was fitted during flight tests.

Top: The first European customer for the EMB-120 was Deutsche Luftverkehrsgesellschaft (DLT), receiving its first example in January 1986. The airline was renamed Lufthansa Cityline in 1992.

The EMB-120 Brasilia grew out of a number of studies made by the Brazilian manufacturer, based on a pressurised Bandeirante development and driven by an increasing need for a larger, 30-plus seat aircraft. EMBRAER officially launched the new aircraft in September 1979, although it was another 10 years before Bandeirante production actually came to an end. EMBRAER began by drawing up its EMB-12X proposal around a twin-engined, T-tailed turboprop with a circular (pressurised) fuselage cross-section. This initial design work gave birth to

the EMB-121 Xingu, a smaller high-speed twin aimed at the executive market. For the airlines, EMBRAER had proposed the 20-seat EMB-120 Araguaia and the even more compact EMB-123 Tapajos. However, the airlines universally wanted a larger aircraft, since demand was outstripping the capacity of the current crop of 19-seat aircraft. The initial concepts were put to one side in favour of a 30-seat aircraft that became the EMB-120 Brasilia.

EMBRAER's new airliner had a low-mounted unswept wing and a swept fin. It employed a conventional semi-monocoque/

stressed-skin structure, with some composites found in the wing, tailplane leading edges, flaps, ventral fins, nose and tailcone. Power was provided by two 1,500-shp (1118-kW) Pratt & Whitney PW115 turboprops, each driving a four-bladed Hamilton Standard 14RF propeller. The two-crew cockpit was built around Collins ProLine

II digital avionics, to which the improved EFIS-86 and MFD-85 display systems were later added. The cabin was fitted out for 30 passengers (plus an attendant) in three-abreast seating.

First flight

The prototype EMB-120 made its initial flight on 27 July 1983.

United Express/WestAir operated a fleet of 20 EMB-120RTs, each configured to carry 30 passengers on US commuter routes. United Express was split into its constituent parts in 1998 and a number of the Brasilias were absorbed into Great Lakes Airlines.

Wearing both its pre- and post-delivery registrations, this aircraft is seen prior to becoming the first EMB-120 to be delivered to Australian carrier Flight West Airlines in May 1990. The airline later received seven more examples for operations in Queensland.

In all, three flying prototypes, two static test aircraft and one pre-series production Brasilia were dedicated to the development programme. With the basic PW115 engines, the EMB-120 received its Brazilian certification on 10 May 1985, followed by FAA type approval on 9 July 1985. The first customer, Atlantic Southeast Airlines of the USA (a member of the Delta Connection feeder network), put the Brasilia into service in October 1985, having taken ceremonial delivery of the second prototype at the Paris Air Show in June 1985.

Improved performance

Initial production EMB-120s had a maximum take-off weight of 10,800 lb (23810 kg). The EMB-120RT (Reduced Take-off) introduced more powerful 1,800-hp (1342-kW) PW118 engines, in early 1986, to improve performance at a higher gross weight of 11,500 lb (25353 kg). Maximum cruising speed was also increased, and

most aircraft have now been brought up to this standard. An 18-seat corporate model was handed over to United Technologies of the USA in the same year. Late in 1987, a 'hot-and-high' version became available. This had improved PW118A engines which maintained maximum output up to a temperature of ISA+15°C at sea level. Empty weight was also reduced by 858 lb (390 kg) through increased use of composites. The first customer was Utah-based Skywest Airlines, another member of the Delta Connection.

EMBRAER investigated improved-performance versions of the Brasilia under the designations EMB-120X and Improved Brasilia. These studies led to the increased-weight, extended-range EMB-120ER Brasilia Advanced, which was announced in 1992. The Advanced did not incorporate any major structural changes, but range was extended after an increase in allowable take-off

weight – now 26,433 lb (11990 kg). This also permits increased passenger baggage limits, a very popular move in the US market. The Advanced features interchangeable leading edges on its flying surfaces, improved flaps, new seals to cut interior noise, a redesigned flight deck, increased cargo capacity and a number of cabin improvements. Cabin lighting, ventilation and baggage space were all improved, while EMBRAER also developed a passive noise and vibration reduction system.

The Brasilia Advanced became available in May 1993, when the first deliveries were made to Skywest, and it is now the standard production variant. Earlier models can be brought up to ER standard with a simple retrofit. The first customers for such an upgrade were Belgium's DAT and Luxair. Alongside the improved passenger version, three cargo versions are still available. These include: the all-freight EMB-120C, based on the

ER with an 8,818-lb (4000-kg) payload; EMB-120 Combi, a mixed-configuration version capable of carrying 19 passengers and 2,425-lb (1100-kg) of cargo; and the EMB-120QC (Quick-Change), convertible in 40 minutes to an all-freight or all-seating configuration.

By June 1999, EMBRAER had delivered a total of 350 Brasilias and the type was in service with 32 operators in 13 countries. On busy commuter routes, each aircraft spends an average of 6.87 hours in the air each day, the fleet leader (the 10th production aircraft) had amassed some 33,711 flying hours, and the worldwide Brasilia fleet had spent over 4,000,000 hours in their air. When, in the early 1990s, EMBRAER made the daring decision to make a regional jet its next project, it used the EMB-120 as a starting point. The first jet to emerge, the hugely successful EMB-145 (now the ERJ-145) uses a stretched Brasilia fuselage, combined with a new wing and a revised tail section. The smaller ERJ-135 is again based on a similar structure. Several other essential components are also common between the jets and the EMB-120. EMBRAER has become one of the very few manufacturers in the regional airliner business to translate success with turboprops into success with jets. For this, EMBRAER can thank the EMB-120.

The Brasilia's biggest market was the USA, due to its massive commuter and feederliner demand. The type's sales success with airlines such as Skywest allowed the development of today's ERJ series of aircraft, which continue to score major sales in this sector.

EMBRAER ERJ 145/135

Basic appeal

EMBRAER has established a firm foothold at the high-power end of the regional jet market. With its ERJ 145, 140 and 135, it has produced three innovative airliners, sold under the twin slogans of 'Back to Basics' and 'Everything you need. Nothing you don't'.

EMBRAER studied a number of follow-on projects to the Bandeirante and Brasilia to maintain a foothold in the regional aircraft market. The most advanced of these was the pusher turboprop CBA-123, but the trend towards jet aircraft persuaded EMBRAER to change direction. Its first twin-jet design was a low-risk development of the Brasilia, with a stretched fuselage for 45 passengers, wing-mounted Allison GMA 3007 turbofans, and the same straight wing. However, wind tunnel tests revealed significant performance shortcomings, leading to the

adoption of a supercritical swept wing. The 7,246-lb (33-kN) thrust engines were also moved to the rear of the fuselage and capacity increased to 50 seats at the behest of potential customers.

The estimated US$300 million development costs were beyond EMBRAER's means, however, and it took on board a number of risk-sharing partners, which took a one-third share, plus some 70 risk-share suppliers for another 10 per cent of the cost. EMBRAER itself contributed one third, with Brazilian institutions providing the remainder.

Assembly of the first prototype (PT-ZJA) began in October 1994,

To minimise risk, development costs for the EMB145 were split between a number of companies. The ensuing savings ensured that the aircraft's US$15 million price tag was competitive compared to rivals such as Canadair's Regional Jet.

and this made its maiden flight on 11 August 1995. Three further pre-production aircraft were flown on 17 November 1995 (PT-ZJB), 14 February 1995 (PT-ZJC) and 16 April 1996 (PT-ZJD). FAA and Brazilian CTA certification was obtained on 16 December 1996, with European JAA certification following on 15 May 1997. On 10 March, the FAA had approved the EMB-145 to operate safely in

a cold-weather environment.

The first North American carrier to fly the EMB-145 jetliner, Continental Express, began regular revenue flights on 6 April 1997, initially linking its Cleveland, Ohio, hub to destinations in six US states. During the year, several new models were developed to meet requests from customers, and the designation was changed to ERJ-145 to reflect the regional jet (RJ) terminology now widely used by the industry, while a further revision to ERJ 145 occurred latterly.

The new models differ primarily in take-off weight and improved payload/range performance. These include: the

Seen here, pre-delivery, over Brazil, is City Airline's first ERJ 145. The aircraft now flies with Sweden's Skyways Express. EMBRAER based its construction programme on total sales of 400 ERJ 145s.

Right: PT-ZJA was the prototype ERJ 135 – the shortened version of the 145. During flight testing, the aircraft reached a ceiling of 37,000 ft (11278 m) and a maximum operating speed of Mach 0.78.

ERJ 145EU, increasing take-off weight from the 42,330 lb (19200 kg) of the standard model to 44,070 lb (19990 kg); the ERJ 145ER, with a further increase to 45,415 lb (20600 kg); and the ERJ 145EP, heavier still at 46,275 lb (20990 kg). The ERJ 145MR introduced the AE3007A1 engine with increased thermodynamic thrust and a take-off weight of 48,500lb (22000 kg). At the Paris Air Show in June 1997, EMBRAER also announced a new long-range ERJ 145LR version, which differs from the MR in having an additional 1,786 lb (810 kg) of fuel, giving a range of 1,600 nm (1,840 miles; 2963 km). Ultimately, EMBRAER has bowed to the demand for even greater range with the ERJ 145XR, able to fly 50 passengers some 2,000 nm (2,303 miles; 3706 km).

Protecting the Amazon

Border invasions, illegal mineral exploration, deforestation and drug-smuggling in the vast and sparsely populated Amazon region of Brazil prompted the Brazilian government in 1990 to create the Amazon Surveillance System (SIVAM) as part of the Amazon Protection System (SIPAM). In March 1997 a SIVAM contract was given to EMBRAER to develop and build eight surveillance and remote-sensing systems, based on the ERJ 145. Five of the EMB 145SA (incorporating the Ericsson Erieye AEW&C system) surveillance version were

produced, along with three EMB 145RS aircraft for remote-sensing operations.

As the EMB 145 AEW&C, the EMB 145SA is also being targeted at other potential customers in Latin America, Europe and the Far East, with orders from customers including Greece and Mexico. Likewise, the EMB 145RS has been developed for export as the EMB 145RS/AGS electronic reconnaissance and intelligence gatherer. Other military developments include the EMB 145MP/P-99 multi-role maritime aircraft.

Smaller still

On 16 September 1997, EMBRAER announced the development of a new regional jet for 37 passengers, designated ERJ 135. The new jet was based heavily on the EMB-145 design, sharing its Rolls-Royce Allison AE3007A3 engines and main systems, cockpit, wing and tail assembly, and having the same cross-section fuselage, albeit 11 ft 6 in (3.5 m) shorter. EMBRAER targeted a market forecast of 500 units over 10 years for the aircraft. It converted one of the four EMB-145 prototypes to the ERJ 135 configuration by replacing two of the central fuselage sections with a shorter single section. The first aircraft was rolled out on 12 May 1998 and made its maiden flight, ahead of schedule, on 4 July.

After two flights and a total of five hours in the air, the full

operational envelope had been explored, including all gear and flap configurations, longitudinal and directional stability at the extremes of the centre of gravity, and full stalls at clean and full-flap configurations. A second prototype took to the air on 24 September 1998 and Brazilian certification was granted in June 1999, FAA in July 1999 and JAA in October 1999. The first aircraft was delivered, to Continental Express, in July 1999. The ERJ 135 has a take-off weight of 41,895 lb (19000 kg) and a

typical range, with 37 passengers and baggage, of 1,190 nm (1,369 miles; 2200 km). The ERJ 135 also formed the basis of a successful business jet, the EMBRAER Legacy, which continues to sell strongly.

Interestingly, the ERJ 135 was joined by another downsized ERJ 145 variant when EMBRAER responded to calls for a capacity midway between the ERJ 135 and ERJ 145, to produce the ERJ 140. By summer 2005, almost 900 ERJ 145-family aircraft were in service.

EMBRAER 170 series

Looking to expand its regional airliner business, EMBRAER realised that the next step was to develop a higher-capacity aircraft with the potential for future 'stretches' built in. Abandoning the winning formula established with the ERJ 145, the company decided on a very high technology design based on a conventional-looking airframe. The resulting EMBRAER 170 suffered a number of delays relating to its advanced cockpit systems and other equipment, but eventually completed a successful first flight on 19 February 2002. The first customer machine was delivered to US Airways in February 2004, with LOT Polish airlines receiving its first machine soon after. Seating 70 to 78 passengers, the 170 has been joined by the 78- to 86-seat 175, which was certified in December 2004, the 98- to 106-seat 190 which was due for certification in August 2005 and the 118-seat 195, which is due to gain certification around mid-2006. In June 2005, total orders for the series stood at 187 (EMBRAER 170, with 66 delivered), 19 (175), 177 (190) and 29 (195).

Fokker
F27 Friendship/50

Dutch twin

First flown in 1955, the F27 exceeded Fokker's expectations in terms of sales, becoming one of the world's most successful twin-turboprop airliners, and leading to the new-generation Fokker 50.

Following World War II, Fokker was keen to develop a design to target the DC-3 replacement market. Hampered by a lack of funding for its new project, in 1948 Fokker sent designers to Boeing and Canadair to validate the concept. In contrast to the North American companies, Fokker intended to adopt a turboprop powerplant, giving advantages in terms of weight, smoothness and reliability.

Initial response

Building on its pre-war civil aviation experience, in August 1950 Fokker introduced its P.275 design. This incorporated a high aspect ratio wing, 32 seats, and offered optimum efficiency in cruising flight. The Armstrong Siddeley Mamba engine was considered, before Fokker opted for the Rolls-Royce Dart.

In 1952, the P.275 – now redesignated F27 – went ahead with advanced features such as the extensive use of fibreglass for unstressed parts and pressurisation.

In 1953, after Dutch government approval and funding, the go-ahead was given for two prototypes, plus static and fatigue test airframes. Concurrently, Handley Page was tailoring its similar four-engined Herald in response to the requirements of global operators.

Above: The first prototype Fokker F27 (PH-NIV) had 1,400-hp (1044-kW) Dart 507 turboprops and a 73-ft (22.25-m) long fuselage, features that were revised on the second prototype.

Top: NLM Cityhopper, later absorbed by the Dutch national carrier KLM, flew the Friendship in its Mk 200, 400 and 500 guises, the example illustrated being an F27 Mk 500.

The piston-engined competitor appeared in 1955, as Fokker began talks with Fairchild in the US with a view to a licence agreement in Maryland. Resisting the US firm's desire for piston-engines, Fokker persuaded Fairchild to sign its deal on 26 April 1956.

The first prototype F27 began trial flights on 24 November 1955, helping to clinch the Fairchild deal.

The fifth F27 Friendship off the production line was delivered to Aer Lingus on 19 November 1958. A Mk 100 airliner with Dart 511 turboprops, the aircraft went on to serve for over 25 years, with operators which included NZ National Airways Corporation and Air New Zealand.

In Australia, Trans Australia Airlines (TAA) persuaded Fokker to strengthen the F27's wing and add a modernised interior with four more seats. TAA ordered six aircraft on 9 March 1956, following orders by Aer Lingus and Braathens.

Fairchild, marketing the aircraft as the F-27 in the US, received orders from West Coast, Bonanza and Piedmont. Sales over the next two years continued apace, but 1958 saw only eight Fokker and 16 Fairchild orders. With costly tooling now complete the first production F27 flew on 23 March 1958, followed by the first F-27 on 14 April. West Coast flew the first commercial service on 28 September 1958. Orders picked up in 1959, keeping the Amsterdam production line busy. Later developments saw major sub-components being built across Europe, while the American production line closed in July 1973, after producing 173 aircraft, despite the introduction of the FH-227 (with stretched 52-seat fuselage) after the merger of Fairchild and Hiller in 1964.

Increased range

Requiring increased range, several customers prompted Fokker to develop the standard Friendship 200 model (Dart 528 engines) with increased fuel capacity. Subsequently, this aircraft was re-engined with the 2,280-ehp (1700-ekw) Dart 532-7 (and later 536-7R) and, from the early 1980s, hush kits were supplied, significantly reducing noise, in particular that of the notoriously loud first-stage compressor. By now the Dart was becoming aged, with poor fuel economy by modern standards. However, Rolls-Royce decided not to proceed with a replacement leaving the F27 apparently stranded with uncompetitive engines in a marketplace that was, by the 1980s, dominated by newer turboprop designs. As a stop-gap measure, Rolls-Royce had introduced its upgraded Dart 551

The American-built FH-227 (illustrated), which first flew on 27 January 1966, featured a 6-ft (1.83-m) fuselage stretch. In total, 79 of the variant were produced. Fokker also built a stretched F27 variant, the Mk 500, which flew in November 1967.

engine and this became available as a retro-kit for earlier airframes.

Fokker watched the situation with disquiet, as the F27 approached the early 1980s with diminishing sales. With the company focusing on its F28 jetliner, it appeared likely that the Friendship would disappear. However, with a new interest in local-service turboprop airliners emerging, the stage was now set for the appearance of an F27 successor, which began life as the P.335, before appearing in 1985 as the Fokker 50.

Fokker 50

In 1983 on the F27's 25th anniversary in service, Fokker announced the Fokker 50 (F50). Similar in size and configuration to the F27, the F50 (so-called because of its seating configuration) featured new Pratt & Whitney PW120 series engines with six-bladed propellers, substantial use of composite materials and a completely redesigned Honeywell EFIS cockpit. The wing was also much improved and featured small 'Fokklets' (or winglets). From a

passenger's point of view, a less satisfactory change was the removal of the F27's large windows in favour of an increased number of smaller ones.

The first two prototypes were modified from F27s, and Fokker's official documentation and some registration certificates referred to the F50 as the F27-050. Ansett Transport Industries placed the launch order for 15 aircraft. The first flight took place on 28 December 1985, followed by the first production F50 on 13 February 1987. Deliveries commenced to Lufthansa CityLine on 7 August 1987, although the first revenue service was made by DLT. The baseline model was the Fokker 50 Series 100 powered by PW125B engines. Depending on the seating configuration, which can range from 46 to 68, the Series 100 was further divided into the Fokker 50-100 (with four doors) and Fokker 50-120 (three doors).

By early 1993, Fokker was delivering the F50 Series 300. This PW127B powered, hot-and-

high version was first ordered by Avianca, and was available in F50-300 and F50-320 models. Fokker also considered a stretched version as the Fokker 50 Series 400.

In 1993 DASA acquired 51 per cent of the Fokker company, which by this time was suffering from financial difficulties. However, in January 1996 DASA withdrew its financial investment and the company was declared bankrupt in March. Fokker was unable to find a saviour and once outstanding orders had been fulfiled all manufacture of the F50 ceased.

Production totalled 205 Fokker 50s and four military Fokker 60s, but had the company remained liquid the aircraft would undoubtedly have gained many additional customers.

Major purchasers of the Fokker 50 included Air UK (nine), Ansett (12), Austrian Airlines (eight), Avianca (10), DLT/Lufthansa CityLine (34), KLM Cityhopper (10), Maersk Air (eight), Malaysia Airlines (11), Philippine Airlines (10) and SAS Commuter (22).

Sudan Airways received its first two Fokker 50s in August 1989, and has four of the type in service today. PW125B engines combined with the Dowty six-bladed composite propellers endow the F50 with a 12 per cent greater cruising speed than that of the F27.

Fokker's 70 was fighting for orders in a fiercely competitive marketplace when the company went bankrupt. Competition from rival types such as the 146/RJ family and CRJ contributed to Fokker's downfall.

The Fokker 100 and 70 – the JetLine as they became known – were logical follow-ons from the successful F28 series. These next-generation aircraft proved popular, particularly with established Fokker customers. However, the Dutch manufacturer found itself hamstrung by high production costs and a difficult market, factors that eventually drove it to bankruptcy.

AirUK received 17 Fokker 100s. The carrier has since become part of the KLM group and 15 F100s continue to fly under the KLM cityhopper uk banner.

F70/F100
A new Fellowship

By the late 1970s Fokker was already searching for a new design to replace its F28 Fellowship. The obvious first step was a stretched 100- to 130-seat 'Super F28' and plans were drawn up to offer such an aircraft by 1984. However, airlines were then still wary of 'small' jets and Fokker felt that there were better sales prospects for a larger aircraft. The 'Super F28' design became the 150-seat F29, though exactly what this aircraft would be remained unclear. At one stage, Fokker was believed to be discussing the use of Boeing 737 fuselage sections. Fokker then joined forces with McDonnell Douglas on the MDF 100 design, but this was quietly abandoned in the late 1980s. Fokker was left to come up with the design and funding for a new aircraft of its own, returning to the proven formula of the F28 for its inspiration.

In November 1983 Fokker announced that it was working on a 100-seat F28 development. This aircraft was launched as the Fokker 100 (F100), alongside the turboprop Fokker 50 (a developed F27 Friendship). The $14.9-million F100 would be available for delivery in early 1987 and Fokker predicted a market for 750 aircraft.

The new aircraft used an F28 airframe, stretched by 18 ft 10 in (5.51 m) compared to that of the F28-2000. It would carry up to 107 passengers. The F100, also had a new, longer wing, a 'glass' cockpit and Rolls-Royce Tay turbofans. Early versions were powered by the 13,850-lb (61.6-kN) Tay 650-15 engine, but these were later replaced by uprated Tay 650-15s, offering 15,100 lb st (67.19 kN).

Partners and customers

Fokker went into partnership with several other European manufacturers and a few US companies, all of which supplied F100 components.

The launch customer was Swissair, which ordered eight aircraft to replace early-model DC-9s, in July 1984. Fokker then endured a wait of almost a year before another airline signed for the F100. This was KLM, which ordered 10 aircraft in May 1985. The up-engined version was launched with an important order from American Airlines in August 1985. American initially ordered just 10 aircraft, but this total was later revised upwards to an astonishing 75.

American Airlines' final four F100s out of a once sizeable fleet are for sale. The excellence of the Dutch product allowed it to make considerable headway into the US market, where airlines have a reputation for choosing 'home-grown' aircraft.

KLM's mainline fleet briefly included a handful of F100s (illustrated).

Fokker was forced to make several changes to the F100 on the production line as a result of customer demands. These included adding a full six-screen Collins EFIS cockpit (with a Honeywell FMS) and increasing the operating weights. The manufacturer also suffered from manufacturing delays caused by launching two major new aircraft projects in parallel. As a result, the predicted first flight was delayed from mid-1986, and certification was pushed back to autumn 1987. The prototype F100 finally made its maiden flight on 30 November 1986.

First deliveries

The F100 was finally certified by the Dutch authorities on 20 November 1987. Swissair took delivery of its first aircraft on 9 February 1988 and placed the type into service on 3 April. The first F100 to fly with the uprated engines took to the skies on 8 July 1988, and its

arrival triggered the 75-aircraft order from American Airlines in February 1989. The more powerful F100 was certified on 30 May 1989 and the first delivery was made to USAir on 1 July. USAir (now US Airways) went on to acquire 40 F100s.

Fokker 70

Fokker examined several developments of the F100 – most notably the 80-seat Fokker 80 and the larger Fokker 130 – before settling on the 70-seat Fokker 70 in 1992. This aircraft would be equivalent in size to the F28-4000, powered by the Tay 620 engine and would launch the development of the Fokker JetLine family of regional jets. However, Fokker became mired in discussions with its new owner, DASA, which took over in 1993. As a result, F70 development and marketing were hampered and the programme went ahead without any firm orders. The second

F100 prototype was cut down to produce the first F70, which made its first flight on 2 April 1993. The F70 programme was formally launched at the 1983 Paris Air Show, where Sempati Air and Pelita Air Services announced combined orders for 15, with five options. British Midland became the European launch customer on 16 November 1993 when it signed a long-term lease for five F70s and four F100s. In the US, Mesa Air became the first customer, on 10 December 1993, when it signed for two (with options on six more).

Into liquidation

During 1994, the F70 had a very successful flight-test programme, the aircraft proving to be faster and quieter than expected. FAA and Dutch type approval was awarded on 14 October 1994. The first production aircraft was delivered to the Ford Motor Company, as a

corporate shuttle, on 25 October 1994. The first delivery to an airline was made to Sempati Air on 9 March 1995.

On 9 June 1994 Fokker delivered its 250th jet to an American airline – the 75th for American Airlines – but since the DASA takeover, the company was finding things increasingly difficult. A crowded marketplace and cut-throat competition was hitting its well-built, but expensive aircraft. By 1996 the workforce had been cut in half, but Fokker could still make the savings demanded to keep it competitive. Then, in January 1996, Daimler-Benz (as DASA had become) withdrew its investment. When no other buyers came forward, Fokker was forced to declare bankruptcy on 15 March. Limited production continued under the liquidators, mostly finishing off uncompleted aircraft, but the end of Fokker brought an end to the Fokker Jetliners. The last F100 was delivered to TAM Brasil on 21 March 1996 and the last F70 went to KLM cityhopper on 18 April 1997. In all, 280 F100s and 45 F70s were built.

Right: In addition to its noticeably shorter fuselage, the Fokker 70 omits a pair of overwing emergency exits when compared to the F100.

Left: The main light-alloy structure of the F100 has a 45,000-cycle crack-free life, while the control surfaces, fairings and the cabin floor are of composites. Externally, however, the aircraft is similar to the F28 Mk 4000. Like Fokker, Air Inter has ceased trading.

Ilyushin

Il-76 'Candid'

Multi-role transport

The Il-76 is the most versatile airlifter to emerge from the Soviet Union. It combines outstanding rough field capability with jet performance, while carrying a substantial payload.

When the Il-76 (ASCC codename 'Candid') first emerged in the early 1970s, it was dismissed as yet another Soviet copy of a Western aircraft. In this case, the Il-76 bore a striking resemblance to the C-141 StarLifter, but the truth was not quite as straightforward. For a start, the undercarriage gave true rough-field capability, which was routinely used in military service.

Under the glazed navigator's station in the nose the Il-76 had a ground-mapping radar, allowing it to operate autonomously, by day or night, and well outside controlled airspace. The cargo hold was equipped with four overhead hoists and the rear ramp could lift a load of up to 30 tonnes, allowing the maximum hold volume to be exploited. The Il-76 could carry a load of 40 tonnes from a normal runway

and 33 tonnes off a grass, dirt or packed snow strip.

The Il-76 was the Soviet Union's first truly strategic airlifter, but it was never portrayed as such. When the aircraft made its Western debut at the Paris Air Show of 1971, and again in 1973, it was presented as a purely commercial aircraft. By 1973, Il-76s in Soviet service had begun to adopt Aeroflot markings, but there was no question that the big freighter was intended 'simply to resupply remote areas of the USSR where there are no runways', as one Ilyushin representative put it. More so than any of its predecessors, the Il-76 had a primary military role. However, Ilyushin did develop civilian versions of the aircraft, Il-76s that were not as obviously militarised as their siblings. These aircraft were seen on Aeroflot

Seen prior to the break-up of the Soviet Union, this Il-76TD is painted in an Arctic-support Aeroflot scheme.

Although carrying Aeroflot markings, this line-up of Il-76s was used for military purposes. The second and fourth aircraft from the camera are Be-976 missile-tracking aircraft, the third machine is an Il-76VPK command post, and the nearest aircraft is a standard Il-76T.

services around the world, mostly on resupply flights to friendly nations, but so too were the military versions, and the line between the two is almost non-existent.

The basic military version of the 'Candid' was quickly followed by the Il-76M 'Candid-B'. This version had more fuel and a higher gross weight, but retained obvious military features such as the rear gun turret and paradropping equipment in the hold. At the same time, Ilyushin did develop a nominally civil version of the basic aircraft, the Il-76T 'Candid-A' (T meaning *trahnsportnyy* – transport). This aircraft had no gun turret, no rear paratroop doors, an extra fuel tank and a maximum payload of 48 tonnes. Ilyushin next produced an increased-weight/extended-range version of the Il-76T, the Il-76TD 'Candid-A',

which had uprated D-30KP Srs 2 engines, yet more fuel and a maximum payload of 50 tonnes. The wings and landing gear were strengthened and the prototype first flew in 1982. What is noteworthy about the Il-76TD is that it flew before the similarly improved military equivalent, the Il-76MD 'Candid-B'. And, despite the seemingly clear division between 'armed' military Il-76M/MDs and unarmed Il-76T/TDs, Ilyushin went on to completely confuse matters by

building Il-76T/TDs with gun turrets and Il-76M/MDs without.

False identities

The origin of these aircraft, which have become known as 'falsies', is unclear. It is thought that the Il-76T/TD 'falsies' were a convenient way of concealing the military mission of export aircraft – most of the civil 'falsies' served with Iraq, in the colours of Iraqi Airways. On the other hand, no explanation has yet been offered as to why 'falsie' Il-76M/MDs

Intended to compete with the Antonov An-70 for sales to CIS and foreign customers, the Il-76MF incorporates new engines, a front and rear fuselage stretch and modern avionics.

were built without gun turrets. Several of these aircraft were exported, to Cuba and Iraq, and it is the Il-76's export customers who have led the way in placing the type into 'civil' service. Most have a military role, but wear civilian colour schemes. In Cuba, two Il-76MDs wore full Cubana colours, but were operated on behalf of the air force. In Iraq, most of the 38 Il-76T/TD/M/MDs wore Iraqi Airways markings. North Korea's three 'falsie' Il-76MDs are operated by the national airline, Air Koryo. Perversely, Libya's Il-76Ms were

painted in Libyan Arab Airlines markings, while its Il-76TDs were not. Syria's Il-76Ms have always worn Syrian Air markings, or at least a quasi-civil scheme.

Countries like Azerbaijan, Belarus and the Ukraine took over substantial numbers of Il-76s after the break-up of the Soviet Union. Although these were all originally military aircraft, many are now operated by commercial firms; some are even operated by the commercial 'arms' of air force units and several Western companies have leased Il-76s from Russian brokers.

Aviaenergo uses one Il-76TDs on cargo-carrying duties from its Moscow base. The company also operates two Il-62Ms, two Tu-154Ms and a Tu-134.

Il-76TD 'Candid-B'

The Il-76 has no direct Western equivalent (although comparisons with the C-141 are inevitable). Aeroflot's Il-76s were used for both civilian and military tasks, on both internal and worldwide operations. The aircraft were capable of being fitted with comprehensive infra-red countermeasures to deter heat-seeking missiles.

Tail section
The variable-incidence tailplane has aerodynamically balanced tabbed elevators and is set in a T-tail arrangement. The rudder is also aerodynamically balanced and, like all flight controls, is hydraulically boosted with emergency manual revision.

Wing structure
The wing is constructed in five sections with the centre section being the width of the fuselage. The other four sections of the wing are set at 4° anhedral.

Powerplant
The Il-76TD is powered by four Aviadvigatel D-30KP-2 turbofans, each delivering up to 26,455 lb st (117.7 kN), housed in individual pods beneath the wings. Each engine has a service life of 6,500 hours, with an intermediate service after 3,000 hours. All the engines are fitted with a clamshell-type thrust reverser, giving a minimum landing run of 2,950 ft (900 m). A new version of the Il-76TD, the Il-76TD-90VD, flew for the first time on 5 August 2005. Powered by PS-90A76 turbofans, the new machine is the subject of two orders from Volga-Dnepr for delivery later in the year. The new engines can also be retrofitted to older airframes, and while Silk Way plans to re-engine at least one Il-76TD, Volga-Dnepr may re-engine its whole fleet.

Cargo hold
The hold has an available volume of 8,310 cu ft (235.3 m³) and is available with a reinforced titanium floor or folding roller conveyor panels. Access is through two outward-opening clamshell doors, with an upward-hinged ramp able to lift a 30-tonne load.

Flight crew
The Il-76's standard crew of seven includes pilot and co-pilot in side-by-side seating in the cockpit, navigator in the glazed nose section, radio operator, supernumerary and two freight handlers.

Undercarriage
The steerable nosewheel has two pairs of wheels attached to a central oleo and retracts forward into the fuselage. The main landing gear has two units in tandem on each side, each unit with four wheels on a single axle. During retraction, the mainwheel axles rotate around the leg to lie parallel to the fuselage axis.

Ilyushin
Il-86 'Camber'/Il-96
Russia's airbus

A fleet of 11 Il-86s is maintained by Aeroflot. The aircraft are configured to carry 20 first-class and 296 tourist-class passengers and have retained their thirsty NK-86 engines despite negotiations to re-engine them with CFM56s.

The Il-86 was the Soviet Union's first attempt at a modern widebodied airliner, but it was not a success. The aircraft failed dismally in meeting the expected performance levels, and just over 100 were built. Its successor, the modernised Il-96, promised to be a far better and more versatile aircraft, but a lack of funding halted its development.

The driving force behind Ilyushin's Il-86 was the 1980 Moscow Olympic Games. The Soviet authorities wanted to have a new prestige airliner in service to take passengers to the games, and the Ilyushin Design Bureau was awarded the task. Ilyushin was the natural choice as it had produced the Il-62 – the backbone of Aeroflot's long-range fleet, and the aircraft which the Il-86 was intended to replace. The first plans for a Soviet widebody were revealed as early as the 1971 Paris Air Show, but little progress was made, due largely to the lack of a suitable turbofan engine. Ilyushin's early designs resembled a fattened-up Il-62, with the same four-jet configuration and T-tailed layout as its predecessor. However, the structural limitations of the rear-engined layout, when combined with new, larger engines, were unacceptable, and the Il-86 that finally emerged had a conventional podded underwing engine design.

Initial discussions for a new widebodied airliner began between Ilyushin and the Soviet Ministry of Civil Aviation following the launch of Boeing's 747 in 1966. After a long design gestation, the prototype made its maiden flight on 22 December 1976.

Double-decker

The Il-86 (ASCC codename 'Camber') was designed to accommodate up to 350 seats, with an unusual two-deck design. Passengers could carry on their own luggage and coats, stowing them on the lower deck, before climbing upstairs to be seated. This system was intended to allow the Il-86 to operate from the USSR's under-developed airports, which lacked modern baggage- or passenger-handling facilities. The Il-86's

Above: AJT Air International operated five Il-86s (including three ex-Aeroflot examples) from Moscow-Sheremetyevo. With a 350-seat layout, the aircraft were used on both scheduled and charter services.

Below: Transeuropean Airlines was one of a number of Russian charter airlines established since the deregulation of the airline industry. This Il-86 was leased by the airline for high-density routes.

With a cargo door forward of the wing on the port side, the Il-96T is capable of carrying standard international freight containers and pallets.

Above: The Il-96-300 was designed to resolve the performance difficulties of the Il-86. The aircraft has distinctive winglets, a shorter fuselage and more efficient Aviadvigatel PS-90A turbofans.

Right: Heavy emphasis has been placed on the Il-96M's Western engines, avionics and systems and low unit cost of US$75 million in the so-far unsuccessful attempts to attract Western airlines.

timetable was dictated by the availability of its new Kuznetsov NK-86 high-bypass turbofans – the first such engines to be built in Russia. The first prototype entered assembly during 1974, but did not make its maiden flight until 22 December 1976. The first Il-86 underwent its flight test trials at Moscow's Zhukhovskii airfield, where it was eventually joined by the first production Il-86. This aircraft was rolled out in 1977 and made its maiden flight on 24 October.

By this time, the Il-86 was running well behind schedule and it was clear that it would not be in quantity service for its 1980 target. Aeroflot took delivery of its first aircraft on 24 September 1979 and the Il-86 entered service on 26 December 1980 – well after the Olympics had concluded.

The Il-86 was designed to handle Aeroflot's high-density 'tourist' routes, such as Moscow-Leningrad or Moscow-Kiev. It was also intended to fly prestige international routes, including transatlantic services, on which it would replace the ageing Il-62M – but this soon proved to be problematic. When it was launched, Ilyushin claimed

a maximum range of 3,420 miles (5000 km) for its new airliner, but these figures were later scaled back to 2,235 miles (3600 km) with an 88,185-lb (40000-kg) payload. Most evidence pointed to a failure to achieve even that level of performance. The East German state airline refused to take delivery of the Il-86s it was offered, and quoted its maximum range as just 1,550 miles (2500 km) – Interflug went on to order three Airbus A310-300s to augment its Il-62 fleet. The Il-86 flew its first international service from Moscow to East Berlin on 3 July 1981. On their routes from Moscow to east coast destinations in the USA, Aeroflot Il-86s had to make two regular fuel stops at Shannon Airport, Ireland, and again in Gander, Newfoundland. Sometimes, headwinds would even force an intermediate stop in Luxembourg.

In the early 1980s, Ilyushin's general designer G. V. Novozhilov spoke of at least 200 Il-86s being built, but production ceased in 1994, at a total of just 104. About 70 remain in service today. They are spread among airlines in Russia and the former CIS republics.

Il-96 family

Although it is outwardly similar to the Il-86, the Il-96 is a new aircraft in every respect. The Il-96 introduced Aviadvigatel (formerly Perm) PS-90A turbofans, a new supercritical wing of greater span and slightly reduced sweep, and improved structure and materials to give lower weight and longer life. New avionics and systems are provided, including a triplex fly-by-wire control system. Internal fuel capacity is doubled by comparison with the Il-86, while reduced drag also contributes to the new aircraft's dramatically increased range. The lower deck of the Il-96 is purely for cargo and luggage, and passengers enter only at cabin level.

The basic production version seats up to 300 passengers and is designated Il-96-300, but the mixed-class layout that is normally used seats 235. The prototype made its maiden flight on 28 September 1988. Russian state certification was achieved on 29 December 1992. Deliveries began to Aeroflot in 1995 and proceeded at a very slow rate. By August 2005 Aeroflot had 12 aircraft. Another three were in service with Domodedovo Airlines, along with two operated by the Russian government.

Ilyushin also developing the stretched Il-96M (originally the I-96-350). This version had Pratt

& Whitney PW2337 turbofans, a smaller tailfin and a cabin that could accommodate up to 375 passengers. The prototype Il-96M was converted from the first Il-96-300 and flew on 6 April 1993. The first production aircraft was rolled out in April 1997. The first deliveries (of 17 on order) were due to Aeroflot in 1998 and a further six were on order for TransAero, but a severe shortage of funds held back the programme. The all-freight Il-96T was also developed, with a 15-ft 11-in x 9-ft 5-in (4.85- x 2.87-m) cargo door fitted on the port side. It flew on 16 May 1997. The first Il-96T customer was to be Aeroflot, with three on order, followed by Volga Dnepr. However, the US-engined Il-96M/T aircraft eventually came to nothing.

Instead, Ilyushin reworked the aircraft with Russian avionics and PS-90 engines as the Il-96-400 airliner and Il-96-400T freighter. Aeroflot now expects to take four Il-96-400Ts in 2006 to replace DC-10 freighters, while Atlant-Soyuz and Volga-Dnepr will receive four Il-96-400s by 2007. Aeroflot has also taken a further six Il-96-300s and on 26 July 2005 Ilyushin, trading as the Voronezh Joint-stock Aircraft Manufacturing Company, unveiled the first of two Il-96-300VIP aircraft for Cubana.

Ilyushin Il-114

Turboprop hope

The first prototype Il-114 made its maiden flight at Khodinka on 29 March 1990. A decade and a half later Ilyushin is still struggling to progress with the programme, with a lack of funding being cited as the principal reason for the delays in production.

The Il-114 was an advanced regional turboprop designed to meet Russia's domestic air transport needs during the late 1980s. Developments of the aircraft saw the addition of Western engines and avionics to improve its chances in the export market. However, drastic funding shortfalls have imposed severe delays on the development programme and the Il-114 is barely in airline service.

This Il-114 was one of two pre-series aircraft purchased by Uzbekistan Airways in 1994. After each had flown 300 hours, both were grounded pending the establishment of an overhaul plant.

In the former USSR travelling by air was the quickest (and sometimes the only) way to gain access to the huge number of remote destinations scattered across the interior of the country. Aeroflot had a major responsibility to serve these airfields, over what would generally be described as 'regional routes'. What it needed was a tough passenger and freight aircraft that could operate in austere conditions from unprepared airfields. This came in the form of the Antonov An-24, an unrefined aircraft that fulfiled its function admirably, but was never designed with passenger appeal in mind.

During the early 1980s several Soviet design bureaux drew up plans for an An-24 replacement. The equivalent Western aircraft were several generations further advanced in terms of their technology, design functionality, operating economics and simple comfort – all of which were becoming increasingly important factors for Aeroflot. Despite its relative lack of experience in designing small turboprop airliners, Ilyushin's twin-engined Il-114 emerged as the front-runner in this competition.

However, even though design was finalised as early as 1986, the prototype did not make its maiden flight until March 1990.

ATP lookalike

The Il-114 closely resembles the BAe ATP in outline. It is a conventional low-wing design, with a swept fin and rudder. Power is provided by a pair of 2,466-shp (1839-kW) Klimov TV7-117S turboprops driving six-bladed Stupino SV-34 low-noise propellers. For the first time in such a Russian-designed aircraft, the Il-114 makes substantial use of composite materials. The flight deck is fitted with a five-screen EFIS, featuring colour CRT displays and two data input panels. In the passenger version, the main cabin is configured for 64 seats.

The Il-114 was produced in co-operation with the TAPO plant in Tashkent, Uzbekistan. The first prototype was built at Ilyushin's Khodinka facility, in Moscow, and made its maiden flight on 29 March 1990. The first production aircraft flew on 7 August 1992 and a flight test schedule involving the first five series production Il-114s was drawn up. Unfortunately, the second prototype was lost in an accident on 5 July 1993, which

In passenger configuration, the Il-114 is designed to carry 64 passengers at 30 in (76 cm) seat pitch. Overwing emergency exits are provided along with a galley, cloakroom and toilet at the rear of the cabin and overhead baggage racks on either side of the central aisle.

Just as the ATP is receiving a new lease of life as a freighter, Ilyushin's best hope of commercial success with the Il-114 may lie in its freighter versions.

brought about the withdrawal of all Russian government funding. As a result of this loss, a major delay was suffered and, coupled with problems in the TV7 engine development programme, the Il-114 did not receive its Russian type certification until 26 April 1997. A pair of TV7-engined aircraft was received by Vyborg North-West Air Transport in 2002/03 and remains in service.

Cargo variants

Ilyushin hoped to build several versions of the Il-114. The basic passenger version was joined by the Il-114T freighter. This all-cargo version has already been ordered by Uzbekistan Airways and is fitted with a 10-ft 10¼-in x 5-ft 10-in (3.31-m x 1.78-m) cargo door in the rear fuselage. The cabin has a removable roller floor, maximum take-off weight is set at 51,805 lb (23500 kg) and the first aircraft flew on 14 September 1996. Ilyushin and Pratt & Whitney Canada signed a joint venture agreement in 1997 to develop and market the aircraft. Customer deliveries were due

to begin in 1998 and Uzbekistan Airways began operating two examples on service trials during the latter part of the year, but none has yet entered official revenue service.

A second cargo version – designated Il-114N200S – incorporating a rear-loading ramp has also been designed, but none of this variant was built.

Ilyushin also developed the Il-114-100 (known until 1997 as the Il-114PC) – a Westernised version powered by two Pratt & Whitney Canada PW127H turboprops driving Hamilton Standard propellers and equipped with Sextant avionics. This export-dedicated version was initiated by a joint venture between Ilyushin and Pratt & Whitney in June 1997, and the first aircraft in an order for 10 from Uzbekistan Airways were delivered in December 2002. Subsequent problems with the supply of Russian components delayed further deliveries until late 2004. The ninth production Il-114 was converted to act as the -100 demonstrator and it first flew on 26 January 1999.

The Il-114-100 has increased range and performance, when compared to the TV7-powered version, and Ilyushin has discussed a freighter version designated Il-114-100T. Ilyushin has also proposed a PW127-powered version with 74 seats, dubbed the Il-114MA. It has additionally drawn up plans for the Il-114M, powered by uprated TV7M-117 turboprops. These would permit an increased maximum take-off weight, comparable to that of the -100 version, but without the hard currency expenditure on foreign-supplied engines.

Military applications

Plans for two dedicated military versions have also been drawn up – the Il-114P maritime patrol aircraft and the Il-114FK survey/reconnaissance platform. The Il-114P would be built around the Leninetz Sea Dragon mission system and drawings of the aircraft reveal a revised nosecone to accommodate a sea-search radar, an optional MAD tailboom and bulged observation windows in the rear

cabin. It is intended that two underfuselage and two underwing hardpoints would carry a variety of stores. Like the Il-114T, the Il-114P is fitted with a large port-side freight door. The aircraft is intended for military or paramilitary duties or for use in civil emergencies and has a projected endurance of some 10 hours.

Announced in 1996, the Il-114FK is intended as a replacement for the An-30 in Russian military service and resembles the older Antonov in its redesigned glass nose. The Il-114FK would also be capable of carrying a podded SLAR radar and Elint systems.

To date, Ilyushin's progress with the Il-114 has been slow and only a handful of aircraft have been built. Two Il-114Ps were 'ordered' by Uzbekistan Airlines, and entered service in 1998. These aircraft had to be withdrawn from service once the 300-hour overhaul limit had been reached on their engines – as no proper maintenance procedure was in place.

Ilyushin/TAPO and Iran's national aircraft manufacturing company at Isfahan had discussed the establishment of a licence-production line at Isfahan for the Il-114, but these plans apparently stalled.

The introduction of PW127H engines improves the Il-114-100's range and economy, but also leads to a significant increase in price.

Lockheed L-1011 TriStar
Development

N1011, the prototype TriStar, remained with Lockheed throughout its working life. In March 1968 Lockheed chose the British RB.211 engine to power the L-1011. The S-duct intake of the centrally-mounted engine precluded the fitment of optional engines without incurring huge extra cost, a problem which did not affect the rival DC-10.

Lockheed's entry into the widebody airliner market was one of the most advanced aircraft of its day, yet it never achieved sufficient sales to recoup its huge development costs. At one point the type almost sank Lockheed and Rolls-Royce – two of the most famous names in aviation – into oblivion.

Lockheed began studies into a widebody airliner in early 1966, based on a far-reaching requirement laid down by American Airlines for a 250-seat airliner to fly on US domestic routes. In the event, American went on to buy the rival DC-10, but Lockheed's design attracted the interests of Eastern, TWA and Air Holdings Ltd, the latter a financial consortium handling overseas sales. A combined total of 144 orders was sufficient to launch the L-1011 programme on 1 April 1968. The date was to prove prophetic, for the L-1011 became a major loss-maker for Lockheed, with just 250 aircraft being built.

Initially designed with two engines, the L-1011 became a three-engined aircraft (giving rise to the popular name TriStar) as a result of a scaling-up of the original requirements. Work on the first prototype began in early 1969 in a newly-built facility at Palmdale, California, from where the aircraft undertook its first flight on 16 November 1970.

Financial struggle

By this time Lockheed was in deep financial trouble, largely through cost overruns incurred by the C-5 Galaxy contract, and by its huge investment in the TriStar. Government money propped up the L-1011 programme while thousands of workers were laid off and the production effort

Festooned with strain gauges, this was the static test airframe. Tests with it proved the 'fail-safe' concept of the structure and showed that the airframe was good for at least 115,000 flight cycles and 210,000 hours (at less than two hours per flight).

slowed to a trickle. Worse was to follow: on 4 February 1971 Rolls-Royce, supplier of the L-1011's RB.211 engines, collapsed. This was again due to cost overruns on a fixed-price agreement, this time concerning the government-funded recovery of research and development costs. After much wrangling between governments, airlines and the two manufacturers, the UK government nationalised the engine company, which became Rolls-Royce (1971) Ltd, and new contracts were forged. The TriStar programme could continue, but the delays had dealt a blow to the long-term prospects of the type from which it would not recover.

Into service

Eastern received its first TriStar on 5 April 1972 and, following the award of FAA Type Certification on 14 April, flew the

Ten TriStars are seen at Palmdale during trials in 1972, the furthest aircraft being the prototype. Orders began to pick up during the year, following the bleak prospects and financial crises of 1971, when only two firm orders were placed.

The TriStar was measurably quieter than the 747 and DC-10, a fact plugged by Lockheed's marketing department. To reinforce the message, Eastern Air Lines rechristened its aircraft as 'Whisperliners'. This is the second TriStar to be built, used for flight trials before being delivered to the airline in 1973.

first scheduled service on 26 April. TWA acquired its first aircraft on 9 May. Deliveries got into their stride over the next two or three years, with important customers such as Air Canada, Delta, All Nippon and British Airways acquiring the type. Indeed, the initial TriStar 1 version, tailored to the medium-haul US domestic market, outsold the rival DC 10 10. However, McDonnell Douglas had followed up its medium-haul DC-10 version with the long-haul Series 30 almost immediately, while Lockheed had no competition to offer. The effects of the 1970-71 financial crisis had caused any development of a long-range TriStar or more powerful RB.211 engines to be put on hold. Such studies had been made in the late 1960s, under the L-1011-2 and L-1011-8 programmes, but it was to be the mid-1970s before any

attempts were made to provide a meaningful rival to the DC-10-30.

Increased weight

The first TriStar 1 derivative was the 100, which had an increased maximum take-off weight allowing greater fuel loads. The result was a considerable degradation in field performance, particularly in hot and-high conditions. The advent of the increased-thrust RB.211-524 allowed this situation to be redressed in the L-1011-200. Subsequent conversions to L-1011-50, -150 and -250 variants further increased weights and ranges.

More important was the TriStar 500, which emerged as a true long-haul variant with a shortened fuselage and extended wingspan. These aircraft offered true intercontinental performance at economic operating costs, but

only 50 were built as most potential customers were already flying the DC-10-30. Further development studies were aimed at creating a family of TriStars offering several fuselage lengths and range/payload options. Some, like the Series 400, were aimed at breaking into the Airbus A310/Boeing 767 market. None of these was built.

Throughout its career the TriStar remained at the forefront of technological advance. It introduced a below-deck galley, although later variants returned to a traditional main deck unit. The No. 1 aircraft tested many new

features, the most important being active control which was incorporated into the L-1011-500. Late in its life, it flew as the 'Advanced TriStar' with automatic brakes, automatic take-off thrust, cockpit CRTs and an all-moving tailplane.

Global recession in the early 1980s forced the inevitable demise of the TriStar. With outstanding orders for 21 aircraft, Lockheed announced the termination of TriStar production in December 1981. The 250th and final aircraft, a TriStar 500 for the Algerian government, made its first flight on 3 October 1983.

Active Control

The ACS (Active Control System) was developed with the aim of improving cruise fuel efficiency. It employed a system which detected aerodynamic loads on the wings and automatically moved the ailerons up or down to counteract the load. This allowed the wings to be extended in span without the need for a structural redesign, increasing wing aspect ratio and improving cruise economics. The result was a significant reduction in fuel flow and greater comfort. Tested on the prototype, ACS was applied to production 500s shortly after the first deliveries.

Three big US airlines accounted for 110 of the 161 L-1011-1s built, Eastern buying 37, Delta 35 and TWA 38. TWA's aircraft performed sterling work on high-density US domestic services from the airline's main hub at St Louis.

Above: The first aircraft was fitted with a variety of new features, several of which found their way on to production aircraft. Although it retained the original-length fuselage, it effectively served as the prototype for the TriStar 500. Its final guise was as the Advanced TriStar. It was eventually withdrawn from use in August 1986.

TriStar in service

The TriStar sold well initially, especially in its medium-haul Series 1 variant. The 17 airlines described here are those which bought TriStars from new. Many of these aircraft have given sterling service with their original owners.

Eastern Air Lines

Launch customer for the TriStar, Eastern bought 37 TriStar 1s although some were sold before delivery. One was lost in the notorious Everglades crash of 29 December 1972, shortly after the type had entered service. Financial problems caused Eastern's demise in January 1991, its fleet being grounded. Many of the TriStars were later picked up by other operators, notably Delta.

Delta Air Lines

Delta was the largest customer for the TriStar, acquiring 44 new aircraft from October 1973, mainly for trunk routes within the US. Further aircraft were also bought second-hand. The TriStar 1s were later augmented by 500s for the transatlantic route, and six of the earlier machines were brought to TriStar 250 standard.

Air Lanka

The national carrier of Sri Lanka began TriStar operations in 1980 with a leased Air Canada TriStar 1, followed by purchases of second-hand aircraft in 1982. That year the airline ordered two TriStar 500s, which were delivered in August/September 1983. This pair, and two second-hand Series 100s, flew on to be replaced by Airbus A330s and A340s from 1994.

Trans World Airlines

One of the launch customers, TWA ordered 38 Series 1s for service on its US transcontinental routes. Several aircraft were subsequently modified to Series 50 standard and used for some transatlantic flights. One aircraft was lost in TWA service when it caught fire on the ramp at Boston. The fleet was heavily utilised between its service entry in 1972 and final retirement in 1997.

Pacific Southwest Airlines

PSA ordered two TriStar 1s in high-density configuration for its Los Angeles-San Francisco route, with options on a further three. The first was delivered in July 1974 although the TriStars were grounded in 1976 due to the world fuel crisis. The three optional aircraft were never delivered, instead being sold to LTU.

Pan American

Pan Am came late to the TriStar, buying 12 Series 500s in 1978 for its thinner intercontinental routes. In 1986 United acquired some of Pan Am's overseas routes and briefly operated the aircraft before most were sold to Delta or to the Royal Air Force.

Air Canada

Canada's national flag-carrier initially bought 10 TriStar 1s, which entered service in January 1973 on high-density routes between Canada and the US. They were later upgraded to TriStar 100 configuration and used for some transatlantic services. Six TriStar 500s were also acquired, primarily for the transatlantic services, these being retired in 1993 in favour of Boeing 767s.

Gulf Air

The multinational airline of Bahrain, Oman, Qatar and Abu Dhabi bought seven TriStars from new and added a further five second-hand. These were a mix of Series 100s and 200s. Five Series 200s remained in service beyond 1998.

Cathay Pacific

Based in Hong Kong, Cathay adopted the TriStar as the mainstay of its fleet for services in the Far East. Only two Series 100s were acquired from new, but the airline built up a fleet of second-hand aircraft.

BEA/British Airways

Originally ordered for BEA, the first of nine TriStar 1s was delivered to British Airways in October 1974. The fleet was further bolstered by eight TriStar 200s and six TriStar 500s. Several of the aircraft were upgraded to Series 50 or 100 and used by subsidiary Caledonian.

Saudia

Saudia's TriStar fleet comprised 16 new-build aircraft and two second-hand. They were a mix of Series 1, 100 and 200, although all were raised to Series 200 status. A much-publicised accident in 1980 due to a cabin fire cost the lives of more than 300.

British West Indian Airways

'Boo Woo', registered in Trinidad and Tobago, acquired four TriStar 500s for its Caribbean-London services, the first delivered in 1979. They were replaced by A340s.

TAP Air Portugal

TAP ordered five TriStar 500s for its long-range routes, the first arriving in 1983. The final three on strength were used primarily for charter work and leasing out.

All Nippon Airways

This major Japanese airline acquired 21 TriStar 1s in three batches, the first entering service in December 1973. The fleet was used mainly on the high-density routes within Japan.

Alia – Royal Jordanian Airlines

Alia ordered eight TriStar 500s, some of the last aircraft built. The first was delivered in September 1981. In 1986 the airline was renamed Royal Jordanian Airlines.

LTU Lufttransport-Unternehmen

LTU's new TriStar purchases totalled six aircraft, two of which were TriStar 500s. The airline operated holiday charters between Germany and the Mediterranean. A further seven second-hand aircraft were also been operated, including ex-PSA aircraft with the lower cabin entrance and underfuselage

Court Line

Inclusive-tour operator Court Line acquired two TriStar 1s (one yellow and one purple) for holiday package work. The first arrived in March 1973 in time for the summer season. Court Line went out of business in August 1974, a victim of the world fuel crisis.

Special missions

Replaced in many airline fleets by newer types, TriStars trickled onto the second-hand market. As well as being bought by airlines (also detailed here), **the TriStar has found itself converted by some operators for freight carriage and a number of unusual missions.**

Royal Air Force

The best known of the 'special mission' TriStars are the tanker/ transport aircraft acquired by the Royal Air Force. Their purchase was made in the immediate aftermath of the Falklands War. Faced with supporting a garrison over 8,000 miles (12874 km) away, the RAF's lack of long-range strategic transport was exposed and, while a full-sized runway was built at Mount Pleasant, the RAF acquired in 1982 the six TriStar 500s operated by British Airways. Marshall of Cambridge converted four of the aircraft to K.Mk 1 standard (illustrated) with a twin Flight Refuelling Hose Drum Unit (HDU) installation under the rear fuselage (above right), additional underfloor fuel tanks and a refuelling probe. The first of these tankers flew as such on 9 July 1985. Subsequently, two of these aircraft, plus the other two ex-BA machines, were converted to KC.Mk 1 standard, this retaining the tanker equipment of the K.Mk 1 but adding a large cargo-loading door in the port side of the forward fuselage and a freight handling system. In 1984 three further TriStar 500s were acquired from Pan Am. Two were converted to all-passenger C.Mk 2

standard for trooping flights. The third aircraft was originally earmarked for K.Mk 2 tanker conversion, but in the event remained as a troop transport, designated C.Mk 2A to reflect some equipment changes. All nine aircraft fly with Brize Norton-based No. 216 Squadron. The C.Mk 2/2As are used for worldwide trooping flights, and also operate the scheduled Falklands flights (via Ascension). The K.Mk 1s and KC.Mk 1s are used for a variety of tasks, and are of great use for supporting tactical aircraft deployments, being able to carry spares and ground support crews in addition to providing tanking while on the 'trail'. The RAF is currently bringing its fleet to a common cockpit standard.

L-1011F cargo conversions

In the late 1980s, with surplus aircraft becoming available, the TriStar became a natural candidate for freighter conversions. Features of the modification are a large port-side upward-opening cargo door, a 9 *g* crashworthy bulkhead behind the flight deck, blanking of cabin windows, strengthened cabin floor and various roller freight-handling systems. The first conversion (a TriStar 1) was performed by Pemco, flying initially on 7 May 1987 with a 9-ft 4-in x 14-ft 2-in (2.84-m x 4.32-m) door. Marshall of Cambridge later became the main supplier of cargo conversions, offering an L-1011F based on the TriStar 200 with a 9-ft 8-in x 12-ft 11-in (2.94-m x 3.94-m) door. American International Airways (illustrated) was the launch customer, with Arrow Air and Millon Air following.

Flying hospital

One TriStar 100 was purchased by Operation Blessing for conversion by Lockheed Aeromod Center at Tucson as the world's largest self-contained flying hospital. Intended to provide emergency relief throughout the world, the Flying Hospital had an operating theatre, pre-/post-op area, patient examination room, surgical preparation area, two dental/ear-nose-throat examination rooms, reception and a pharmacy. To cater for prolonged ground operations, it had its own auxiliary ground power units and water purification system.

VVIP Transport

Excellent range, cruise comfort, reliability and a capacious cabin made the TriStar 500 a natural candidate for a governmental VVIP transport. Three aircraft have been outfitted for such duties, with luxury interiors and extra communications equipment. Shown above is JY-HKJ, the personal transport of King Hussein of Jordan. Other VVIP TriStars were two aircraft flown by the VIP transport division of Saudia. One of these was the last TriStar built. In August 2005, at least four TriStar 500s remained on VVIP duties.

Space launcher

The most unusual use of the TriStar is that of a launch platform for the Orbital Sciences Pegasus XL low-cost space booster, originally tested on a NASA NB-52. Air-launched from the TriStar at about 38,000 ft (11580 m), the Pegasus then climbs into space to place a small satellite (up to 1,000 lb/454 kg in weight) into orbit. Marshall performed the conversion on an ex-Air Canada TriStar 100, which first flew in its new guise on 12 July 1993. On 3 April 1995 Pegasus made its first powered launch from the TriStar. The most recent successful Pegasus XL launch from the TriStar was on 15 April 2005.

Second-hand commercial users

Having achieved a high level of reliability and efficiency with its original customers, by the late 1980s the TriStar was due for replacement, the airlines being tempted by the new highly efficient types on offer, notably the Boeing 767 and Airbus A330/340. The first major fleet to announce re-equipment was that of Gulf Air, which announced a 767 order in 1989. Cathay Pacific ordered A330s the same year. A steady flow of TriStars then became available for purchase by other airlines. This process was accelerated by the air transport crisis induced by the Gulf War of 1991. While existing customers such as Delta seized the opportunity to increase their own fleets, the majority of aircraft went to charter operators or low-cost airlines. United briefly operated six TriStar 500s to cover its new-found routes after the demise of Pan Am, while Hawaiian Airlines also used the type on scheduled services. Major charter operators included Air Atlanta, AirOps, Blue Scandinavia, Caledonian Airways (originally BA's subsidiary), Peach Air and Royal. Canadian operators Air Transat and Worldways picked up several for transatlantic charter work, while in the United States American Trans Air built up a sizeable fleet for low-cost/charter work. In addition to regular charter work, a small number of TriStars (notably those of Air Atlanta and AirOps) were used on wet-lease work, standing by to fill gaps in the schedules of other charter carriers. As such, aircraft were often positioned on standby during the summer season at regular holiday departure points such as Manchester and London-Gatwick.

In 2005 the worldwide commercial TriStar fleet stood at around 21, the majority operated by Air Transat (three, all for sale) and ATA Airlines (formerly American Trans Air).

TriStar 100, Worldways Canada

TriStar 50, American Trans Air

TriStar 50, leased by Rich International

TriStar 100, Air Sweden, stored at Tucson

McDonnell Douglas
DC-10

Development

Dogged by an undeserved bad press after several serious accidents, the DC-10 nevertheless sold in considerable numbers and was, for some time, the best-selling US widebody after Boeing's 747.

The 'Big Ten' can trace its origins back to Douglas's proposals for a 650-seat aircraft to fill the USAF's 1965 CX-HLS requirement for a very large logistic transport, a contract won by Lockheed with a design that became the C-5 Galaxy.

Undeterred, Douglas set about salvaging something from the project, and from the 650-seater derived a new design aimed squarely at the 250-seat widebody market. This market had already been spotted by Lockheed (US domestic carrier, American Airlines, was the potential launch customer), which intended to exploit it with its new L-1011 TriStar.

Meanwhile Douglas, unable to fund its continued existence as a separate entity, merged with McDonnell Aircraft to form McDonnell Douglas. The 'Douglas Commercial 10' thus became a McDonnell Douglas product and was officially launched in February 1968, having gained 50 orders, with promises of more.

First flight

The first DC-10 Series 10 took to the air on 29 August 1970. The distinctive trijet design had capacity for up to 380 passengers and was powered by three General Electric CF6 turbofans. The initial deliveries

The only DC-10s to be built with engines other than General Electric CF6s were the 42 DC-10-40s purchased by Northwest Orient and Japan Airlines. Initially, the long-range Series 40 was known as the Series 20, hence the titles on this aircraft, N141US, the first of Northwest Orient's fleet.

With much pomp and ceremony, officials representing the two launch customers for the DC-10, United Airlines and American Airlines, take delivery of their first aircraft on 29 July 1971. United retained two 'Big Tens' as freighters in 2005.

were made simultaneously in July 1971 to US carriers, American Airlines and United Airlines, with domestic services

beginning the following month. In all, 122 DC-10-10s were built, including Series 10CF combi freighters with side cargo doors.

The long-range Series 30 was the best-selling DC-10 variant. I-DYNA Galileo Galilei was the first of Alitalia's eight examples and was delivered in early 1973. After nine years with the Italian carrier, the aircraft was sold back to McDonnell Douglas and leased to Aeromexico.

The DC-10's potential as a freighter was exploited towards the end of its production life, principally by FedEx which amassed a fleet of more than 30 Series 30CF combi freighters and Series 30AF all-freight aircraft. The DC-10-30CF formed the basis of the USAF's KC-10A.

Series 40

In early 1972, the first DC-10-40 (originally known as the Series 20) was completed and flown. This variant was powered by Pratt & Whitney JT9D engines at the request of Northwest Orient. With a longer range, the 42 examples completed were delivered to Northwest Orient and JAL.

Within four months of the first flight of the Series 40, the first Series 30 was ready. This variant was developed alongside the Series 40 with transatlantic routes in mind and, upon its launch in 1969, had been ordered by airlines in the European KSSU group, namely KLM, Swissair, SAS and UTA. As it operated at higher weights than previous versions, the DC-10-30 sported an extra undercarriage leg beneath its centresection, a greater wingspan and more powerful CF6 engines. Swissair put the Series 30 into service across the Atlantic on 15 December 1972.

Engine failures plagued the first few months of DC-10 operation while problems with an underfloor cargo door culminated in the crash of a Turkish THY Series 10 near Paris in March 1974, in which all 346 on board were killed. In June 1979, an American Airlines DC-10-10 crashed on take-off at Chicago's O'Hare airport. The FAA grounded the type and, in an unusual move, withdrew the DC-10's type certificate. By the end of the year, operations had resumed, but the DC-10 was again in the news in November, when an Air New Zealand Series 30 on a sightseeing flight over Antarctica crashed in white out conditions, with the loss of all 257 passengers aboard. Although none of these tragedies could be attributed to any major inherent flaw in the airliner's design, the DC-10's reputation never fully recovered.

The final DC-10 variant was the Series 15, certificated in 1981.

Based on the lightweight DC-10-10, the Dash-15 was tailored for 'hot and high' operations. Only seven were built, for Mexicana and Aeromexico, for operations from Mexico City.

Top-selling model

The Series 30 was to be the best-selling of the DC-10s – 266 of the 446 aircraft completed were of this variant. Between 1982 and 1988, a small number of DC-10-30ERs, with extra fuel and improved CF6 engines, was built, along with 28 Dash-30CF combi freighters and nine DC-10-30AF pure freighters. Most examples of the latter variants were delivered to Federal Express. The last commercial DC-10 off the production line was a Series 30 delivered to Nigerian Airlines in 1989.

Meanwhile, the Series 30CF freighter served as the basis for McDonnell Douglas's contender to satisfy the USAF's off-the-shelf ATCA (advanced tanker/cargo aircraft) requirement, a contract awarded to McDonnell Douglas in 1977. Sixty aircraft, known as KC-10A Extenders, were built allowing the DC-10 production line to be kept open into the late 1980s, pending the development of a next-generation design.

A number of variants were proposed, but most failed to leave the drawing board, including a downsized 'DC-10 Twin' to compete with the Airbus A300. However, a stretched version – first sketched by designers in the 1970s, when it was known as the DC-10-60, but shelved during the recession of the early 1980s – showed promise and was revived in 1982. The new design was designated MD-100, then MD-XXX and it ultimately entered production in the 1990s as the MD-11.

Left: Within the proposed DC-10-60 series were the -61, -62 and -63 models, each having varying degrees of 'stretch'.

Below: In 1981, this Continental Airlines Series 10 became the first widebodied airliner to be fitted with winglets. A NASA/McDonnell Douglas test programme studied their drag-reducing effects and this led to the planned fitting of similar devices on the proposed Series 60 and its successor, the MD-11.

Major operators

A total of 446 DC-10s was built between 1970 and 1988. Most were delivered to major airlines, which retained their fleets for another 20 years. This cross-section of DC-10 operators covers the major operators that purchased the type new from McDonnell Douglas.

American Airlines

The original customer for the DC-10 was American Airlines. The final DC-10 design was driven by American's requirement for an 'airbus' to serve its long-haul domestic routes. On 19 February 1968 American signed up for 50 DC-10-10s (orders and options). The DC-10-10 was handed over to American in July 1971 and entered service on the Los Angeles-Chicago route on 5 August. An American DC-10-10 was tragically involved in a crash at Chicago O'Hare in May 1979 which did much to harm the DC-10's reputation – and sales prospects. American's DC-10-10s nevertheless provided sterling service until the early 1990s, when the fleet was progressively withdrawn from use. The last DC-10-10 was delivered to American in 1980, but in 1981 the airline started to acquire used DC-10-30s, beginning with ex-Air New Zealand aircraft.

FedEx Express

FedEx has built up a large fleet of freighter-configured DC-10-30CF/Fs since it took delivery of its first aircraft in 1984. Today, FedEx has a fleet of 26 DC-10-10F/-30Fs and 41 ex-American and United Airlines DC-10-10/-30s converted for cargo carriage under the MD-10 programme.

KLM

KLM was part of the European KSSU airline grouping which played a major part in the DC-10 story. KSSU (KLM, SAS, Swissair and UTA) was formed by a committed group of Douglas airliner customers who together formed a major European purchasing bloc. The group was the launch customer for the DC-10-30 and signed up for an initial 36 aircraft on 7 June 1969. KLM itself acquired 11 DC-10-30s between 1973 and 1975 and all were named after famous composers. The DC-10 remained in KLM service into the mid-1990s, when it was replaced by the McDonnell Douglas MD-11. The DC-10s were then acquired by the manufacturer, as part of the MD-11 deal, and found their way into (leased) service with several airlines including American, Northwest and Krasnoyarsk Airlines.

British Caledonian

The Gatwick-based charter airline, better known as 'B Cal', took delivery of its first two DC-10-30s in 1979. The DC-10 fleet expanded during the 1980s, until 'B Cal' was taken over by British Airways in 1988. Although it did not fit with the BA fleet, it remained a cost-effective type to operate and eight remained in service for some time.

CP Air

Canada's CP Air (Canadian Pacific Airways) acquired 12 DC-10-30s between 1979 and 1982. In April 1987 CP Air and Pacific Western Airlines merged to form Canadian International (later simply Canadian/Canadien) which had a DC-10 fleet of 11 aircraft.

Japan Air Lines

On 28 December 1973 JAL announced an order for six Pratt & Whitney JT9D-powered DC-10-40s, becoming only the second customer (after Northwest Orient) for this version. Deliveries took place between 1976 and 1983. A total of 20 entered service with JAL and seven remain in service.

Lufthansa

In 1973 the first of Lufthansa's nine DC-10-30s was delivered. The DC-10 survived in Lufthansa service until 1994, when the last aircraft were leased out and sold on.

National Airlines

National was a well-known US carrier and an early DC-10 customer. It took delivery of its first nine DC-10-10s in 1971/72, followed by more (-10s and -30s) in 1973/75. In 1980 National merged with Pan American, which continued to operate some of the DC-10s until 1984. The DC-10s were then sold on to American Airlines.

Northwest Orient Airlines

Northwest Orient (today simply Northwest Airlines) was the launch customer for the DC-10-40 (originally the DC-10-20), and one of only two operators of the type. On 30 October 1968 Northwest placed an order for 14 aircraft with 14 options, eight of which were later converted to firm orders. Between 1972 and 1974 the airline accepted 22 aircraft, 21 of which remain in service today. One of Northwest's DC-10-40s was destroyed by fire, on the ground at Chicago in 1986. Between 1991 and 1997 Northwest expanded its DC-10 fleet, buying or leasing an additional 17 DC-10-30s – including eight former Swissair aircraft and three from Korean Airlines. As a result, Northwest retains 22 DC-10-30s in August 2005, five of them DC-10-30ER machines.

Scandinavian Airlines System (SAS)

SAS acquired its DC-10s in two distinct tranches. Between 1974 and 1976 five DC-10-30s were acquired from the manufacturer. These were followed, between 1984 and 1987, by an additional seven second-hand aircraft. Another six aircraft were acquired by the SAS charter subsidiary, Scanair (later Premiair). Phase-out of the DC-10 began in 1987 and the last aircraft left the SAS fleet in 1991.

Swissair

On 15 December 1972 Swissair became the first of the KSSU airlines (see KLM entry for more details on KSSU) to place the DC-10 in service. Between 1972 and 1982 Swissair took delivery of 15 DC-10-30s. Swissair later replaced its DC-10s with MD-11s, beginning in 1991. Seven of its aircraft were sold on to Northwest Airlines between 1991 and 1994, while two more went to Continental.

Thai Airways International

In the mid 1970s Thai briefly leased five DC-10-30s and then acquired another five of its own in 1987/1988. Indeed, in 1988 Thai became the last formal customer for the DC-10, when it took delivery of the final DC-10-30ER on 26 May. Today, all have been retired.

United Airlines

United followed American's lead, becoming the second DC-10 customer when it placed an order for 60 aircraft (30 firm and 30 options) in April 1968. Between May 1972 and March 1980 United took delivery of 37 DC-10-10s. As of August 2005, United had two DC-10-30Fs in service.

VARIG

16 DC-10s have seen service with VARIG. None remain in use today.

Western Airlines

Western was one of the many carriers that expanded rapidly in the United States during the 1970s, after the US airline market was deregulated (allowing greater competition). Western began DC-10 operations in 1979 with DC-10-10s, but it was swallowed by its larger rival Delta Air Lines in 1987. Delta briefly operated the DC-10s, before disposing of them to leasing companies.

DC-10 variants

The DC-10 began life as a Douglas project and was one of a generation of US airliners (including the Boeing 747) that owed its existence to the US Air Force's 1965 CX-HLS airlifter programme. The DC-10 airliner that emerged in 1968 was a McDonnell Douglas product, **after those two companies merged in 1967. Production continued from 1968 to 1989. In 1997 McDonnell Douglas merged with the Boeing Company, and was effectively taken over. Thus the DC-10 has been subsumed into Boeing corporate history.**

DC-10 Series 10

The basic model DC-10 Series 10 (or DC-10-10) was built as a wide-bodied high-capacity airliner for domestic US trunk routes. It was similar in role and concept to Lockheed's TriStar 1 – and both were intentionally smaller than Boeing's 747 whose future success was anything but assured at that time. The DC-10-10 was 182 ft 3 in (55.56 m) long with a wingspan of 155 ft 4 in (47.36 m) – almost identical figures to those of the TriStar. The Series 10 could accommodate up to 380 passengers in a 10-abreast configuration, but a load of 250-300 was more usual. The DC-10-10 was powered by three General Electric CF6D/-6D1 turbofans, each rated at 40,000 lb (178 kN) and 41,000 lb (182.5 kN) respectively. The Series 10 was built as a relatively short-range aircraft for the USA, but some aircraft were fitted with additional fuel tanks giving them transatlantic endurance. The type was certified by the FAA on 29 July 1971 and the first deliveries were made to American Airlines and United Airlines simultaneously. The DC-10-10 entered service with American on 5 August 1971, on the Los Angeles-Chicago route. Over 90 per cent of all DC-10-10 production was sold to five airlines in the US, with American and United between them accounting for 76 per cent. A total of 122 was built before production ceased in 1982.

DC-10 Series 10CF

Nine convertible cargo/freight models of the DC-10-10 were built from new, followed by two additional conversions from existing aircraft. The CF was identical to the basic Series 10 but was fitted with a large (102-in x 104-in/2.59-m x 3.56-m) cargo door to port and a cargo handling system, including a roller floor, restraint nets, etc. The Series 10CF offered over 16,000 cu ft (453 m³) of cargo space – enough for 30 standard 88-in x 88-in (2.22-m x 2.22-m) pallets. The first aircraft was delivered to Continental Airlines in 1974.

DC-10 Series 15

The Series 15 was a development of the Series 10, intended for 'hot and high' operations and was produced specifically to meet a requirement from the Mexican airlines Aeromexico and Mexicana. Only seven were produced, between 1981 and 1982, and the final two examples served with the Minneapolis-based holiday carrier Sun Country Airlines. The DC-10-15 was powered by uprated 46,500-lb (207-kN) CF6-50C2F turbofans. These new engines allowed the DC-10-15 to operate from an 11,000-ft (3353-m) runway at 8,000 ft (2438 m) AMSL (above mean sea level) and carry 275 passengers and baggage over 3,750 nm (6940 km; 4,312 miles).

DC-10 Series 20

The Series 20 became the Series 40 (q.v.) but the prototype of this re-engined DC-10 model flew with 'DC-10 Series 20' titles before it was renamed in 1972.

DC-10 Series 30

The Series 30 was the most successful of all DC-10 variants. It was developed as a long-range version of the DC-10-10, with more powerful engines and increased operating weights. The new engines were General Electric CF6-50C/C1/C2s which were rated at between 51,000 lb and 52,500 lb (227 kN and 233.6 kN) of thrust. Maximum take-off weight could be as high as 580,000 lb (263088 kg), some 40 per cent higher than that of the DC-10-10. To cope with the weight of the airframe a distinctive two-wheel undercarriage bogie was added, under the wing centre section, between the existing main gear assemblies. This spread the DC-10-30's weight, allowing it to stay within airfield load limitations. The DC-10-30 also had an extended wing with a span of 165 ft 4 in (50.4 m). The DC-10-30 typically operates with between 220 and 260 seats, though Germany's holiday charter airline Condor did have aircraft configured for 370 passengers. The launch order for the DC-10-30 came from the KSSU group of KLM, SAS, Swissair and UTA, which ordered a total of 36 aircraft on 7 June 1969. The DC-10-30 first flew on 21 June 1972 (the third major variant, following the DC-10-10 and -20) and deliveries began to KLM and Swissair in November 1972. On 15 December 1972 the type entered service with Swissair, on its transatlantic routes. The DC-10-30 sold consistently to numerous operators, but only in small numbers to each. The largest operator of passenger aircraft, Swissair, only acquired 13 examples from the production line. A total of 156 basic model DC-10-30s was built, not including the DC-10-30ER, DC-10-30AF/CF and KC-10A variants (described separately). The last of the 446 DC-10s to be built was a DC-10-30 (the 266th DC-10-30 if all sub-types are included). It was built for Nigeria Airways, and was delivered in 1989.

DC-10 Series 30CF and AF

Like the DC-10-10CF before it, the DC-10-30CF was a convertible passenger/freight version of the DC-10-30. It added the same cargo door and cargo system to the Series 30 airframe. A total of 28 DC-10-30CFs was built at Long Beach and several conversions of existing airframes have since been undertaken. The first DC-10-30CF was delivered to Trans International Airlines (TIA) in March 1974. Most of the -30CFs had several owners but the bulk of the fleet saw out its time in service with FedEx Express (formerly Federal Express). It was Federal Express which was behind the development of the all-freight DC-10-30AF in the mid-1980s. This was a pure freighter version, also referred to as the DC-10-30F. Nine DC-10-30AFs were built and the first was delivered in May 1986. Distinctively, the DC-10-30AF has no cabin windows. Between November 1991 and November 1992 Sabena converted three of FedEx's DC-10-30CFs to -30AF standard.

DC-10-40

At the insistence of Northwest Orient Airlines, McDonnell Douglas developed a DC-10-30 fitted with Pratt & Whitney engines. This was the JT9D-powered DC-10-40, which began life as the DC-10-20. Northwest Orient was an early customer for the DC-10, but specified Pratt & Whitney engines for commonality with its Boeing 747s. The prototype DC-10-20 flew on 28 February 1972. A total of 42 DC-10-40s was built for just two customers, Northwest Orient (JT9D-20) and Japan Airlines (JT9D-59A). The first delivery was made to Northwest Orient on 10 November 1972 and the type entered service on 13 December. The JAL order came much later, in 1973, when more powerful versions of the JT9D became available. JAL's DC-10-40s were delivered between March 1976 and 1981.

DC-10 Advanced Freighter Conversion/MD-10

In September 1996 FedEx and McDonnell Douglas announced the DC-10 Advanced Freighter Conversion, to convert passenger DC-10s to freighters and to modify FedEx's existing DC-10 freighters to a common standard by fitting them with the Advanced Common Flightdeck (ACF). The ACF was added to the newly converted freighters, and all of the modified aircraft are known as Boeing MD-10s. FedEx Express acquired a substantial number of early-model DC-10s and fitted them with the standard 102-in x 104-in (2.59-m x 3.56-m) cargo door of earlier freighter versions, fitting them out for total freight operations. A total of 70 FedEx DC-10s was covered by the contract, with a further 50 options. In August 2005, FedEx Express had 41 MD-10 conversions in service.

DC-10-30ER

Five CF6-50C2B-powered DC-10-30s were built with additional fuel tanks in the rear cargo hold for extended range (ER) operations. Seven were later modified to the same standard. These tanks could hold either 1,530 US gal (5791 litres, 1,274 Imp gal) or 3,200 US gal (12,113 litres, 2,665 Imp gal) of fuel. First deliveries were made in 1982 to Swissair and Finnair.

DC-10 cargo conversions

In 1990 Italy's Aeronavali was certified to undertake cargo conversions to existing DC-10-10s, DC-10-30s and DC-10-40s using all of Douglas's original drawings, parts and standards. Since then Aeronavali has rebuilt DC-10 freighters for various customers, including DAS Air Cargo, Gemini Air Cargo, ILFC, Aeroflot and FedEx. Aeronavali was an important modification centre for the MD-10 programme.

KDC-10

The Royal Netherlands Air Force acquired two DC-10-30CFs from Dutch cargo charter airline Martinair and converted them, in 1994/95, to act as tanker/transports – in a similar fashion to the KC-10A. The two Dutch aircraft were fitted with a refuelling boom and the unique RARO (Remote Aerial Refuelling Operation) system. The palletised RARO system allows an operator in the cabin to control the refuelling using a TV monitor, and does away with the need for a boom operator's station. The KDC-10s can also be fitted with wing-mounted hose drum units (HDUs). The first modified KDC-10 (T-264, formerly PH-MBT) flew in July 1995 and was delivered to No. 334 Squadron in August. The second followed in February 1995.

KC-10A Extender

From its original roots as a military design, the DC-10 came full circle when the USAF selected a version of the DC-10-30CF to fulfil its ATCA (Advanced Tanker Cargo Aircraft) competition, in December 1977. The airframe was fitted with an air-to-air refuelling boom, and a boom operator's station, at the rear of the fuselage. An air-to-air refuelling receptacle was also added above the cockpit. The underfloor cargo doors and all but two cabin windows were deleted. The resulting aircraft was designated KC-10A Extender. The USAF acquired a total of 60 KC-10As, which were delivered from March 1981 to November 1988. One aircraft was destroyed in a fire in 1987, but the other 59 remain in everyday service.

McDonnell Douglas

MD-11

DC-10 successor

McDonnell Douglas spent a lot of time examining the aircraft that would succeed its popular DC-10, but through a combination of poor timing and bad luck, it failed to quite hit the mark. The MD-11 was not a substantial improvement over the DC-10, though it did boast new technology and design features.

In tried-and-trusted form, McDonnell Douglas used one of its existing aircraft – the DC-10 – as the basis for the MD-11. The new, larger aircraft would be an advanced technology trijet, with extended range, modern engines and digital avionics. Work had begun on such an aircraft as early as 1978, when McAir began to examine its options for a DC-10 'stretch'. The plan was to introduce an aircraft in the early 1980s to compete with the Boeing 747 and to pre-empt the efforts of Airbus. A proposed DC-10 Series 60 was drawn up in three different versions: DC-10-61, aimed at the US domestic market, using the wing of the DC-10-30 with a larger, heavier fuselage; the transatlantic DC-10-62, with a shorter fuselage and extended wing with winglets; and the DC-10-63, that coupled the Series 62 wing with the Series 61 fuselage. Each of these aircraft would have been larger than the MD-11 of today, though their

MTOWs would have been roughly equivalent. However, despite early optimism, customer interest in the Series 60 proved to be illusive and, as time passed, the aircraft began to look increasingly dated. As fuel prices climbed, McAir shelved its DC-10 developments and began to look at an all-new design as the next way forward.

New proposals

In 1982 the resultant MD-100 proposal was unveiled. This aircraft retained the trijet configuration and was approximately the same size as a

Above: VASP was an early operator of the MD-11 airliner, leasing two examples in the spring of 1992. Success in service subsequently led to VASP leasing a further six.

DC-10. Differences included its two-crew flight deck and Pratt & Whitney PW2037 or Rolls-Royce RB.211-535 engines (both as found on the Boeing 757). Like the Series 60, the MD-100 failed to gain much interest and, remarkably, McDonnell Douglas began to reconsider a 'quick and easy' DC-10 derivative once more. This led to the MD-XXX of 1984, an aircraft that was little more than a DC-10-30 with General Electric CF6-80C2 or Pratt & Whitney PW4000 engines. A fuselage stretch was proposed and, by the end of the year, MDC had adopted the MD-11 title for its new project.

The first MD-11 to enter service with Finnair is seen at the official roll-out in 1990. The type entered service at the end of the year on Finnair's Helsinki-Tenerife route.

With the MD-11 came a whole family of proposed aircraft – the MD-11X-10ER, the MD-11X-20 and the MD-11X-MR. The -10ER would have a DC-10-sized fuselage while the others would both be stretched. In July 1985 the McDonnell Douglas board of directors gave the go-ahead for the MD-11 to be offered to the airlines and a launch date was suggested for early 1986. A market for 1,400 aircraft in the class of the MD-11 was foreseen,

The third MD-11 to fly, N311MD was part of the three-aircraft test programme which resulted in the aircraft's certification with PW4460 engines in November 1990.

Left: The DC-10 ancestry is readily evident in the MD-11's layout. Although a number of loyal Douglas/McDonnell Douglas customers ordered the type, performance figures never reached the initial predictions and production was halted.

Right: The first MD-11 to fly was N111MD, which took to the air on 10 January 1990. After participating in the flight test programme the aircraft was delivered to Federal Express as an MD-11F in June 1991.

with McAir hoping to make at least 300 sales. First deliveries were scheduled for 1989.

By October 1985 several changes had been made to the MD-11 design and the family options had been chopped, since little interest had been shown in the short-range MD-11X-MR or the short-fuselage MD-11X-10ER. The MD-11's overall fuselage stretch was also reduced. The two-crew cockpit and CF6-80C2/ PW4000 engines were retained.

Initial orders

The MD-11 received its formal go-ahead on 30 December 1986, when McDonnell Douglas announced commitments for 82 aircraft from 12 customers. However, few of these were firm orders and, of those that were, events conspired to block several of them. By the end of 1987 the official figures comprised 30 firm orders and 47 commitments. Such low figures quickly attracted criticism, as did the fact that no major orders from a US carrier had been won. Along with the passenger version came two cargo versions and it was as a freighter that the MD-11 would eventually find its most successful niche.

The baseline MD-11 was built around a DC-10-30 fuselage with two plugs inserted fore and aft of the wing section. The MD-11 has an overall length of 200 ft 11 in (61 m) when fitted with PW engines, or 201 ft 4 in (61.30 m) when fitted with GE turbofans. One difference from the DC-10 comes with the addition of the MD-11's aluminium and carbon-fibre winglets. These are credited with reducing overall drag by 4 per cent. The MD-11's fin and tailplanes are revised, with reduced sweep and area, again to reduce drag. Engine options came in the form of the 61,500-lb st (273.6-kN) CF6-80C2D1F or 60,000-lb st (270-kN) PW4460. Rolls-Royce proposed a Trent 665 option for the MD-11, but the one customer for this solution, Air Europe, collapsed in 1991 before deliveries could begin and the Trent was quietly dropped from the MD-11 programme.

On the flight deck the MD-11 is configured with a six-screen EFIS cockpit and an advanced flight management system. In the cabin, it can be fitted with up to 405 seats in a single-class configuration, though a more typical layout is 293 seats in three classes.

Hand-in-hand with the all-passenger MD-11 (sometimes referred to as the MD-11P) came three other variants: the MD-11C Combi, MD-11F Freighter and the MD-11CF Convertible Freighter. The Combi is fitted with a side cargo door, on the port side of the fuselage. The side cargo door was developed by Alenia, at its Aeronavali facility – one with great experience in developing cargo conversions for aircraft like the DC-8 and DC-10. The Combi configuration allowed up to 214 passengers and six standard cargo pallets to be carried in the main cabin. Structurally, the aircraft can handle up to 10 pallets and 120 passengers.

The MD-11F has a slightly smaller side cargo door when compared to the MD-11C. This improves the structural integrity of the aircraft and gives it a higher maximum landing weight. The MD-11F is unmistakable through its lack of cabin windows, and absence of all passenger access doors.

The MD-11CF offers a user the ability to switch the aircraft from all-passenger to all-freight configurations, giving maximum flexibility with one airframe. The CF has the same side cargo door as the MD-11F and can be converted from all-passenger to all-cargo configuration in 35 hours.

Delta Air Lines placed an order for 15 MD-11s in 1988, seven of which remain in service with the airline today. They are powered by PW4460 turbofans and were delivered between 1992 and 1994.

MD-11 in service

Typical of many operators, Eva Air of Taiwan found the MD-11 more suitable as a freighter than as a passenger-carrying type. The airline currently operates 12 MD-11Fs.

The MD-11 was never a 'best seller' and its very public difficulties hurt its order book severely. Though the freighter versions are seen as invaluable by those lucky enough to have them, this was not enough to save the production line, which closed in 2000.

World Airways, based at Charleston, South Carolina, currently operates a fleet of 13 MD-11s, including four MD-11F freighters. All of the aircraft were acquired on long-term leases.

The MD-11 was launched on 30 December 1986, with 82 announced 'commitments', of which many were never firmed up. In fact, only 11 firm orders were placed in 1986. The next tranche of orders came in March/April 1987 as deals were struck with Finnair (two), Swissair (six, plus four in December) and Alitalia (one). Alitalia also became the launch customer for the MD-11C Combi, with an order for five, while FedEx launched the MD-11F Freighter, with an order for two.

As the first MD-11 entered the assembly phase in March 1988, the order book stood at just 31 aircraft. At the same time, it was announced that the slow delivery of components from suppliers would delay the first completion by a month, to February 1989, with the maiden flight now rescheduled to April. During 1988 McDonnell Douglas received orders from Thai International (four), FedEx (two), China Airlines (four), Delta Air Lines (nine), China Eastern (four, plus one MD-11F), Finnair (two), Garuda (six), ILFC (three, plus two MD-11Fs), LTU

(three) and VARIG (four). The Delta order was, at the time, the most significant. Its full terms included nine firm orders and 31 options, but it also marked the first MD-11 purchase by a major US airline.

In 1989 the slow pace of orders continued, with signings by FedEx (two MD-11Fs), Swissair (two), American Airlines (15), LTU (one) and EVA Air (two, plus three MD-11Fs). The order from American was the first of two that would see it become the largest operator of MD-11s in passenger service. Also in 1989 Air Europe announced its order, but the airline went out of business before these aircraft were ever built. Air Zaïre also announced orders that were never fulfiled.

The first MD-11 took to the air on 10 January 1990 – eight months behind schedule. This CF6-powered aircraft launched the flight-test programme and to speed up the process, McDonnell Douglas had the MD-11 certified as a derivative of the DC-10, rather than a completely new type. FAA type certification was awarded on 30 November 1990, with certification of the PW4460-powered MD-11 following on 19 December. The first customer

LTU International Airways operated four PW4462-powered MD-11s – first ordered in 1988 – until the aircraft were sold to Swissair in the late 1990s.

After acquiring the four ex-LTU examples, Swissair had a total fleet of 19 MD-11s by 1999. However, the fleet was sold to FedEx, which converted them into MD-11F freighters.

delivery of an MD-11 was made to Finnair on 29 November 1990. Finnair placed the aircraft into revenue service on 20 December 1990. The first PW4460-powered MD-11 was delivered to Korean Airlines on 25 January 1991.

1990 was a good year for the MD-11 as several (comparatively) large orders rolled in from important customers. These included deals with American Airlines (11), KLM (10), Japan Airlines (10), Korean Airlines (one), FedEx (two MD-11Fs), Delta Air Lines (two) and GATX Capital (one). The next year, business dropped sharply, with orders placed by Delta Air Lines (two), FedEx (five MD-11Fs) and Martinair Holland (three MD-11Fs).

Improving performance

The reason for the decline in interest soon became clear. Though it was only in the earliest days of its service life, the MD-11 was already suffering serious problems. The aircraft was falling well short of its promised payload/range performance, through a combination of aerodynamic flaws and poor engine operating economy. The brochure figures for the MD-11 quoted a maximum range of 7,000 nm (8,050 miles;

12955 km) with 293 passengers and a 61,000-lb (27670-kg) payload, but even before the flight test programme was complete McDonnell Douglas knew that the aircraft would not perform as advertised. Much of the problem could be traced to higher than expected fuel consumption by both engine types – which was falling between 4 and 9 per cent outside the contract specification. The MD-11 was also overweight and suffered from excess drag. To try to solve the problem, McAir implemented a multi-phase performance improvement package (PIP) that reduced drag, reconfigured the wing and other external surfaces and boosted take-off weight, allowing more fuel to be carried, and reduced overall empty weight.

As the various phases of the PIP were introduced, the MD-11's

range began to creep upwards. Both engine manufacturers developed their own powerplant PIPs and Delta Air Lines introduced a novel auxiliary fuel tank arrangement which could be fitted in the cargo hold, replacing two LD3 containers. By 1996 McDonnell Douglas believed that it had reached the limit of what was possible without profound airframe changes and that performance had been boosted by some 8 per cent. This put the MD-11 back into the 7,000 nm bracket, but the damage had been done. For example, a vital order from Singapore Airlines for 20 aircraft was lost, as the MD-11 could not meet SIA's range requirements.

Cargo versions

In the specialist cargo market the MD-11F was beginning to shine. The first MD-11F was delivered on 29 May 1991, to FedEx, while Alitalia took delivery of its first MD-11C Combi on 27 November 1991. Martinair Holland became the launch customer for the MD-11CF, on

26 August 1991, with an order for three aircraft (with two options). The first Convertible Freighter was delivered in December 1994. During the mid-1990s McDonnell Douglas announced several dramatic developments of the MD-11, including twin-engined derivatives and extended-range versions. The MD-11ER was announced in 1994 as an aircraft that would be 'the longest-range 300-seat airliner in revenue service'. Capable of carrying 298 passengers over 8,295 miles (13350 km), the MD-11ER was developed in direct competition to the Boeing 777 and Airbus A340. However, as sales of the basic aircraft declined, plans for the ER died some time before the takeover of McDonnell Douglas by Boeing in August 1997.

After the takeover, despite some hopes that the MD-11F would be saved, after a small flurry of late orders, Boeing announced – in June 1998 – that all MD-11 production would cease during 2000. Some 200 MD-11s were built.

The MD-11F received a welcome boost in 1996 when Lufthansa Cargo ordered five aircraft, with options on a further seven, in an order worth over $550 million. A total of 19 is now in service, all powered by General Electric CF6-80C2D1F turbofans.

VARIG of Brazil leases 15 MD-11s which are utilised on a number of the airline's long-haul routes. They are configured to carry either 12 first-, 49 business- and 180 economy-class passengers, or six, 49 and 230, respectively.

The clean lines of the Super 80's significantly stretched fuselage quickly set it apart from the earlier DC-9 models.

McDonnell Douglas MD-80 family

DC-9 successor

By the end of the 1970s the DC-9 had been flying for 15 years and McAir decided to open a new chapter in its story. The stretched MD-80 family maintained its forerunner's sales records and spawned a new family, the MD-90/Boeing 717.

In 1973 the Douglas Aircraft Company division of the McDonnell Douglas Corporation, which was then finalising design of the DC-9 Series 50, began looking to the next major development of its versatile airliner. A number of proposals was considered, all based on quieter, more fuel-efficient, re-fanned versions of the JT8D engine which had powered all DC-9s to date.

Several options were discussed with potential customers and eventually evolved into the DC-9 Super 80, which was launched in October 1977 when an order for 15 aircraft was received from Swissair. While bearing a clear

resemblance to its DC-9 forerunners, the Super 80 was to all intents and purposes an entirely new aircraft. McDonnell Douglas recognised this fact by dropping the DC-9 title in favour of the designation MD-80, a generic term for the entire series of contemporary twinjets.

Compared with the DC-9 Series 50 which it succeeded, the Super 80/MD-80 had a fuselage lengthened to 147 ft 10 in (45 m) by means plugs forward of the wing and in the rear fuselage. The cabin provides accommodation for 137 passengers in typical mixed-class configuration and up to 172 in high-density layout. Underfloor cargo volume was

increased. The MD-80 series wing incorporated a new centre-section and an extension at each wingtip.

The engine selected for the MD-80 was the 18,500-lb st (83.25-kN) JT8D-209 high-bypass ratio turbofan, with a further 750-lb st (3.38-kN) Automatic Power Reserve (APR) available in engine-out situations. Enlarged, acoustically-treated nacelles were designed to accommodate the engines, enabling the aircraft to meet FAA Federal Air Regulation Part 36 noise emission standards

as well as the more stringent ICAO standards.

A key feature of the MD-80's advanced two-crew flight deck was its Sundstrand digital electronic integrated flight-guidance and control system, incorporating speed command with digital full-time autothrottles and Sperry CAT IIIA autoland. A Honeywell Electronic EFIS with CRT screens was available optionally in place of electro-mechanical flight instrument displays. An electronic Performance Management System (PMS), similar to that previously developed for the DC-10, was introduced as standard from 1983, coupling through the autopilot and autothrottle systems to control automatically the aircraft's pitch attitude and engine thrust to give optimum speed and fuel

Above: The prototype Super 80 was equipped with a stall recovery parachute. It would have been deployed in the event of the aircraft entering an unrecoverable deep stall.

Below: By far the biggest operator of the MD-80 has been American Airlines which, at its peak, had 350 examples in its fleet. Today, it retains a huge fleet of MD-82s and MD-83s.

Above: The MD-83 was an extended-range variant of the family. This example served with the now-defunct Minneapolis-based Republic Airlines.

The final member of the MD-80 family was the MD-88. Equipped with a 'glass' cockpit and constructed of composite materials, this variant was sold in the greatest numbers to Delta Air Lines, which retained a large fleet in 2005.

efficiency in climb, cruise and descent.

First in line

The first aircraft in the Super 80/MD-80 series, an MD-81, made its maiden flight on 18 October 1979. The first of launch customer Swissair's aircraft was delivered on 12 September 1980, flying its inaugural revenue service from Zurich to Frankfurt on 5 October.

On 16 April 1979 McDonnell Douglas announced development of the MD-82. Powered by 20,000 lb st (00-kN) JTOD-217 turbofans with 850-lb st (3.83-kN) APR, was model is generally similar to the MD-81, but was optimised for operation from 'hot-and-high' airports and has a higher maximum take-off weight of 147,000 lb (66679 kg).

On 12 April 1985 McDonnell Douglas signed an agreement with the China Aero-Technology Import/Export Corporation (CATIC) and the Shanghai Aviation Industrial Corporation of the People's Republic of China for the sale of 26 MD-82s for use by the Civil Aviation Administration of China. Five aircraft had already been supplied for use by China Eastern Airlines and China Northern Airlines. This agreement provided for licence assembly of all but one of the 26 aircraft by the Shanghai Aircraft Manufacturing Factory (SAMF),

Right: Hawaiian Airlines leased two MD-81s from United Aviation Services for two years, but has since returned the aircraft. This Pacific carrier now uses the Boeing 717 and 767.

using components and sub-assemblies shipped from Long Beach. A further 20 aircraft were added to the agreement in April 1990.

Announced on 31 January 1983, the MD-83 is a long-range development of the MD-80 series, externally similar to the MD-81/2, but powered by 21,000-lb st (94.5-kN) JT8D-219 engines. It has an additional 1,160 US gal (4391 litres) of fuel in two cargo bay tanks, and a maximum take-off weight of 160,000 lb (72576 kg). It was first flown on 17 December 1984 and entered service early in 1986 with launch customers Alaska Airlines and Finnair. Finnair's first MD-83 made the longest non-stop flight ever recorded by an MD-80 series aircraft during its delivery flight on 14 November 1985, flying the 3,920 miles (6308 km) from Montreal, Canada to Finnair's base at Helsinki in 7 hours 26 minutes.

The only version of the basic MD-80 series to display a major airframe change was the MD-87, announced on 3 January 1985. This had a fuselage shortened by 16 ft 5 in (5 m), seating 109 passengers in mixed-class or 130 in single-class accommodation. The MD-87 was first flown on 4 December 1986; deliveries to

launch customers Austrian Airlines and Finnair began in October 1987.

The fifth member of the MD-80 family, designated MD-88, was announced on 23 January 1986, following receipt of a launch order for 80 aircraft (subsequently increased to 110) from Delta Air Lines. Similar to the MD-82, this version is powered by 21,000-lb st (94.50-kN) JT8D-219 engines and featured an EFIS flight deck, flight management system (FMS), inertial reference system (IRS), and windshear detection system as standard. Increased use was made of composite materials in the airframe, and its 142-passenger, five-abreast seating cabin interior was extensively redesigned with

a wider aisle and new overhead storage bins. The MD-88 first flew on 15 August 1987, received FAA certification on 9 December and entered service with Delta on 5 January 1988.

In addition to airliner variants of the MD-80 series, McDonnell Douglas also built MD-83 and MD-87 Executive Jets. Designed to individual customer specifications, these are typically configured to carry 20-30 passengers and have maximum ranges of 4,100-4,500 nm (4,718-5,179 miles; 7593-8334 km).

A total of 1,191 aircraft of the MD-80 series was ordered by operators ranging from Adria Airways through Continental to Venus Air. Late in 1999, however, Boeing, which by then controlled McDonnell Douglas, brought production of the family to a close.

Above: Powered by two 20,000-lb st (90-kN) JT8D-217C turbofans, the MD-87 was the first aircraft in the series to offer an EFIS, an attitude and heading reference system (AHRS) and a head-up display as standard in its avionics/flight deck configuration.

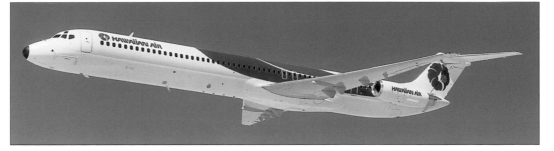

The -80s today

Above: Continental's huge fleet includes dwindling numbers of MD-80 series aircraft, including MD-81s, -82s (illustrated) and -83s. The airline has retired its DC-9-31 and -32 aircraft.

The book has now been closed on the MD-80 story, following the delivery of the last aircraft by Boeing in 1999. The production life of Long Beach's 'Super 80' lasted 20 years and spanned two continents. It is a tribute to the quality of the basic design that most MD-80s were acquired by airlines that already had many happy years of DC-9 experience.

The 'Super 80' title did not follow on from the earlier DC-9 designations and reflected the fact that these latest developments would be a family of new aircraft for the 1980s. There was never an actual type designated DC-9-80. Instead, the first production variant was the DC-9-81 (and this was the form that appeared on all aircraft construction plates right until the end of MD-80 production).

Initial sales were slow, with just 100 orders logged in the five years after the programme was announced in 1977. This situation improved remarkably during the early 1980s, when sales rose to an average of 125 a year. The DC-9-80 was launched on the back of 36 orders and options from Swissair, Austrian Airlines and Southern Airways (though the latter never actually proceeded). The first customer for the type was Swissair, with an order for 15 aircraft. The Swiss

national carrier took delivery of its first DC-9-81 on 13 September 1980, placing it into service on 10 October, on the Zurich-London-Heathrow route. Swissair's first two aircraft were used by McDonnell Douglas for the DC-9-80's flight test programme and, during this process, both were rendered undeliverable. The very first DC-9-81 was damaged and retained by the manufacturer until 1990, when it was finally sold on. The second aircraft was actually damaged beyond repair in an incident at Yuma on 19 June 1980. Both of these aircraft were replaced further down the delivery schedule and different DC-9-81s were handed over to Swissair in December 1981 and March 1982. After Swissair, DC-9-81 deliveries continued to Austrian Airlines, Austral Lineas Aereas, Muse Air, AirCal, TOA

Top: In either 164-seat high-density, or 131-seat layouts, the MD-82 remains the backbone of Alitalia's fleet. Note the 'Super 80' titles on the engine nacelles of this aircraft.

Domestic Airlines (later Japan Air System), Pacific Southwest Airlines/PSA (later merged with USAir, now US Airways), Hawaiian Airlines and Inex Adria Airlines. Other operators included Sun Air, Harlequin Air, Avioimpex, SAS, Aeromexico, Continental Airlines, Midwest Express and Spirit Airlines.

First Super 80 variant

In 1979 McDonnell Douglas announced the first variant in the Super 80 family, the DC-9-82. This version was almost identical to the DC-9-81, but was fitted with more powerful engines for 'hot-and-high' operations. The launch customer was officially Aeromexico, but Inex Adria later swapped two of its existing

Super 80 series orders to become DC-9-82s. The first delivery was made to the USA's Republic Airlines (later merged with Northwest Orient, now Northwest Airlines) on 5 August 1981 and the first Inex Adria aircraft followed on 11 August. Aeromexico received its first DC-9-82 on 14 December 1981. Other operators included AirCal, Jet America Airlines (later merged with Alaska Airlines), Frontier Airlines, VIASA, ALM Antillean Airlines, New York Air (later merged with Continental Airlines), Martinair Holland, American Airlines, Trans World Airways/TWA, Alitalia, Austrian Airlines, Ozark Airlines (later merged with TWA), Alisarda, Continental Airlines, Finnair, Far

While the MD-87 will remain an important type in Iberia's fleet for a few years, the type is set to be ousted following a major Airbus purchase by the Spanish national carrier.

SAS remains a major McDonnell Douglas twinjet operator. This MD-81 is typical of the earliest examples of the MD-80 series to enter service.

Eastern Air Transport, Nouvelair Tunisie, Sun Air, Air Philippines, Beiya Airlines, Pacific Airlines, U-Land Airlines, Meridiana, SAS, Spanair, Midwest Express and Spirit Airlines.

MD-82s built under licence in China remained in service with China Eastern Airlines, China Northern Airlines and China Northern Swan Airlines into the 21st century.

In January 1983, McDonnell Douglas launched the next version in the family, the DC-9-83. This extended-range, higher gross weight aircraft was aimed at holiday charter airlines and other specialist operators flying long, thin routes. In June 1983 McDonnell Douglas finally dropped the illustrious 'Douglas Commercial' (DC) prefix in favour of 'MD'.

First of the 'MDs'

The Super 80 series thus became the MD-80 family, the DC-9-81 became the MD-81 and the DC-9-82 the MD-82. Launch customer for the MD-83 was Alaska Airlines, which took delivery of its first aircraft in February 1985. Other MD-83 operators included Finnair, American Airlines, Korean Airlines, Nouvelair Tunisie, Far Eastern Air Transport, British Island Airways, Aero Lloyd, Air Liberté, AOM French Airlines, Austrian Airlines, Eurofly, Meridiana, SAS, Spanair, Aerolineas Argentinas, Aeromexico, Air Jamaica, Allegro Air, Austral, Avianca, BWIA,

Finnair has a reduced fleet of MD-82 and -83 (illustrated) aircraft remaining in service.

Continental Airlines and Midwest Express.

Shrinking the -80

Introduced in 1985, the MD-87 featured the first significant change in the basic MD-80 design. The short-fuselage MD-87 was an MD-80 'shrink', designed to replace ageing short DC-9s. The first orders were won from Finnair and Austrian Airlines in December 1984 and the first aircraft were handed over on 1 November 1987 and 27 November 1987, respectively. A total of 75 MD-87s had been delivered to 10 customers when production ceased in 1992. Other current operators include Austrian (one, for sale), Iberia, Japan Airlines Domestic, SAS and Aeromexico.

The final member of the MD-80 family was the MD-88.

Developed specifically for Delta Air Lines, the MD-88 added an advanced technology EFIS cockpit to the basic airframe of an MD-82 or MD-83. Delta itself chose the new designation, and launched the programme with orders and options for 80 aircraft. The first MD-88 was delivered on 19 December 1987 and entered service on 5 January 1988. Delta later increased its total by converting earlier deliveries to MD-88 standard. Other MD-88s currently serve with Onur Air, Aerolineas Argentinas, Aeromexico and Midwest Airlines.

The 1,000th MD-80, MD-83 N960AS, was delivered to Alaska Airlines on 23 March 1992. An MD-83 (N596AA) handed over to American Airlines on 11 June 1992 became the 2,000th twinjet to be delivered by McDonnell Douglas.

The final countdown

Following the August 1997 acquisition of McDonnell Douglas by Boeing, a shadow was cast over the future of the entire MD airliner series. Uncertainty reigned for nearly a year until May 1998, when

Boeing announced that it would phase out production of the MD-80 (and the MD-90, which shared the same final assembly line). In a ceremony held at Long Beach, California – home of the Douglas airliners – Boeing handed over the last MD-80 to TWA on 21 December 1999. The aircraft was an MD-83 and the 26th MD-80 delivered to TWA that year. It brought the number of MD-80s operated by TWA to 102, and the aircraft was christened *Spirit of Long Beach*.

In 1933 TWA had taken delivery of the very first twin-engined airliner built by the Douglas Aircraft Company, the (one and only) DC-1. Douglas Aircraft, McDonnell Douglas and Boeing delivered 1,191 MD-80s from 1979 to 1999. In 2005 remaining MD-80 operators included American Airlines, Delta Air Lines, Alitalia, SAS, Continental Airlines, Iberia, Alaska Airlines, Aeromexico, Finnair, Japan Airlines Domestic, Spanair, Meridiana, China Southern Airlines, Austrian Airlines and Avianca.

Alaska Airlines was launch customer for the MD-83, its first being delivered in 1985.

Raytheon 1900
King Air-based commuterliner

A conventional machine of efficient design, the Beech 1900 was cleverly produced to fill a recognised gap in the market place.

With its King Air twin-turboprop executive aircraft well established, Beech decided that a new market existed for turboprop commuter airliners. The company's first move was to reintroduce its Model 99 Airliner into production during 1980. It was soon apparent that the large number of airlines now feeding passengers into the services of the main US carriers could use an aircraft of greater capacity, and to fill this requirement Beech developed the Model 1900.

The new aircraft used a wing based on that of the Model 200 Super King Air, while its tail section, cockpit and nose section were lifted directly from the Super King Air.

New fuselage

Quite clearly, the Model 1900 would need a new fuselage with cabin space for a maximum of 19 passengers and their baggage. The pressurised fuselage was of aluminium construction and featured a small vortex generator ahead of each wing root leading edge. Initially installed as retractable surfaces, these vortex generators are among a number of aerodynamic 'tweaks' that have been applied to the 1900 airframe during its evolution and add to the type's distinctive, if somewhat untidy, overall appearance.

Regular orders from feederlines such as Continental Express allowed Model 1900D deliveries to reach almost 700.

The flightdeck was comprehensively equipped with Honeywell EFIS as standard, while avionics included a Bendix RDR-160 weather radar. A pair of Pratt & Whitney Canada PT6A-65B turboprops flat rated at 1,100 shp (820 kW) powered the aircraft.

Prototypes

Three flying prototypes were constructed, along with one aircraft for static test and another for fuselage pressure cycle testing. The first of the fliers completed its successful first flight on 3 September 1982,

Above: Of the three flying Model 1900 prototypes, the third was used for an range of systems and reliability testing, as well as acting as the type demonstrator.

Right: Thanks to its standard cargo door, the 1900C makes an ideal basis for freighter conversion. This machine has its cabin windows blanked off.

Above: Additional aerodynamic surfaces sported by 1900C-series aircraft include 'tail-lets' beneath the tailplanes and large horizontal 'stabilons' either side of the rear fuselage.

Below: This view of the Model 1900D prototype emphasises the type's increased fuselage depth, especially when compared to the 1900C pictured left. Note also the aircraft's winglets and prominent ventral strakes.

and FAA certification was gained on 22 November 1983.

The first of the production models was the Model 1900C Airliner, the first example of which was delivered in February 1984. The 1900C's versatility was improved by the addition, as standard, of a 52-in (1.32-m) square cargo door. In addition, both the forward and rear cabin doors featured integral airstairs and there were baggage compartments in the rear fuselage and in the nose. Drawing on its extensive experience with executive aircraft, Beech also offered an executive version of the 1900C as the Model 1900 Exec-Liner. Construction of both models finally reached 72, with production slowing from October 1991 after the withdrawal of the special conditions under which the aircraft had been certified.

'Wet-wing' 1900C-1

The most successful of the 1900Cs was the 1900C-1, however, an aircraft which was built to a total of 173 before production ended in 1993. The C-1 has a 'wet-wing' – its internal wing structure is sealed to act as an integral fuel tank – giving a total capacity of 685 US gal (92593 litres). This model also formed the basis for the 1900C's limited military sales. In March 1986 the USAF ordered six 1900C-1s, extending its C-12 designation system for the King Air to include the 1900C-1 as the C-12J. The C-12Js initially replaced Convair C-131 Samaritans with the ANG, but two were later transferred to the

US Army. Egypt purchased six 1900C-1s for the electronic surveillance and maritime patrol roles. Two of the machines were equipped for maritime reconnaissance. The final military customer was the Republic of China Air Force, which took 12 aircraft from early 1988. They are primarily employed on utility transport duties, although two were modified for radar/ navigational aid calibration duties.

High-roof 1900D

At the March 1989 US Regional Airlines Association meeting, Beech announced its intention to produce a new Model 1900 variant. By virtue of a 1-ft 2-in (0.36-m) increase in fuselage depth, the cabin could now be made obstruction free, since the wing mainspar now passed beneath the cabin floor. On all previous 1900's passengers had been forced to step over the spar as they walked through the cabin. The higher roof line of the new aircraft gave the machine a decidedly odd look, but increased cabin volume by

28.5 per cent. Externally, winglets were added to improve 'hot-and-high' performance, while large ventral strakes were added beneath the rear fuselage to improve directional stability and turbulence penetration. Powered by 1,279-shp (953-kW) PT6A-67D turboprops, the first Model 1900D prototype made its maiden flight on 1 March 1990. Certification was granted in March 1991 and the first aircraft was delivered to Mesa Airlines in November 1991. Since 15 February 1994, Beech has traded under the name of its

owner Raytheon and in summer 2005 this company had a dedicated used Model 1900 sales facility. A Model 1900D Executive aircraft was also offered and could be configured either as a business aircraft or corporate shuttle. Military deliveries were restricted to a single 1900D received by the US Army in March 1997 for use by its Chemical and Biological Defense Command. Model 1900D airline orders included a 16-aircraft contract for Air New Zealand subsidiary Eagle Airways.

Above: Model 1900C-1s remain in service with the US military as the C-12J. Little is known, however, of an order placed in 2000 for six Sigint-configured Model 1900Ds for Algeria.

A number of export orders have been won by the 1900, this 1900D flying with Canada's Air Creebec. The design is made more attractive by an optional UltraQuiet system for the cabin.

Left: Although Saab remained disappointed in 340/2000 sales to the end, the manufacturer made significant inroads into the lucrative US market.

Saab 340

Sweden's feederliner

Produced initially in co-operation with Fairchild in the US, the Saab 340 eventually became an all-Swedish project, achieving significant sales and spawning the even more advanced Saab 2000.

The Saab 340 began life as the Saab-Fairchild 340A, a joint venture between the Swedish company and the American company responsible for the sales, manufacture and further development of Swearingen's Metro and Merlin. Saab had begun working on a high-winged civil/military twin turboprop (the Saab 1084) some time before, but growing costs led the Swedish company to look for a foreign (and preferably American) partner.

A preliminary agreement was signed with Fairchild Republic in June 1979, and a joint team (consisting of about 50 engineers from each company) began work at Fairchild's Long Island facility. The Saab 1084 was refined into a low-winged, 35-37 passenger aircraft for airline use only, with considerable emphasis on the use of advanced technology in the airframe, engines and systems to achieve low operating costs. The airframe thus used a high proportion of composites, and even many of the alloy components were bonded rather than conventionally rivetted. This gave low weight and better corrosion resistance. Fairchild selected an extremely advanced low-drag aerofoil for the wing, while the engines were 1,700-shp (1268-kW) General Electric CT7s with composite four-bladed Dowty propellers. The aircraft was fitted with all-digital avionics which have been compared to those used on much larger contemporary airliners like the Boeing 757 and 767, with a sophisticated autopilot and flight director. But while extremely advanced in its details, the Saab-Fairchild 340A was entirely conventional in its overall appearance, with only its swept tailfin distinguishing it from much older aircraft like the BAe 748 or NAMC YS-11.

Shared production

Fairchild took responsibility for wing, nacelle and empennage design, with Saab taking care of the fuselage as well as production, systems integration, flight test and certification. The aircraft would be legally Swedish, with initial certification by the Swedish Civil Aviation Board.

The existence of the Saab-Fairchild 340 project was revealed at a press conference on 25 January 1980, the same day that the two companies finally signed a formal agreement to produce the new aircraft. Saab built a 269,000-sq ft (24990-m^2) factory for production of the new aircraft, taking a SwKr350 million loan from the Swedish government, which would be repaid in the form of a royalty on each Saab-Fairchild 340A.

Of these, the first four 340s, SE-ISA was the second completed and was later revised as the first 340B. SE-ISB was the pre-production machine, SE-E04 was the fourth 340 and the first for Comair, while -ISF was the first prototype.

Left: This Saab 340A was delivered to Formosa Airlines in August 1988 as one of the first of the type configured with 37 seats. The revised cabin layout was designated as the Generation II interior by Saab.

Below: This Mesaba Airlines Saab 340B Plus was the 300th aircraft of the 340 family to be built and it was flown for the first time on 22 April 1992. The basic 340B marked a considerable improvement over the 340A and, as such, Saab made the modifications included in the new standard available as a retrofit.

The first of five prototypes and early production aircraft (SE-ISF) made its maiden flight on 25 January 1983, and the aircraft received its Swedish certification on 30 May 1984. The aircraft entered scheduled service with Switzerland's Crossair (which had placed an order in November 1980) on 14 June 1984, and with Comair of Cincinnati in October 1984. Saab assumed overall control of the programme on 1 November 1985, and in 1987 took over wing and empennage construction from the 110th aircraft onwards. The aircraft was thereafter simply known as the Saab 340.

After 159 Saab 340As had been built (including three prototypes), production switched to the 'hot-and-high' Saab 340B, with more powerful CT7-9B engines and increased tailplane span. The prototype 340B made its maiden flight in April 1989,

and deliveries began in September 1989. A stretched, scaled-up, 50-58 passenger derivative with 4,152-shp (3096-kW) Allison AE2100A turboprops was launched at the end of 1988 as the Saab 2000, with Westland, CASA, and Valmet as major sub-contractors. The prototype first flew on 26 March 1992.

Latest variant

The next variant was the Saab 340B Plus, which introduced some of the high-technology features developed for the Saab 2000, including a new interior, active noise suppression and optional extended wingtips. The first was delivered to AMR Eagle/Wings West in April 1994.

Named New Horizons and delivered in 1990, this 340B still flew with its original owner, the Australian carrier Hazelton Airlines, in late 1999.

The 340B Plus is available specially equipped for gravel runway operation, with strengthening and special coatings on parts of the undersides. Like all 340 variants, the B Plus carries 35 (or 37) passengers as standard, with eleven rows of three seats (two to starboard, one to port), plus two rear-facing seats one behind the other at the forward end of the cabin on the starboard side. Alternatively, the aircraft can

carry 19 passengers in a combi passenger/freight layout.

More than 450 Saab 340s were delivered (at least 290 of these being Saab 340Bs or Saab 340B Pluses). The biggest 340 operators were US regionals, principally members of the American Eagle and Northwest Airlink groups of companies which, between them, operated more than 250 aircraft. Crossair's 14 aircraft total seems modest by comparison, though the Swiss carrier became the largest operator of the Saab 2000, with 32 aircraft. These sales figures are regarded as 'disappointing' by Saab, and efforts were made to sell the Saab 2000 production tooling (most notably to the Shanghai Aircraft Manufacturing Company). Saab reportedly views its future in civil aviation as lying in collaborative projects with much larger companies like Airbus or Boeing and currently builds components for the Airbus A320 series, A340-500/-600 and A380. Saab also maintains a leasing arm for the 340/2000 range and conducts maintenance and modification work, the latter including 340 freighter conversion.

The family resemblance is obvious in this shot of the third Saab 2000 and a Saab 340B (actually the 340th built). Outstanding as the Saab 2000 was, it failed to sell in a market that had become fixated on regional jets.

Saab 2000

Saab is no longer an airliner manufacturer. After 16 years at the top, the Swedish company was forced to call it a day when sales slumped and the regional airliner market moved on. Saab had pinned its hopes on the Saab 2000, a revolutionary high-speed turboprop, which it hoped would take over from where the smaller, slower Saab 340 had left off.

Saab had ridden the crest of a wave with the 340 during the 1980s but, as the 1990s unfolded, the 340 was seen as too small and too slow. To counter this, the Saab 2000 was conceived as a super-fast 50-seat regional aircraft, that would link city pairs at jet-like speeds but at a fraction of the operating costs.

Like the 340 before it, the Saab 2000 concept was driven largely by Crossair, which signed up as the launch customer when the programme was launched in December 1988.

The Saab 2000 had all the appearance of a stretched 340, but there were many subtle and important differences. The fuselage had the same cross-section as the Saab 340, but was 24 ft 10 in (7.55 m) longer. It could accommodate up to 58 passengers, seated in rows of

three. The standard layout was for 50.

A six-screen Collins Pro Line 4 avionics system was selected for the cockpit and the radical reduction of cabin noise became a major design goal. To this end, a pair of 4,152-shp (3096-kW) Allison GMA 2100 turboprops (now AE2100) was selected, each driving slow-speed Dowty R381 propellers with six swept blades. The engines were set out from the cabin to reduce noise, but Saab also developed an active noise reduction system which effectively 'switched off' cabin noise.

Records and delays

Saab spread the development burden of its new aircraft, entering into agreements with CASA to build the wing, Valmet to build the tail unit and elevators, Hispano-Suiza to supply the engine

Above: Crossair was the launch customer for the earlier Saab 340 and the 2000. This is the fourth Saab 2000 built and the first for Crossair, seen prior to delivery.

cowlings and Westland Engineering to build the rear fuselage. The prototype flew for the first time on 26 March 1992. Early on in the test programme all Saab's performance requirements were met or exceeded. Underlining this, a Saab 2000 set a new time-to-climb record of 29,527 ft (9000 m) in 8 minutes 8 seconds, bettering that set previously by an E-2 Hawkeye.

The 2000 was at the forefront of glass cockpit technology when it first flew in March 1992.

Deutsche BA *received five Saab 2000s and held options for a further five examples, which it did not exercise. This aircraft was passed on to Regional Airlines, which today, as Regional, uses six.*

The Swedish division of Scandinavian Airlines Commuter, Swelink, used six Saab 2000s. Gerd Viking *was the fourth delivered.*

SE-001, fitted with a flight-test nose probe, was the first prototype Saab 2000, making its maiden flight on 26 March 1992. It was scrapped in mid-June 1996.

However, the certification timetable was set back by problems with the aircraft's high-speed longitudinal stability, and a new powered elevator control system had to be initiated in late 1993. First delivery dates were thus delayed into the fourth quarter of 1994 – 18 months behind schedule.

Into service

European certification of the Saab 2000 was achieved on 31 March 1994. FAA certification was achieved on 29 April 1994. Deliveries to Crossair finally began on 30 September 1994, and these were followed by the first aircraft for Deutsche BA on 17 March 1995. Other customers included Air Marshall Islands, Regional Air, Med Airlines and SAS.

Saab had proposed using the 2000 as a platform for the Ericsson Erieye AEW radar, carried by Saab 340s in Swedish air force service. However, no Saab 2000s ever entered service in this role. However, the modified Saab 340s (known in Sweden as the S 100B Argus) do incorporate the rear fuselage section of a Saab 2000, as the

latter features an auxiliary power unit which is needed by the AEW&C aircraft.

In airline service, the Saab 2000 suffered from additional early teething troubles, but these were nothing compared to the explosive arrival of competing regional jets, which emerged just as the 2000 was trying to find its feet. EMBRAER and Bombardier forged ahead to create an enormous new market that conventional wisdom had always decreed did not, and could not, exist. It was too much for Saab. Almost overnight, the company went from being a technological pace-setter, to a manufacturer

whose aircraft still had propellers! Saab announced that the 340 and 2000 production lines would close in 1999.

End of the line

Saab 2000 production ceased at 63, though a 64th airframe was laid down on the Linköping line. Crossair was very happy with its aircraft and gave them

the nickname 'Concordino', to reflect their impressive performance. Despite having left the manufacturing business – its final airliner was completed in 1998 – Saab finds that there is still demand for its aircraft.

To meet that demand Saab Aerospace established Saab Aircraft Leasing (SAL) to manage its worldwide fleet.

One of the early Saab 2000s is put through its paces over typical Swedish terrain. Most surviving 2000s are based in Europe.

SATIC A300-600ST Beluga

Beluga '2' is seen arriving at Filton, UK on its inaugural visit in June 1996. BAE Systems' Filton factory produces Airbus wings, which are transported by Beluga to the final assembly plants in Toulouse and Hamburg.

Super Transporter

For many years Airbus components were airlifted between plants by the Aerospacelines Super Guppy. While they were reliable workhorses, and the only aircraft available that could carry large airframe sub-assemblies, they were old and expensive to operate. To solve these difficulties Airbus decided to build its own 'Super Transporter'.

By the late 1980s it was becoming clear that Airbus Industrie's fleet of four Model 377SG Super Guppies – modified from Boeing Stratocruisers by Aerospacelines in the USA – would need replacing. For most of their careers the Guppies were irreplaceable as they carried Airbus parts from factories in the UK, Germany and Spain to the central production line in France. But despite its Allison 501 turboprops, the Super Guppy was still an aircraft of the 1950s. It was not very fast, it was complicated to operate and its costs increased year by year.

Beluga is born

In 1990 Airbus proposed a modification of its own A300 airliner to replace the Super Guppies, using the A300B4 as a baseline. On 22 August 1991 Airbus Industrie's executive committee gave the project its go-ahead, approving the purchase of four 'Super Transporters', with an option on a fifth. Several companies, in Europe and the US, tendered for the development contract, but the successful bid came, in May 1992, from an Aérospatiale/DASA consortium dubbed SATIC (Super Airbus Transport International Company).

The plan to use older A300 airframes was dropped in favour of the slightly larger and more advanced A300-600R structure, which also has a more sophisticated wing. The configuration of the new aircraft was the subject of much debate. A front-loading design was preferred by the users, but in the Super Guppy this had imposed the need to disconnect all electrical, hydraulic and flight control systems each time the swing nose was opened. This increased the chance of system failure and led to lengthy recalibrations before each flight. A side-loading door was the easiest option, but no door could be made large enough to accommodate an A340 wing section, and complicated offset loading positions would have to be developed. The elegant solution to these problems was to build a 'dropped' flight deck, below the level of the cargo hold floor, and install a large but conventional upwards-opening cargo door that allowed direct access to the hold. As a

The Beluga (foreground) was developed to replace the aging Super Guppy (behind). Seen here shortly before its initial flight in September 1994, the first Beluga (c/n 655) underwent 12 months of flight trials before entering service in October 1995.

Left: The Beluga's upward-hinging cargo door and cavernous hold allow the aircraft to carry the fuselage sections or wings of any current Airbus products except the A380, including, as demonstrated here, a pair of Airbus A330 wings.

Below: The Beluga's immense fuselage cross-section disturbs airflow to the tail control surfaces. To counter the problem, the Beluga incorporates an A340 tail section and large endplate fins to give adequate lateral stability.

result, the Beluga can be loaded and unloaded in as little as 45 minutes.

Beluga described

The enlarged cargo hold of the A300-600ST has a usable length of 123 ft 8 in (37.70 m). It is capable of carrying an entire A330/A340 fuselage section. The cargo deck is 24 ft 3 in (7.40 m) wide. Total volume of the cargo hold is 49,440 cu ft (1400 m³). The A300-600ST is fitted with an A340 tail section, extended by a 4-ft (1.20-m) plug, to which is attached the CASA-built horizontal tail. This has distinctive endplate fins for improved lateral stability. In all, the Super Transporter can carry a load twice that of the Super Guppy – 105,310 lb (45500 kg) over a range of 900 nm (1,035 miles; 1666 km). Maximum take-off weight is 337,307 lb (153000 kg). Power is supplied by two 59,000-lb (262.4-kN) General Electric CF6-80C2A8 turbofans, engines more usually found on the A310. It has the standard EFIS two-crew cockpit of the A300-600R.

The aircraft destined for modification were taken straight off the A300 production line, at the wing/central fuselage mating stage. The first airframe entered the modification stage in 1992 and was rolled out on 23 June 1994. The maiden flight occurred on 13 September 1994 and certification was achieved in September 1995. The A300-600ST entered service for Airbus in October 1996. The second aircraft flew in March 1996, the third on 21 April 1997 and the fourth was handed over in July 1998. A fifth aircraft was subsequently delivered. Airbus christened the A300-600ST Beluga – an appropriate title for this great, white whale.

The Belugas were built primarily for Airbus' own needs, but the possibility of leasing them out to other operators, when their schedule allowed, was raised from the beginning. In October 1996 Airbus Transport International (ATI) was established to market the Beluga's unique capabilities commercially. The acquisition of a fifth aircraft

allowed ATI to offer a dedicated aircraft for cargo charters. The first paying customer for the A300-600ST was the European Space Agency, which used the Beluga to carry a 40-ton section of the Alpha Space Station in November 1996. Since then, the Beluga has carried other modules for NASA's International Space

Station, water purification equipment to China following severe flooding in September 1998, and German army CH-53 helicopters serving on peacekeeping duties in Bosnia. SATIC has latterly considered a Beluga development of the A340 to provide even greater lift capability over longer ranges.

Right: The Beluga utilises standard A300-600R wings, engines and landing gear, which helped to keep development and production costs to a minimum.

Below: The A300-600ST (Super Transporter) has been actively marketed to companies looking to lease an outsize cargo aircraft. A fifth Beluga has been acquired to facilitate more charter work.

Swearingen Merlin/Metro
Fleet feederliner

Above: North America was by far the most lucrative market for the 19-20 seat Metro III. This example has been operated by Bearskin Airlines of Canada since March 1992.

Left: Scenic Airlines of Las Vegas, Nevada, utilised both Merlins and Metros in the 1980s and early 1990s. The aircraft were mainly utilised for sightseeing trips over the Grand Canyon.

Designed in the early 1960s, the Merlin/Metro series of light transport aircraft remained in production into the late 1990s.

The spindly fuselage of the Metro has been a regular sight at most US airports, sizeable fleets of the aircraft hurrying between large fields and smaller ports of call to bring passengers into the main hub centres. This commuter traffic constitutes the bulk of the Metro's operations, although an increasing number has been used for cargo carriage, albeit operating in a similar fashion by feeding a central hub from outlying airfields.

Edward J. Swearingen started his little company at San Antonio, Texas, over 35 years ago. His first major work was to build proto-types for others, and to fit more powerful engines to Beech Twin Bonanza and Queen Air aircraft, but he yearned to produce aircraft of his own design. To start with, he took a modified Queen Air wing and Twin-Bonanza landing gear and added twin turboprop engines and a completely new

fuselage and tail. Called the Merlin IIA, the new aircraft first flew on 13 April 1965 and was a winner from the start. It needed few changes, and deliveries began soon after certification in August 1966. This was the starting point for the entire Merlin/Metro family. Structurally, the original Merlin IIA was a completely traditional all-metal stressed-skin machine, with a smooth, flush-riveted exterior. The engines were 550-hp (410-kW) Pratt & Whitney Canada PT6A-20 turboprops, fed from integral tanks in the wing and with bleed-air anti-icing of the inlets. The retractable tricycle landing gear had a single wheel on each leg and, like the flaps, was operated electrically, the only hydraulic item being the wheel brakes. The cabin was fully air-conditioned with a Freon-cycle system, and pressurised by engine bleed. Normal accommodation was provided for

two people on the flight deck and six more (three pairs) in the cabin, with a bulkhead with a sliding door behind the flight deck. Easy access was gained by an airstair door on the left side.

In 1968, when 36 aircraft had been produced, the engines were changed to the 665-shp (496-kW) Garrett TPE331-1-151G. The inlets were located above the spinners of the Hartzell three-bladed propellers, the latter being feathering and reversing, and fitted with a synchrophasing system to reduce noise and 'beat' vibration. Although there were been projects to use PT6A engines, all subsequent production versions of the Merlin/Metro family used various sub-types of Garrett (now Honeywell) TPE331.

Merlin IIB production continued to 1972, but back in 1968 work had begun on a completely redesigned aircraft known as the Merlin III. It had a longer fuselage, and totally new wings with a different aerofoil profile and fractionally greater span, and new landing gears with two small

wheels on each leg. The new, more-tapered wing had double-slotted flaps, and both these and the forward-retracting landing gears were operated hydraulically. Thanks to the use of 840-shp (626-kW) TPE331-303G engines, the all-round flight performance was considerably enhanced. The Merlin III was certificated in July 1970, and was followed in production by the IIIA, IIIB and IIIC, incorporating numerous – mostly minor – improvements, among the most important being the introduction of 900-shp (671-kW) TPE331-IOU-501G or -503G engines, driving four-bladed propellers, giving cruising speeds of up to 355 mph (571 km/h).

In parallel with the Merlin III, the growing Swearingen engineering staff designed the SA-226TC Metro. In most respects, the two aircraft were identical, but the Metro was considerably longer, to seat 19 or 20 passengers. One might have thought such cramped dimensions would have made the long, tube-like Metro unsaleable. Far from it! Airlines all over the

Left: Built for the corporate and business market, the SA-227AT Merlin III had standard accommodation for seven passengers. However, the relocation of seats and couches is possible, using continuous tracks recessed into the floor.

Below: This SA-226TC Metro II was converted from SA-226AT Merlin IV standard and commenced service with US operator Tejas Airlines in September 1977.

world queued to build up fleets of these aircraft, which were cheap to buy, relatively fast and, once passengers are in their seats, comfortable.

The development and marketing of the new aircraft was a joint venture with what was then Fairchild Hiller, and the new wings and various other parts were made at Fairchild's plant at Hagerstown, Maryland. The first Metro flew on 26 August 1969 and, as with previous Swearingen designs, it proved virtually right first time.

Early upgrades

Sales were certainly enhanced by the early switch of production to the Metro II, still designated SA-226TC. This greatly improved the psychological comfort of the cabin by replacing the tiny portholes with upright rectangular windows every bit as large as those found in typical jetliners. Swearingen replaced the 'corporate Metro' by the Merlin IVA, first delivered in 1970. This introduced a modified fuselage with two fewer windows on each side, the interior being normally configured for 12 to 15 passengers, with a toilet and baggage compartment. In 1979 Swearingen became a wholly-owned subsidiary of

Fairchild Industries, but the work remained centred at San Antonio and the company operated as the Fairchild Aircraft Corporation.

It was partly the obvious desire to increase the weights of the Metro/Merlin family that led, in 1981, to a major upgrade. The chief change in this new Metro III version was a dramatic 10-ft (3.05-m) increase in span, providing an increase in useful load of 1,480 lb (672 kg).

While the Metro III was entering production, the design team at San Antonio continued the product improvement process by upgrading the smaller Merlin III into the SA-227/TT41 Merlin 300. In 1983, development began of the Merlin 300, and deliveries of this began at the beginning of 1985. The most obvious change was the addition of 2-ft 5-in (0.76-m) wingtip fences, or winglets.

The corporate version of the Metro III was the Merlin IVC, which included, among other upgrades, certification of a Bendix electronic flight instrument system. Fitted with a luxurious interior which included reclining seats, a couch and sophisticated refreshment and entertainment centres, the Merlin IVC can accommodate between 11 and 14 persons.

Able to seat 25 passengers, the Metro 25 – a higher gross weight modification of the Metro III – had the cargo door deleted, but featured an increased number of windows in the rear of the cabin; here, the extra passengers were accommodated in what was the baggage area. Luggage is housed in a large

underfuselage pannier. A rebuilt Metro III incorporating Metro 25 features began flight tests on 25 September 1989 to assess design features prior to a full production decision. Deliveries began in 1992 and production continued into the late 1990s. In total, over 1,000 of the Merlin/Metro family was produced.

Special missions

Fairchild has offered a number of Special Mission Aircraft based on the Metro III and, subsequently, the Metro 23. These have included the maritime patrol variant with a 360° Litton radar in an underbelly blister and an endurance of over 10 hours, and the anti-submarine variant offered with sonobuoys and a MAD tailboom. In response to a Swedish air force requirement, a Metro III was fitted with an Ericsson PS 890 Erieye AEW radar (below). The aircraft underwent flight trials from 1986, but the Saab 340 was eventually chosen as the mount for the radar. Launched in 1993, the Multi-Mission Surveillance Aircraft (MMSA) (bottom) is capable of performing multiple missions, while maintaining the ability to return quickly to passenger or cargo configuration. Equipment can include a centreline-mounted surveillance pod, mission radar and electronic reconnaissance systems.

The Expediter I is a dedicated cargo version of the Metro III family, with a payload of over 5,000 lb (2268 kg) and a reinforced floor. The first deliveries were made to DHL Worldwide Courier Express in April 1985.

Tupolev Tu-134 'Crusty'

Above: The Tu-134 was the first Soviet jetliner to be delivered to several foreign airlines, initially comprising LOT, Czechoslovak CSA (pictured), Interflug, Malev, Balkan and Aviogenex.

Left: Characteristic features of the Tu-134 (and a trademark of post-war Tupolev designs) are the main undercarriage bogies, 'somersaulting' to lie horizontal within the wing nacelles.

Tupolev's T-tail twin

Once the most important airliner in the Soviet Union, and the airlines of its client states, Andrei N. Tupolev's Tu-134 remains in widespread service today. A distinctive shape, the 'Crusty' is identified by its pronounced T-tail, sharply swept wings, and main gear which folds back into wing fairings.

The lineage of the Tu-134 can be traced back to the Tu-124 'Cookpot', the first turbofan short-haul transport in the world when it entered service on 2 October 1962. The Tu-124 was itself, in turn, a scaled-down Tu-104 'Camel' and the original Tu-104 was simply a re-fuselaged derivative of the Tu-16 'Badger' bomber.

Although an excellent short-haul jet, the Tu-124 was not particularly efficient, with an outdated layout inherited from the Tu-104, dictating a high structure weight and reduced engine efficiency. The Tu-134 (initially designated Tu-124A) design aimed to iron out the

deficiencies of the 'Cookpot'. By adopting a T-tail configuration, the Tu-124A overcame most of the problems of its predecessor, and funding for OKB's 'Cookpot' derivative was cleared by the GVF (civil air fleet) as the Tu-124 was entering Aeroflot service in 1962. The Tu-124A would be of modern design, in the same

class as the Tu-104, but retaining nothing from the design of the original Tu-88/Tu-16 'Badger' medium bomber.

The prototype Tu-124A made its maiden flight on 29 July 1963. After the unveiling of the aircraft on its 100th test flight on 29 September 1964, the airliner's designation was changed to Tu-134. By this date, a number of other development aircraft had flown, although only slow progress was being made, and the airliner suffered the protracted development common to post-war Soviet transports. Too readily written off as a sign of mismanagement and technical

shortfall, the prolonged development and pre-service regime typical of new Soviet aircraft was, in reality, a reflection of the rigorous nature of the aircraft development process under the centralised economy of the USSR.

A large number of production-standard aircraft had been completed before the Tu-134 (which had by now received the uncomplimentary ASCC codename 'Crusty') began scheduled passenger flights with Aeroflot in September 1967, when the airliner began servicing the Moscow-Stockholm route. It was

In early Aeroflot service, the Tu-134 was principally employed on domestic routes, with limited international services to Europe and the Far East. Today's Aeroflot fleet includes 13 examples.

subsequently to become the most familiar airliner in the Eastern Bloc.

New look

Major parts of the fuselage and wing of the production Tu-134 appeared to be similar to those of the Tu-124. The engines of the Tu-124, which had been retained by the Tu-124A prototypes, had been replaced on the production Tu-134 with the new Soloviev D-30 and were now rear-fuselage mounted. The wing centresection was cleaned up in comparison to that of the Tu-124. The efficiency of the flaps was also increased.

Wingspan was increased in comparison with the Tu-124, and the ailerons were divided into two parts. As on the Tu-124, all the undercarriage units retracted to the rear, the characteristic fairings aft of the wings being longer and more pointed. The addition of powerful anti-skid brakes rendered a tail parachute unnecessary.

Fuselage alterations

The change in engine installation required alteration to the rear fuselage, with a considerably larger tail, and the tailplane mounted on top of the fin with a pointed fairing over the junction. As in the Tu-124

Following bankruptcy in 1996, Almaty-based Air Kazakstan's fleet included eight Tu-134A/A-3s, alongside An-24s, Tu-154s, Il-76TDs, Il-86s and two Boeing 737-200s. Tupolev switched Tu-134 production to the 76-seat Tu-134A model in 1970.

'Cookpot', the tailplane was driven by an electric screwjack for trimming purposes. All flight controls were manual, with geared tabs. Spoilers for lift dumping and augmented roll control were increased in power, and the powered air-brake under the fuselage was retained from the Tu-124 in order to steepen the approach. De-icing remained unaltered, with electrothermal tailplane strips and engine-bled hot air for the wings, fin and engine inlets.

The fuselage length of the Tu-124A/Tu-134 was only 5 ft 3 in (1.60 m) longer than that of the Tu-124, but the capacity was increased by over 50 per cent. A major improvement over the Tu-124 was that the main spar box no longer projected into the cabin, allowing a level floor with all seats and windows at the same level. From the start, the

cabin was provided with capacity for 64 passengers: 16 first-class at the front of the cabin, 20 tourist-class in the main cabin and 28 tourist-class in the rear cabin. Cabin noise and vibration were significantly reduced compared to earlier jet airliners. The crew comprised two pilots, a navigator in a glazed nose and one steward. Baggage and cargo were stored behind the flight deck and at the extreme rear of the fuselage.

Service delays

A total of five pre-production aircraft flew, introducing the new D-30 powerplant. A take-off rating of 14,990 lb (66.7 kN) allowed higher operating weights and production aircraft soon followed the Tu-124 from the production line. Most Aeroflot aircraft lacked first-class seating, and, as a result,

the passenger seating was increased to 72, with 44 in the front cabin and 28 in the unchanged rear cabin.

Despite flight testing being relatively problem-free, the Tu-134 did not enter service until 1967. By this time, various modifications had been incorporated into the production Tu-134, including the introduction of inverters to supply most of the main electrical power loads as AC (alternating current). By 1969, the Tu-134 was carrying English Electric CSDs (constant-speed drives), giving unparalleled AC supplies. Another 1969 upgrade provided the Tu-134 with twin-clamshell thrust-reverser doors, dramatically reducing landing distances. A year later, a new rear fuselage APU system was installed, providing enhanced electric power for engine starting and cabin air-conditioning.

Following a 1999 International Civil Aviation Organisation ruling, Russia grounded all aircraft not fitted with Kopsas-Sarsat emergency radio beacons on 1 July 2005. Most of the aircraft affected by this are Tu-134s and Tu-154s. The status of the country's sizeable fleets of these aircraft was therefore difficult to assess at the time of writing.

Above: Formed in 1968 as Genex Airlines, Aviogenex was the air transport division of the Yugoslav General Export organisation, flying passenger charter flights around Europe and the Mediterranean. Four Tu-134A-3s served from 1971-90.

Right: Founded in Moscow in 1997, Skyfield Airlines Limited operated a fleet comprising a single Tu-134A-3 and one Tu-134B-3 (pictured), for executive charter flights.

Tu-134 evolution

The Tu-134 was widely used by East German agencies, and the national airline, Interflug, had 18 examples at its peak. The DDR's government was another major operator, with up to 14 Tu-134s on strength.

Above: This Tu-134A-3 was the personal aircraft of the Soviet commander of the Western Group of Forces in Germany, but was also used for other VIP flights.

Despite entering service 35 years ago, the Tu-134 remains in service with a number of airlines. The break-up of the Soviet Union means that this affordable aircraft assisted in the creation of dozens of new companies.

By 1970, production at Kharkov had switched to the Tu-134A. This had first flown prior to 1970, and it introduced a fuselage lengthened (mainly ahead of the wing) by 6 ft 10 in (2.10 m), overall length going up from 112 ft 6 in (34.35 m) to 122 ft (37.10 m). It retained the 28-seat rear cabin, but made possible various front cabins seating up to 80 in all or, exceptionally, up to 84. Seating throughout remained 2+2 so that, with 84 passengers, 21 rows were needed. The longer

This Tu-134A-3 was modified with underwing sensor pods as the Tu-134SKh (CX) for Agroprom (agriculture industry) use. It first flew in 1983 and could also be used for ice and pollution survey.

fuselage also increased cargo/baggage space by 71 cu ft (2 m³). In addition, the D-30 Series III (or D-32 engine) had an extra zero-stage on the LP compressor, enabling the existing ratings to be maintained with reduced turbine temperature, or under adverse (hot-and-high) conditions, and allowing maximum thrust to reach 15,608 lb (70.24 kN). The main wheels and brakes were also strengthened to handle the increased weights, maximum take-off weight having gone up from 98,104 lb (44500 kg) in the -134 to 103,600 lb (47000 kg) in

the -134A. The most obvious external change was that the fin/tailplane bullet was extended forwards as a long spike to form a VHF radio antenna.

Throughout the life of the Tu-134/-134A, the avionics fit was progressively increased, though it was always fairly basic. Arkhangelski once claimed that the type had the ability to make blind landings in ICAO Category III conditions, but this was certainly erroneous.

Customers

On the whole, the Tu-134 was certainly the best short-haul jet produced at that time in the Soviet Union. As early as 1968, export orders had been signed with Interflug of East Germany, Balkan Bulgarian, LOT of Poland, Malev of Hungary and Aviogenex of Yugoslavia. All these operators later also ordered the Tu-134A, Interflug replacing the earlier type with 20 of the longer model. An additional customer for the -134A was CSA of Czechoslovakia, which bought 13.

Aeroflot might not have required any change, but in 1971 Aviogenex suggested that the retention of the glazed nose had become archaic, and that radar performance, and possibly aerodynamic drag, might be improved if the Tu-134A were to be redesigned in line with Western transports, with a scanner antenna of different shape looking ahead from the nose. The first two aircraft for this operator were already on the production line, but it was found possible to incorporate the requested changes into the No. 3 aircraft. Subsequently, the more modern nose became an option on all aircraft, and it was immediately adopted for CSA's complete fleet. Several other aircraft were retroactively modified. Even the last batch for Aeroflot was fitted with radar in the nose.

The last batches were of two sub-variants, incorporating further minor improvements. The Tu-134B had a revised flight deck, with no navigator, but retaining an engineer at the side panel. The spoilers were also modified,

Above: Several nations continue to use the Tu-134 for military purposes, the type being primarily operated in the transport and communications roles. The 'Crusty' pictured above was formerly operated by the East German air force.

Above: Aeroflot still operates a small number of Tu-134s for short-and medium-haul routes around the Russian Federation. However, they are slowly being replaced by more modern Western types.

so that the pilot could use them for Direct Lift Control (DLC).

Production of the Tu-134 family ended in around 1984. The total was at least 300, around 200 seeing service on Aeroflot's shorter (up to about 1,000 miles/1609 km) trunk-route sectors for many years. Roughly 100 were exported, including 56 to major airlines in Europe.

Tu-134 today

Stringent noise and pollution controls mean that the ageing Tupolev aircraft are no longer allowed into major European airports such as Charles de Gaulle and Heathrow.

However, in East Europe and in the Russian Federation, the Tu-134 still plays a major part in the transport industry. The type

was a popular choice for the many up-and-coming airlines that formed in the former Soviet states, and small companies like Alania, Aviaekpress-kruiz, Perm Airlines, SAAK and Volga Aviaexpress ordered small numbers of the cheap, plentiful and relatively efficient Tu-134. Some of the bigger companies, such as Aeroflot, Russia State

Transport Company and Tyumen Airlines, operated larger numbers, but began replacing the type with more modern aircraft.

Tu-134s also appeared in the livery of several other airlines outside the former Soviet Bloc, but in summer 2005 only Hemus Air of Bulgaria and Syrianair retained the type.

Tu-134A-3 'Crusty'

Formed in 1968, Aviogenex flew passenger charter flights in Europe and the Mediterranean, in association with Yugotours. The airline operated four Tu-134A-3s alongside a small fleet of American-built aircraft.

Avionics
The original -134 fit included R03-1 weather radar under the nose, the NAS-1A6 navigation system, based mainly on Doppler, and BSU-3P ILS steering when coupled via the AP-6EM-3P autopilot. The latter was replaced in the -134A by the Course MP-1 navigation and landing system, with several Sperry items, including the SP-50 autopilot, VOR and ILS (later duplicated). The radar was changed for the ROZ-1, and the Doppler for the DISS-013.

Seating
The Tu-134A-3 was fitted with lightweight seats of a less bulky shape, enabling 23 rows to be accommodated in an all-tourist layout, seating a total of 96. This gave a seat-mile cost which was 50 per cent lower than that of the original version.

Titles
Each of Aviogenex's Tu-134A-3s was named after a Yugoslavian town: this aircraft was *Titograd*, the others being *Beograd*, *Zagreb* and *Skopje*. They were replaced between 1986 and 1990 by Boeing 737-200s.

Specifications
The Tu-134 has a wingspan of 95 ft 1¾ in (29 m) and a length of of 121 ft 6½ in (37.05 m). Its maximum take-off weight is 103,600 lb (47000 kg).

Radome
The third aircraft delivered to Aviogenex differed from previous Tu-134s in having the original glazed nose and undernose radome replaced by a more conical nose radome. This subsequently became optional on both the Tu-134 and the Tu-134A.

Performance
With its two Soloviev D-30 Srs II turbofans, each rated at 14,990-lb (66.7-kN) thrust, the Tu-134 had a maximum speed of 550 mph (885 km/h) and a range of 1,876 miles (3020 km).

Tupolev Tu-154 'Careless'

Second-generation Soviet jetliner

When Aeroflot came to replace its first-generation jets and turboprops on medium-range, medium-density routes, Tupolev was a natural choice, being the nation's most experienced builder of large jet aircraft. The resulting trijet design drew heavily on previous airliners as well as introducing new features inherited from contemporary Western designs.

Above: CCCP-85000 was the first Tu-154 prototype, which made its maiden flight on 4 October 1968.

Top: In total, 996 Tu-154s of all variants were delivered by Tupolev, many of which remain operational today. The aircraft remains the backbone of Aeroflot's fleet.

Tupolev's Tu-104, Tu-124 and Tu-134 provided the strong background of experience needed to tackle a challenging GVF (civil air fleet) requirement for a larger and much more powerful jetliner to replace the Tu-104 and turboprop-powered An-10 and Il-18. Passenger capacity had to exceed 120, and particularly difficult demands were that reduced payload sectors of up to 3,725 miles (6000 km) had to be flown, and that the new jets should be able to operate from airports with runways no longer than 6,500 ft (2000 m), with a surface of gravel or earth.

From the start there was never much doubt that the new aircraft would generally resemble an enlarged Tu-134, with three engines. The timing was perfect to adopt any good features from

the British Trident and American Boeing 727. From the former it was decided to adopt triplexed (three independent) hydraulic systems. From the 727 came two features never before attempted by the Tupolev bureau, leading-edge slats and triple-slotted flaps.

Like its predecessors, the Tu-154 was given a fuselage of circular cross-section. This was adequate for six-abreast seating and for the wing structure to be

accommodated beneath the floor. It was eventually decided not to fit a rear airstairs door under the tail. Instead, two main doors were fitted on the port side, ahead of the wing, with service doors on the starboard side.

The sharply swept wing had a leading-edge sweep of 40° outboard and an angle on the quarter-chord line of 35°. Structurally, the wing had three

spars, with the spaces between holding the integral tankage. The leading-edge slats were arranged in five sections and the hydraulically-driven trailing-edge triple-slotted flaps in two sections, separated by the main landing gear. Also attached to the wing were airbrakes and spoilers for lower-speed control.

As in the Tu-134, a T-type tail was fitted, but with sweep

In a bare metal finish, this Tu-154 was used for test and evaluation flights. The aircraft was one of the nine pre-production prototype Tu-154s.

Above: An early production machine (the 22nd aircraft) is seen on a test flight, accompanied by another Tu-154. From an early stage, the Tu-154 was designed to operate from semi-prepared airfields.

Below: In 1973 Egyptair became the third export customer when it received eight Tu-154As. However, the loss of one aircraft in a training accident plus the unwillingness of Tupolev to install non-standard interiors, resulted in the aircraft being returned in 1975.

increased to 45° on the leading edges. Triplexed power units drove not only the elevators but also the tailplane, which thus became the primary control surface. Hot high-pressure bled air was piped to de-ice the leading edges of the wings and tail, and the centre engine inlet. The slats were electrically heated.

To meet the severe field-length requirement, considerable engine power was needed, so that although gross weight and seating capacity were lower than for the 727-200, the engine chosen was much bigger and more powerful than its US counterpart. The engine selected was the NK-8-2, a slightly less powerful version of the turbofan already developed by Kuznetsov for the four-engined Il-62. The engines were grouped at the tail with the outer engines toed inward and fitted with cascade-type thrust reversers.

To meet the severe demand for operations from unpaved runways, the main landing gears were designed as six-wheel bogies. Each unit was designed to retract hydraulically to the rear, the bogie somersaulting so that it could lie inverted in the fairing projecting aft of the trailing edge. As in earlier Tupolev jetliners, the twin-wheel steerable nose gear retracted to the rear also.

The first of six development aircraft, CCCP-85000, was flown by test pilot N. Goryanov on 4 October 1968. CCCP-85006 was fully furnished and used for press flights in August 1970. Aeroflot (cargo-only) services began in late 1970. Irregular passenger services were flown to Tbilisi from July 1971, scheduled services began to Mineralnye Vody via Simferopol on 9 February 1972 and the first international service was to Prague on 1 August 1972. Almost all early deliveries had 128 passenger seats, a few having a higher-density configuration for 146

Later versions

From the outset strenuous efforts were made to clear the structure for a 30,000-hour crack-free life. Meanwhile, the designers had, by 1971, completed work on the Tu-154A, first delivered in April 1974 and in regular airline service from mid-1975. Almost indistinguishable from the Tu-154 externally, the -154A introduced the uprated NK-8-2U engine, giving an improved maximum take-off weight. Oddly, most of this increase was taken up by an extra fuel tank in the centre section; the fuel in this tank could be transferred elsewhere only if the aircraft was on the ground. Thus, it was used merely to cut down purchases of fuel in foreign countries. Other improvements included uprated electrical systems, strengthened baggage holds with smoke detectors, passenger seats increased to 168 and an autolanding facility.

In 1977 production switched to the Tu-154B, which was quickly refined in 1980 to Tu-154B-2 standard. This variant again increased maximum take-off weight, and introduced two additional emergency exits to enable passenger accommodation to be raised to 180. The most important change in the B-2 was that the centresection tank was made a normal part of the fuel system, usable in flight. Other changes included improved lateral-control spoilers and upgraded avionics, including French Thomson-CSF/SFIM autopilot and navigation equipment and a new weather radar. A curious feature was the addition of small actuators which, in cross-wind landings, can pivot the front axle of each main landing gear to reduce tyre wear.

The Tu-154B/B-2 was exported to many countries with friendly relations with the USSR.

Of the total of 62 Tu-154A/Bs which were exported, Tarom of Romania operated 12. Tarom's aircraft, which were delivered in 1976, were the more refined Tu-154B-2.

By 1991, a total of 612 Tu-154s of all variants had been delivered to Aeroflot.

Tu-154M & current operations

In the mid-1980s a new version of the Tu-154 entered service, fitted with new, more efficient engines. Designated Tu-154M, the aircraft sold widely to Soviet client states before the end of the Cold War made more advanced Western designs available.

In 1982 the Tu-154C freighter was announced – as far as is known, this version consists entirely of conversions of As and Bs. The main differences include the provision of a large door (measuring 110 in x 73½ in/ 2.80 m x 1.90 m) in the left-hand side of the forward fuselage, the stripping-out of the passenger accommodation to give a clear interior with a volume of 2,542 cu ft (72 m³), and the fitting of special cargo flooring, with ball mats inboard of the door and roller tracks along the main hold.

The maximum cargo load, above and below the floor, is 44,090 lb (20 tonnes).

Tu-154M

A new Tupolev airliner was announced in the early 1980s – the Tu-164 – but this designation was subsequently changed to Tu-154M. By this time, 600 of the earlier Tu-154 versions had been ordered, of which more than 500 had been delivered to Aeroflot. Thus, it may seem to have been a little late to carry out a major update of the -154,

Above: Nicaraguan airline Aeronica received its only Tu-154M in December 1989. It operated for three years before it was grounded due to financial problems and difficulties in obtaining spares.

Top: China is the Tu-154M's most successful export market. In excess of 45 have been acquired by Chinese airlines, including this example seen in Civil Aviation Administration of China (CAAC) service before its transfer to China Xinjiang Airlines in 1991.

especially as the Tupolev bureau was already thinking about a new airliner in this class, which materialised as the Tu-204. Be that as it may, a total revision of

the entire aircraft was requested, and though there are obvious external similarities – apart from the bigger, forward-pointing fairing ahead of the tailplane – it

Right: Between 1984 and 1989, Balkan received eight Tu-154Ms to supplement its fleet of Tu-154Bs and B-2s. The aircraft remained in service despite the airline's acquisition of more modern Western types such as the Boeing 737-500 and 767-200ER.

Left: Large numbers of Tu-154s served with the Soviet Union's national carrier Aeroflot throughout the 1980s and into the 1990s. This Tu-154B was delivered in 1977 and is seen in special markings celebrating the hosting of the Olympic Games in 1980.

is not possible to convert any earlier version to -154M standard.

The most important change is a switch to the Soloviev D-30KU-154-II engine, a newer and more efficient turbofan than the NK-8. Although its take-off rating of 23,380 lb (105.21 kN) is only slightly greater, its mass flow is significantly increased, necessitating enlarged inlets. The centre engine has a plain, instead of a scalloped-shaped nozzle, and the side engines have totally new pods, arranged almost axially and fitted with clamshell reversers. The gas turbine APU, previously above the centre engine, has been moved to the centre fuselage. The slats have been made smaller, yet more efficient, and the outboard spoilers have been considerably enlarged, from three sections on each side to four. As noted, the only obvious change is that the spike fairing projecting ahead of the tailplane is slightly modified, but what is less apparent is that the entire horizontal tail has been redesigned. The span remains unchanged at 43 ft 11½ in (13.40 m), but the surface has been cleaned up and increased in area from 436.50 sq ft (40.55 m²) to 454.24 sq ft (42.20 m²).

What is certainly remarkable is that, over the years, the basic operating weight (the weight of the equipped empty aircraft) has risen from 109,127 lb (49500 kg) in the Tu-154 to 111,938 lb (50775 kg) in the B and to 121,914 lb (55300 kg) in the M version. This largely cancels out the payload/range improvements gained by the extra fuel and newer engines. The maximum take-off weight of the M is 220,459 lb (100 tonnes) yet, while the original Tu-154 could carry a payload of 14,770 lb (6700 kg) with full reserves for a distance of 4,287 miles (6900 km), today's -154M can carry a payload of just 12,015 lb (5450 kg) for 4,100 miles (6600 km).

The Tu-154M was preceded by a Tu-154B-2, which was returned to Kuibyshyev and fitted with the D-30 engines. It began its flight test programme in 1982. Aeroflot took delivery of the first two

production Tu-154Ms on 27 December 1984.

A single Tu-154 was modified to evaluate L/H₂ (liquid hydrogen) as a fuel, with the designation Tu-155. The possibility of an eventual shortage of fossil petroleum could make L/H₂ very important, but it suffers from two major drawbacks. One is that its low density means that, for equivalent heat energy, the tankage has to be much bigger (though the fuel is lighter). The other disadvantage is that L/H₂ boils at -423°F (-253°C), so that it has to be stored at this intensely cold temperature, which causes numerous problems. The test aircraft's centre engine was replaced by a modified type, designated NK-88. This was fed from a carefully lagged tank, filling the rear of the cabin via a pipe in an insulated duct running along

the right-hand side of the rear fuselage. Flight-testing began on 15 April 1988, and it was then expected that the test engine would later also be run on LNG (liquified natural gas).

Versions of the Tu-154M which have appeared in the 1990s have included the Tu-154-100 with new Aviacor interior furnishings, the Tu-154M-LK-1 (two VIP aircraft for head-of-state use) and the Tu-154M/OS version with side-looking synthetic aperture radar for Open Skies Treaty observation flights. Production in 2005 has slowed to a trickle and some new-build aircraft have been placed into storage minus engines and other equipment until buyers are found. Various Tu-154 versions have been exported to the airlines of many countries aligned to the former Soviet Union including Balkan, Cubana, Malev, Tarom, LOT, CSA, Syrianair, CAAC and Aeronica of Nicaragua. Among the latest operators were the Iranian carriers Iran Air Tours, Kish Air, and Bon Air. The 1 July 2005 implementation of the 1999 ICAO ruling concerning emergency radio beacons is likely to be having a serious effect on older Tu-154s.

Tupolev Tu-204/214

The similarity between Tupolev's Tu-204 and the Boeing 757 is clear in this view of one of the four flying prototypes. The most notable feature distinguishing the aircraft from the 757 is the incorporation of drag-reducing winglets.

Russia's new hope

Designed to replace the Tu-154 in Aeroflot service, Tupolev's Tu-204 suffered during the period of the break-up of the Soviet Union. Unfortunately, even with the integration of Western avionics and engines, the aircraft has struggled to gain vital export orders.

When the Tu-204 first emerged, it resulted in a widespread feeling of déjà vu, but the Tu-204 – while it looked uncannily like a Boeing 757 – was not merely an unlicensed copy of the Boeing twinjet. Intended as a replacement for the Tu-154, the new aircraft was designed to match the latest Western airliners, while still satisfying Soviet requirements. It was drawn up around a pair of Perm-Soloviev PS-90A high-bypass turbofans, and was planned from the start to incorporate a modern glass cockpit and the most sophisticated navigation and flight management systems. The aircraft was optimised for two-crew operation; the Tu-204's designers included a flight engineer's station only to meet Aeroflot requirements, and anticipated selling many two-pilot aircraft to export customers. The aircraft was modern from nose to tail, making use of advanced aluminium-lithium alloys, and composites in its construction, and had a highly advanced supercritical wing. Tupolev envisaged using varying proportions of Western equipment for different customers, with a Rockwell Collins EFIS cockpit virtually standard across the range, except for Aeroflot.

By the time the prototype made its maiden flight on 2 January 1989, Tupolev had received firm orders for 80 and provisional orders for 350 aircraft from Aeroflot (of a stated requirement for 500 of the type), but these later lapsed when the USSR disintegrated, and Aeroflot split into fragments. Some of the fragments of the old Aeroflot within Russia itself placed new orders for small numbers of Tu-204s but, generally, the new Russian and former Soviet civil

Russia State Transport Company operated two PS-90A-powered Tu-204s on VIP flights for the Russian government. By August 2005 it had three PS-90 powered Tu-214s on charge.

operators turned westward for their equipment. Without massive support from Aeroflot, the Tu-204 programme has struggled to turn a profit ever since, despite brave efforts by the company to offer a range of variants tailored to different customer requirements.

Tu-204 variants

The original 214-passenger Tu-204 used PS-90 engines and Russian avionics, as did the original Tu-204C cargo aircraft and the extended-range Tu-204-100. The Tu-204-120 introduced RB.211-535E4 engines (actually with slightly higher fuel burn, but with much greater reliability, and thus lower operating costs), while the -122 was similar but with Rockwell-Collins avionics. Production Tu-204-120s for Kato of Egypt used Honeywell avionics. The Tu-204-200 introduced further increases in fuel and maximum take-off weight, with a strengthened undercarriage. A combi freighter version of the -200 is designated Tu-214, and this became the first 200-series Tu-204 to obtain an order, and to fly. The Tu-204-220 is offered with RB.211-535E4, -535F5 or Pratt and Whitney PW2240 engines, or as the -222 also with Rockwell Collins avionics. The Tu-204-230, with Samara propfan engines remained at the project stage, while shortened, short-

range, 99-166-seat trunkliner derivatives have also been offered. These consist of the Tu-224 with RB.211-535E4 engines and the Tu-234 with PS-90As. The latter aircraft was also known as the Tu-204-300, and a prototype was produced by shortening the fuselage of the very first Tu-204 prototype. Production -300s have been delivered to Vladivostok Avia and KMV is also looking at the type. Further advanced projects include the dual fuel (mixed kerosene/liquid natural gas) Tu-206 and the wholly cryogenically-fuelled Tu-216.

Financial failure?

One should not judge the Tu-204 too harshly, however. The collapse of the old Soviet Union took place almost 15 years ago, and the memory of what its society and economy were like, and how they operated, is fading fast. It is too easy to judge the Tu-204 by normal Western 'capitalist' standards, giving no thought to the unique demands of the system it was designed to serve. For most of the Soviet era, Aeroflot operated a gigantic, heavily subsidised rural 'bus service', taking peasants to market across the vast distances of the USSR, and using austere airfields without the usual 'razzamataz' of luggage conveyors and sophisticated passenger/freight-handling facilities. Carry-on luggage bins were the norm in Aeroflot aircraft, and hand baggage was as likely to consist of a live chicken or a small pig as anything else. Shaving the last percentile point off fuel burn figures was not the most important criterion in Soviet airliner design, whereas rugged dependability and ease of maintenance were highly prized. A Western commercial aircraft manufacturer would pat itself on the back if a particular maintenance procedure could be undertaken by a single, college-educated and expensively trained technician in minutes. Russian practice would prefer a procedure which could be undertaken reliably and without error by half a dozen barely trained mechanics, even if it took them an hour! Manpower was cheap, but skilled man-power was in very short supply.

New generation

Despite the environment in which it was created, the Tupolev Tu-204 did mark a tenuous first step towards modern Western design practice and operating concepts in what was still a Soviet Aeroflot airliner, and in that alone, it was a remarkable, significant and historic aircraft. The type deserved to find a market among Third World airlines, and the carriers of developing nations, where its easy, flexible pricing, operating characteristics, tolerance of austere airfields and undemanding maintenance procedures should have been highly prized. Unfortunately for Tupolev, the same nations whose air forces demand the latest supersonic fighters rather than easier-to-fly, easier-to-operate and more useful armed trainers, also have airlines which want the dubious prestige of operating the latest Boeing or Airbus design. Accordingly, Tu-204 sales have continued to be disappointing, although by the second half of 2005 there were some signs of a resurgence in the Russian market. Many Russian carriers are reporting a scarcity of older airframes and new Tu-204/-214 orders are coming in. There is also renewed interest in the type from China.

The extended-range Tu-204-100 is offered in all-passenger and Tu-204-100C freighter versions. Marketed from 1994, the -100C offers increased payload at the expense of reduced range.

The prototype Tu-204-120, powered by Rolls-Royce RB.211-535E4 turbofans, was the sixth Tu-204 built and made its maiden flight in August 1992. The first production example flew in March 1997.

Index

ABX Air 127
ACF (Advanced Common Flightdeck) 159
ACS (Active Control System) 149
ACS Cargo 13
Adria Airways 165
Aer Lingus 33, 67, 80, 85, 138
Aero Caribbean 45
Aero International 50, 51
Aero Lloyd 167
Aeroflot
  Antonov 42–3, 44, 45, 47
  Boeing 85
  Ilyushin 142, 145
  Tupolev 44, 178, 178, 180, 182, 183, 183,
    184, 185, 186
Aerolineas Argentinas 20, 67, 167
Aeromexico 166, 167
Aeronavali 126, 127, 159
Aeronica 184
Aerospace Technologies 109
Aerospacelines Super Guppy 174, 174
Aérospatiale 16, 22, 50, 174
  Caravelle 72, 76, 128–9
African Eagle 53
AHRS (Attitude and Heading
    Reference System) 165
Air 2000 100
Air Açores 60
Air Afrique 21, 67
Air Algerie 87
Air Berlin 87
Air Canada
Airbus 26, 27, 33, 35, 37
  Boeing 79
  Douglas 126, 132
  Lockheed 149, 150
Air China 87, 97
Air Creebec 169
Air Dolomiti 52
Air Europa Express 61
Air Europe 99, 100, 162
Air Foyle 47
Air France
  Airbus 10, 11, 22, 27, 27, 28, 34, 35,
    36, 37, 39
  ATR 52
  Boeing 67, 72, 91, 115
Air Greenland 124, 125
Air Guinea 43
Air India 19, 67, 95
Air Inter 22, 27, 28, 31, 32, 33
Air Jamaica 20, 167
Air Karakstan 179
Air Lanka 33, 36, 37, 151
Air Liberte 167
Air Littoral 53
Air Mali 120
Air Marshall Islands 173
Air Mauritius 36, 37, 63, 103
Air New Zealand 138, 155, 169
Air Phillipines 167
Air Sweden 153
Air Transat 153
Air Transit Canada 121
Air UK 54, 139
Air Wisconsin 58, 60
Air Zaire 162
Airborne Express 127
Airbus 31
  A3XX 38

A300 10–15, 102
A300-600 13
A300-600F 13, 13, 14
A300-600R 12, 13, 14, 104, 174, 175
A300-603 15
A300-605R 15
A300-622R 14, 15
A300B 16–17
A300B1 10, 11, 12
A300B2 12, 15
A300B2-1C 14, 15
A300B2-103 15
A300B2-300 12
A300B2-320 12
A300B2K 13, 15
A300B2K-3C 15
A300B4 11, 12, 13, 13, 174
A300B4-2C 15
A300B4-103 14, 15
A300B4-203 14, 15
A300B4-601 15
A300B4-605 15
A300B4-605R 14
A300B4-606R 15
A300B4-620 15
A300B4-622R 15
A300B4 SX-BEE 13
A300B9 30
A300C4 12
A300C4-200 15
A300C4-203 15
A300C4-600 13
A300C4-620 15
A300F4-200 13
A300F4-203 15
A310 16–21, 30, 102
A310-100 17
A310-200 17, 17, 19, 21
A310-200F 19, 19
A310-300 18, 19, 20, 21, 104
A310-342 20
A310-600 19
A318 26–7, 27
A319 26–7, 75
A320 8, 22–5, 24, 24–5, 83, 84
A321 24–5, 25, 28, 75
A321-100 24
A321-200 25
A330 7, 28, 28–33, 29, 31, 32, 38, 106
A330-200 29, 31, 33
A330-300 29, 29, 31, 31, 33
A330-321 32
A330-342 32
A340 7, 28, 29, 29, 31, 34, 34–7, 36, 39,
    106, 163
A340-200 31, 35, 36, 36
A340-211 35
A340-300 35, 36, 36–7
A340-300E 35, 37
A340-300X 35
A340-311 34, 37
A340-400 35
A340-500 35, 37
A340-600 35, 35, 36, 37
A340-8000 37
A380 7, 9, 38, 38–9, 39
Corporate Jetliner (ACJ) 27
F-WZLI 18
SA-1 22
SA-2 22

TA9 30
TA11 30
AirCal 166
Airlines of Britian (AoB) 60
Airtech see CASA
Airtours International 100
AirTran 71
AirUK 140
Ajax 47
AJT International 144, 185
Alaska Airlines
  Boeing 74, 87, 87
  McDonnell Douglas 165, 167
Alenia G222 50
Alia 151
Alisarda 166
Alitalia
  Airbus 25
  Boeing 91
  Douglas 129, 131
  McDonnell Douglas 154, 162, 166, 166
All Nippon Airways
  Boeing 75, 105, 107, 115
  Lockheed 149, 151
Allegheny Airlines 133
Allegro Air 167
Allied Signal 54
Allison engines
  501 174
  AE2100A 171
  AE3007A1 137
  AE3007A3 137
  GMA 2100 172
  GMA 3007 136
ALM Antillean Airlines 166
Aloha 99
Alyemda 124
Amazon Protection System 137
AMC 70
American Airlines
  Airbus 13, 14
  ATR 50
  Boeing 63, 67, 73, 87, 92, 98–9,
    100, 100, 103
  Fokker 140
  McDonnell Douglas 154, 155, 156, 162, 163,
    164, 166
American Eagle 50, 52, 61, 171
American Transair 100
ANA 89
Ansett New Zealand 59, 73, 139
Ansett World Wide Aviation 100
Antonov
  An-10 'Cat' 43
  An-12 'Cub' 42–3
  An-24 'Coke' 44, 44–5, 45, 146
  An-26 'Curl' 44, 45
  An-30 'Clank' 45, 147
  An-32 'Cline' 45
  An-70 143
  An-124 'Condor' 9, 46, 46–7, 47
  An-225 Mriya 'Cossack' 9, 48–9
Antonov, Oleg 42
AOM French Airlines 167
Arkansas Air Transport International 9
Armée de l'Air 19, 41
Arrow Air 127
Asiana Airlines 33, 83, 104, 105
Astar Air Cargo 127
ATI (Airbus Transport International) 127, 175

Atlantic Southeast Airlines *125*, 135
ATR (Avions de Transport Régional) *50, 51*
  42/72 50–3
Austral Lineas Aereas 166, 167
Austrian Airlines 36, 37, *82*, 166
AVENSA *132*
Aviadvigatel engines
  D-30KP-2 *143*
  PS-90A *145*
Aviaenergo *143*
Avial Aviation *43*
Avianca 67, *80*, 167
AVIC
  II SAC 43
  XAC Y-7 45
Aviogenex *178*, 180, *181*
Avioimpex 166
Avro
  RJ 54–9
  RJ70 *58*
  RJ85 *58*
  RJ100 *58*
  RJ115 *58*

BAC 22
BAC 111 76, 129
BAe *10*, 22–3, 61
  146 51, 54–9
  146-200 *8*
  146-300 *52*, 58–9
  Airbus 16, 17, 31, 32
  ATP/Jetstream 61 *50, 51*, 60–1
  P132 *61*
  Super 748 60
BAe Asset Management *55*
Bahrain *37*
Balkan Bulgarian *43*, 43, *178*, 180
Bavaria International Leasing Company 71
BEA *151*
Bearskin Airlines *176*
Beech *see* Raytheon
Beiya Airlines 167
Belairbus 17
Belgian Forces 19
Best *129*
Biman Bangladesh 60, 61
Binter Canarias *40, 52*
BITE (Built-in Test Equipment) *23*
BOAC *63*, 63, 65, *67*
Boeing
  247 *106*
  300 62
  367-80 *62*, 62, *64*, 64, *66*, 67
  377 Stratocruiser 62
  387-80 *68*
  400 62
  707 7, *9*, *62*, 62–9, *63*, 88, 102
  707-100 66, *68*
  707-121 *64*, 65
  707-200 *68*
  707-220 *64*
  707-300 *63*, 67, *68, 69*
  707-320 65
  707-320B 65
  707-400 *63*, 67, *67, 69*
  707-700 *69*
  717 64, 70–1
  717-100 71
  717-200 71
  720 24
  727 *63*, 64, 72–5
  727-22 *72, 73*
  727-100 *72*, 74–5
  727-200 *73, 74*, 75
  727-300 98

737 7, 8, 71, *76*, 76–87, *77*
737-100 *76*, 77, *78*, 80
737-200 76, 77, 78–81, *81*
737-300 *77, 82*, 82–3, 84
737-400 *74*, 77, 82–3, 84, *84*, 85
737-500 *77, 82*, 82–5
737-600 86–7
737-700 *86*, 86–7
737-800 *25*, 86–7
737-900 86–7
737 Advanced 77, *79*, 79, 80
747 'Jumbo Jet' 7, 28, 38, *88*, 88–97, *89*, 160
747-100 *90*, 91
747-200 *8*, 91, 92
747-200B *93*
747-300 91
747-400 *37, 39*, 39, 91, 93, 95
747-400 Advanced 93
747-436 94–5
747SP 37, 93, 96–7
757 *75*, *98*, 98–101, *100, 101*, *186*
757-200 84
757-200X 101
757-300 100, *101*
757-300X 101
767 34, *37*, *102*, 102–5
767-200 103
767-300 101, 104
767-300ER 104
767-400ER *105*, 105
767ER 103
777 *7*, 9, *29*, 106–15, 163
777-200 107, *109*, 112, *112*
777-200 LRD 113
777-200ER 107
777-200LR 112, 115
777-300 113, 115
777-300 LRD 113, 115
777-300ER 115
777F 115
787 Dreamliner 9, 33
7127 *53*
76738E *104*
Business Jet *87*
C-40A Clipper 87
C 135 71
E-4 89
F-86 Sabre *90*
MD-80 167
MD-95 *71*
MD-100 160
T-38 Talon *106*
YAL-1A 89
Bombardier 173
  CRJ *52, 53*, 116–17
  Dash 8 Q 118–19
Bon Air 185
Bonanza Airlines *132*, 139
Bouillion Aviation Services 87
Braathens SAFE 80, *81*, 85
Braniff International 67, *96*
Brit Air *52*, 117
Britannia Airways *102*
British Aerospace Aviation Services 13
British Airways
  Airbus *17, 22, 24*, 27
  ATR *52*
  BAe 60
  Boeing 67, 80, *85, 89, 94, 98*, 104, *106*, *112*, 114–15
  Lockheed 149, *151*
British Antarctic Survey 121
British Caledonian *17*, 67, *101, 151, 156*
British Eagle 67

British Island Airways 167
British Midland
  Airbus *24*
  BAe 60
  Boeing 83
  de Havilland Canada *125*
  Fokker 141
British Regional Airways 61
British Transglobe Expedition 121
British West Indian Airways *151*
British World Airlines 61
Brunei *37*
Brymon Airways 125, *125*
Buran 48
BWIA 37, *131*, 167

CAAC (Civil Aviation Administration of China) 43, *45*, 80, *97*, *184*
Canadair
  Challenger 116
  Regional Jet 116–17, *136*
Canadian Airlines *118*
Canadian Forces 19, 19, *119*, *124*, 125
Canadian Pacific Airways *156*
Canmmacorp 126
CASA 17, *22*
  C-295 40, *41*
  CN-235 *40*, 40–1, *41*
  CN-235M *41*, 41
  Saab 171, 172
category IIIA landings 85
Cathay Pacific
  Airbus *8, 32*, 32–3, 37
  Boeing *107*, 112, *114*, 115
  Lockheed *151*, *153*
CATIA CAD/CAM 106
CFDSs (Centralised Fault Display Systems) *23*
CFM International engines
  CFM56 24, 34, *69*, 77, 81, 82, 126
  CFM56-2 82, 126, 127
  CFM56-3 82
  CFM56-3B-1 83
  CFM66-3B-2 83
  CFM56-3C 83
  CFM56-5-A1 *23*
  CFM56-5A5 *26*
  CFM56-5B *25*
  CFM56-5B6/2 *27*
  CFM56-5C2 35
  CFM56-5C4 35, *37*
  CFM56-5S1 34
Champion Air *75*
China Aero-Technology 165
China Airlines 14, 67, 162
China Eastern Airlines
  Airbus *14*, 36, 37
  Boeing 71
  McDonnell Douglas 162, 165, 167
China Northern Airlines 165
China Southern Airlines *39*, 71, 100, *115*
China Southwest 100
China Xinjiang 100, *184*
Chinese Forces 169
ChryslerBenz Aerospace Airbus (Dasa) 13
CIS *143*
Citiexpress *60*
City Airlines *137*
Cityflyer Express *52*
Cityhopper *138*, 139
CityLine 139
closed-circuit records 47, 48
Comair 117, *170*, 171
Conair *12*
Condor Flugdienst 100, 101, *101*
Continental Airlines

Boeing 66, *67*, 67, 87, 100, *105*
Douglas *132*
McDonnell Douglas *155*, *166*, 166, 167
Continental Express 136, 137, *168*
Convair
880 63, 66
990 66
Court Line *151*
Crossair 59, 171, *172*, 172, 173
CSA Czech Airlines *7*, 85, *178*, 180, 185
Cubana 185
Cunard Eagle 67
Cyprus Airways *23*, 24, *25*
Czech Air Force *185*

Dan Air 55
DASA 139, 141
Airbus 25, 174
Dassault
Falcon 20 *53*
Mercure 22
de Havilland Canada
CC-132 *124*, 125
DHC-6 Twin Otter *53*, 120–1
DHC-6 Twin Otter Series 200 *121*
DHC-6 Twin Otter Series 300 121, *121*
DHC-7 Dash 7 122–5
DHC-7 Dash 7 Series 110 *123*
DHC-8 Dash 8 50, 125
de Havilland DH.121 Tristar 72
Delta Air Lines
Boeing 71, 85, 87, 98, 100, *102*, *105*
Douglas 126, *128*, *132*
Lockheed 149, *150*
McDonnell Douglas *70*, *157*, *161*, 163, 165, *165*, 167
Deutsche Airbus *22*
Deutsche BA *173*
distance records 37
DLT 116–17, 139
Domodedovo Airlines 145
Dornier Do 228 *53*
Douglas
D-2086 129
DC-3 62
DC-8 *7*, *9*, 62, 63, 64, 126–7
DC-8-60 126
DC-8-61 126
DC-8-71 126–7
DC-8-72 *127*
DC-8-73F *127*
DC-9 *7*, 55, 76, 80, 128–33, 166
DC-9-10 *128*, 128–9, 130, *132*
DC-9-15 128–9, *129*, *132*
DC-9-20 *130*, 130–1, *132*
DC-9-30 128–9, *129*, 130, 131, *132*, 132–3, *133*
DC-9-40 *130*, 130–1, *131*, *133*
DC-9-50 *130*, 130–1, *131*, *133*, 164
DC-9-51 *130*
DC-9-80 166–7
DC-9 C-9A *133*
DC-10 *7*, 10, 34, 149
DC-73CF *126*
Dragonair *33*, 33

East German Air Force *181*
Eastern Air Lines
Boeing 74, *99*
Douglas 129, *132*
Lockheed 148, *149*, *150*
easyJet 87
ECAMs (Electronic Centralised Aircraft Monitors) 13, *23*
EFIS *165*

Egypt *37*
Egypt Air
Airbus *14*, *36*, 37
Boeing *62*, 67
Tupolev *183*
El Al 67
EMBRAER 173
EMB-120 Brasilia 134–5
EMB-145 116, 135
ERJ 135 136–7
ERJ 145 *136*, 136–7, *137*
ERJ 170 *137*
Emery Worldwide Airlines *127*
Emirates *21*, 33, *39*, *113*
ENAER CN-235 *41*
Engine Alliance GP7200 39
Ethiopian Airlines *53*, 67
Etihad Airways *39*
ETOPS (Extended Range Twin-engine Operations) 13, 33, 111
Euralair 114
Eurocity Express *125*
Eurocypria Airlines *25*
Eurofly 167
Eurolot *53*
Europa-Jet 74
Eurowings *26*
Eva Air 115, *162*, 162
Executive Jet 67

FADECs (Full-Authority Digital Engine Controls) *23*, 59
Fairchild
F-27 139
Special Mission Aircraft *177*
Fairchild Hiller FH-227 139
Far Eastern Air Transport 166–7
FBW (Fly-by-Wire) *24*, 107, 109
Fed Ex
Airbus 13, *13*, 14, *17*, 19, *19*, *39*
Boeing 75
McDonnell Douglas *155*, *156*, *159*, *161*, 162, 163, *163*
FFCC (Forward Facing Crew Cockpit) 17
Finnair *131*, *133*, *160*, 162, 165, 166, *167*
flap systems *11*, 12
flight decks *23*
Flying Colours *101*
Flying Tiger *66*, 67
Fokker
50 *52*
100 *52*
F27 Friendship 138–9
F28 *53*, 55, 140
F50 50, *53*, 139
F60 139
F70 *53*, 140–1
F100 *52*, *53*, 55, 140–1
Formosa Airlines *171*
freighters *8*, 9
French Forces *127*
Frontier Air Lines 80, 166

Garrett TPE331 176
Garuda 33, 162
GATX Capital 163
GE Capital 87
General Electric engines 39
CF6 91, 103, 154, 162
CF6-32 98, 99
CF6-50 10
CF6-50C *15*, *158*, *159*
CF6-80 47, *105*
CF6-80A2 104
CF6-80C2 19, 30, 160

CF6-80C2A2 18
CF6-80C2A5 14
CF6-80C2A8 175
CF6-80E1 33
CF6D *158*
CF34-3A 116
CJ805-23 128–9
CT7 170
CT7-7 40
CT7-9B 171
GE90 107, 110
GE90-77B 114–15
GE90-110B1 113
GE90-115B 110, 113
Germania *83*, 87
Ghana Airlines 43
Gill Airways *53*
GPA Ltd 100
GPWS (Ground-Proximity Warning System) *116*
Great China Airlines *119*
Greenlandair Charter 121
Grumman 126
Gulf Air
Airbus 24, 33, 36, 37
Lockheed *151*, *153*
Gulfstream V 37

Handley Page Herald 138
Hapag-LLoyd 87
Harlequin Air 166
Hawaiian Air 71
Hawaiian Airlines
Douglas *126*, *130*, *133*
Lockheed *153*
McDonnell Douglas *165*, 166
Hawker/Breguet/Nord HBN 100 10
Hawker Siddeley 10, 10, 54–6
Trident 1 74, 75
Hazelton Airlines *171*
Hemus Air 181
Honeywell 54, 59, 176
hush-kits 81, 127

IAE (International Aero Engines)
V2500 23, 24, 34–5
V2500-A5 *26*
V2524 *26*
V2524-A5 27
V2525-D5 70
V2530 *25*
V2530-A5 25
Iberia 11, *14*, 75, *166*
ILFC (International Lease Finance Company) 31, 33, *39*, 87, 100, 162
Ilyushin
Il-62M *143*
Il-76 'Candid' 142–3
Il-86 'Camber' 144–5
Il-96 145
Il-114 146–7
Impulse Airlines 71
Indian Airlines *14*, 24
Indonesia *78*
Inex-Adria Aviopromet *122*, *131*, 166
Interflug 19, *178*, 180, *185*
IPTN *see* CASA
Iran Air Tours 185
Iran Aseman Airlines *53*
Iranair 67
Iraqi Airlines 67
IRBMs (Intermediate-range Ballistic Missiles) 46
Irish Air Corps 41, *41*
Ivchenko engines , AI-24 44

JADC (Japan Aircraft Development
    Corporation) 108, *108*
JAL (Japan Air Lines)
    Boeing 71, 75, 93, *104*, 104, 115
    McDonnell Douglas *154*, 155, *156*, 163
Japan Air Lines Domestic 75
Japan Air System *15*, 70
Japan Aircraft Manufacturing Co. Ltd 108
jet airliners 7
Jet America Airlines 166
JMC Airlines 100, *101*
John Wayne Airport *8*

Kingfisher Airlines *39*
Kish Air 185
Klimov TV7-117S 146
KLM
    Airbus *17*
    Boeing 87, 92
    Fokker *138*, 139, 140, *140*, 141
    McDonnell Douglas 155, *156*, 163
KLM UK *52*
KMV 187
Korean Air Lines
    Airbus 13, *15*, 33, *39*
    Boeing 115
    McDonnell Douglas 163, 167
Kosmos *42*
Krüger flaps 12, *13*, 15
Kuwait Airlines 36, 37
Kuwait Airways 13, *15*, *21*, 67
Kuznetsov NK-86 145
Kyrgyzstan Airlines 25

LanChile 25
landing categories 85
largest aircraft, twin-aisle 13
Lauda Air 104, *116*
Little Rock-Adams Field *9*
Lockheed
    C-5 Galaxy 148
    C-5A Galaxy 88
    C-141 Starlifter 142
    Flying Hospital *153*
    L-100 Hercules *53*
    L-749 72
    L-1011 Tristar 7, 10, 34, 148–53
    L-1011F Tristar *152*
    Tristar 50 *153*
    Tristar 100 *153*
    Tristar 500 *149*, 149, *152*, 153
London City Airport *55*, 125
London City Airways *125*
longest-ranged airliners 35
LOT
    ATR *53*
    Boeing *84*
    Tupolev *178*, 180, 185
Lotarev D-18T 46
LTU International Airways *32*, 100, *151*, *162*
Lufthansa
    Airbus *11*, 11, *15*, *17*, 25, *25*, 27, *28*, 35, 36,
        37, *39*
    Boeing 63, 67, *73*, 73, 74, 76, 78, *78*, 80, 85,
        92, 92
    Fokker 139
    McDonnell Douglas *156*, 163
Lufthansa CityLine *116*, 117, *119*, 134
Luftwaffe 19, *185*
Luxair *85*
Lycoming ALF502 54

Maersk Air 124, 139
Makung Airlines *55*

Malaysia Airlines 139
Malaysian Airline System (MAS) 32, *39*, 67
Malev *178*, 180, 185
Mandala Airlines 41, *62*
Mandarin Airlines *97*
Manx Airlines *60*
Martinair 19, 163, 166
MBB 16, *22*
McAir 161
McDonnell Douglas
    DC-3 72
    DC-6 72
    DC-8 126, 127
    DC-9 see Douglas DC-9
    DC-10 154–9
    DC-10-10 *158*
    DC-10-15 *158*
    DC-10-20 *158*
    DC-10-30 *154*, 155, *158*, *159*
    DC-10-40 *154*, 155, *159*
    DC-10-60 *155*, 160
    DC-10 Advanced *159*
    KC-10A Extender *159*
    KDC-10 *159*
    MD-11 28, 35, 106, 160–3
    MD-80 55, 71, 82, 164–7
    MD-88 *165*
    MD-90 70–1
    MD-95 *70*, 71, 102
    MD-XXX 160
McDonnell Douglas Fokker MDF 100 140
MEA 67
Med Airlines 173
Meridiana 167
Merpati Nusantara Airlines 41, 60
Mesa Airlines 100
Mesaba Airlines *171*
Mexicana 155
Midwest Express 166, 167
missiles 46
Mohawk Airlines 129
Monarch Airlines *100*
Morrocan Forces *41*
Motorola 79
MSA *80*
MTOW (Maximum Take-off Weight) 35
Muse Air *100*

National Airlines *157*
NDs (Navigation Displays) *23*
New York Air 166
noise *8*, 56, 81
non-stop flights 37, 165
Nord 262 50
NorOntair *121*
Northwest Airlines
    Airbus *24*, 32
    Boeing *65*, 67, *92*, 93, 100
    McDonnell Douglas 155
Northwest Airlink 171
Northwest Orient 35, 36, *154*, 157, *159*
Nouvelair Tunisie 167

Olympic Airways 13, *15*, 37, 67, 87
Olympic Aviation *53*, 71
Oman Royal Flight *126*
Ontario Lakes and Forrests 120
Onur Air 167
Orbital Sciences Pegasus XL *153*
Orbiter 89
Orion Airways 84
Ozark Airlines *132*, 166

Pacific Airlines 167
Pacific Southwest Airlines *8*, 58, *150*, 166

Pacific Western *79*
Pakistan International (PIA) *20*, 67, 113, 115
PAL 37
Pan Am
    Airbus *18*
    ATR *51*
    Boeing *62*, 63, *64*, 65, *66*, 67, *88*, 88–9, *92*,
        92, *97*
    Douglas 65
    Lockheed *150*
payload records 47, 48
Pelita Air Services *124*
Pembroke Capital 71
Perm-Soloviev PS-90A 186
PFD (Primary Flight Display) *23*
Philippine Airlines 33, 36, *37*, 139
Piedmont Airlines *83*, *103*, 139
pilot training 28
Polet *47*
Portugalia *136*
Pratt & Whitney engines 39
    Canada PT6 120
    Canada PT6A-20 *121*, 122, 176
    Canada PT6A-27 121
    Canada PT6A-50 *123*
    Canada PT6A-65B 168
    Canada PT6A-67D 169
    Canada PW120A 118
    Canada PW124 60
    Canada PW127G *41*
    Canada PW127H *147*
    JT3 62, 64
    JT3C-6 65
    JT3D *9*, 65
    JT3D-1/3B *68*
    JT3D-3 65
    JT3D-3B 127
    JT3D-7 127
    JT4A 65
    JT4A-3 67
    JT8D 80–1, 129
    JT8D-1 73, *132*
    JT8D-7 78–9, *132*
    JT8D-9 75
    JT8D-209 126, 164
    JT9D 12, *12*, 90, *90*, 103, 155
    JT9D-7A 96
    JT9D-7R4D1 18
    JT9D-7R4E1 18, 19
    JT9D-7RH1 *15*
    JT9D-59A 12
    JT9D7R4D 104
    JT10 128
    JTD8-11 *132*
    JTD8-17 *133*
    JTD8D 131
    JTD8D-11 75
    JTD8D-217C *165*
    JTD8D-219 165
    JTD9D *159*
    PW115 134
    PW118A 135
    PW120 50, 139
    PW121 50
    PW124 51
    PW125B 139
    PW126A 60
    PW127 51, *51*
    PW127B 139
    PW127D 61
    PW2037 98–9, 160
    PW2040 *99*, 100
    PW2240 186
    PW2337 145
    PW4000 30, 104, 107, 110, 160

PW4098 110
PW4168 *31*, *33*, 33
PW4460 *160*, *161*, 162

QANTAS *39*, 67, *91*, 103
Qatar Airways *39*
Qatar Amiri Flight *37*
Queen's Flight *55*

RAF *55*, *152*
Ransome Airlines 124
RARO (Remote Aerial Refuelling Operation) *159*
Raytheon 1900 168–9
Regional Airlines *173*
Regional Airlines of France *136*
Republic Airlines *128*, *133*, *164*
RFG Regional *51*
Rich International *153*
RMPs (Radio Management Panels) *23*
Rocky Mountain Airways 124
Rolls-Royce engines
　Conway *63*, 65, 67, *69*
　Dart 507 *138*
　Dart 511 *138*
　Dart 532-7 *139*
　Dart 551 139
　RB.211 10, 148
　RB.211-524 *91*, 96, 149
　RB.211-524G/H 104
　RB.211-535 98, 99, 160
　RB.211-535E4 *101*
　RB.211-535F5 186
　RB.211535E4 186, 187
　Trent 553 35
　Trent 556 35
　Trent 800 *107*, 110
　Trent 877 114, 115
　Trent 895 110, 115
　Trent 900 39
rough-field operations 79
round-the-world 37
Royal Brunei Airlines *101*
Royal Jordanian Airlines *20*, *151*
Royal Netherlands Air Force *159*
Royal New Zealand Air Force *75*
Royal Saudi Air Force *40*, 41
Russia State Transport 181, *186*
Ryanair 87

Saab
　340 170–1, *172*
　2000 172–3
Saab-Fairchild , 340A 50, 170
Sabena 33, 37, 59, 63, *118*
Sailplane Leasing 85
SAS (Scandanavian Airline Systems)
　Airbus *12*
　Boeing 71, 87
　Douglas *129*, *130*, *132*, *133*
　Fokker 139
　McDonnell Douglas 70, 155, *157*, 166,
　　167, *167*
　Saab *173*
SATA 60
SATIC , A300-600ST Beluga 174–5
Saudi Arabia *37*
Saudi Arabian Airlines *12*, *15*, 67, *70*, 71
Saudia 13, *151*
Scanair *12*
Scandanavian Airlines 87
Scenic Airlines *176*
Schreiner Airways *118*
Seaboard World 67
Separate Access Landing Systems 124

Shaanxi Y-8 43
Shanghai Aircraft Manufacturing Factory
　(SAMF) 70, 165
Shanghai Airlines 100
ShinMaywa 108
Short Brothers 116
Sichuan Airlines 25
Sikorsky S-61 124
Singapore Airlines
　Airbus 35, 36, 37, *39*, 39
　Boeing 115
Skyfield Airlines *179*
Skyways Express *137*
Skywest *135*
SLAMMR (side-looking airborne
　multi-mission radar) 79
Soloviev engines
　D-30 180
　D-30KU-154-11 *185*
South African Airways 12, *13*, *15*, 67, *96*
Southern Air Transport *67*
Southern Airways 166
Southwest Air Lines 80, 84, 85
Space Shuttle 89
Spanair 167
Spirit Airlines 166, 167
SSC (sidestick controller) *23*
STOL (short take-off and landing) 124–5
Sudan Airways *21*, 139
Sun Air 166
Superfans 34, 35, *36*, 36
Swearingen Merlin/Metro 176–7
Swedish Air Force *177*
swept wings 10
Swissair
　Airbus *16*, 27, 33
　Boeing 93
　Douglas 131, *133*
　Fokker 140, 141
　McDonnell Douglas 155, *157*, 162, *163*, 164,
　　165, 166
Syrian Arab Airlines *97*

TAA (Trans Australia Airlines) 73, 120, 139
TACA 25
TAM 25, *26*, 141
TAP Air Portugal 36, 37, 67, *151*
TAPO 146
Tarom *183*, 185
TDA *130*, *131*, 131
Tejas Airlines *177*
Texas International *132*
Thai Airways International
　Airbus *12*, *15*, 19, 32, 33, *39*
　Boeing *114*, 115
　McDonnell Douglas *157*, 162
Thai Forces 19
Thomas Cook Airlines 100, *101*
THT 60
THY Turkish Airlines *21*, 37, *37*, *59*, 87, 155
Titan Airways *53*
TOA Domestic Airlines *15*, *129*, *133*, 166
Transavia Airlines 87, *87*, 100
Transbrasil 98
Transeuropean Airlines *144*
Transport Canada *123*
Tumanskii RU-19-300 45, *45*
Tunisair *86*
Tupolev
　Tu-16 'Badger' 178
　Tu-104 'Camel' 178, 182
　Tu-124 'Cookpot' 178, 179, 182
　Tu-134 'Crusty' 8–9, *44*, 178–81, 182
　Tu-154 'Careless' 8–9, *44*, 182–5
　Tu-154C 184

Tu-154M 184–5
Tu-155 185
Tu-204/214 186–7
Tu-234 187
turbofan engines 7, 9
TWA
　Airbus 27
　Boeing 63, *66*, 67, 71, 73, *74*, 100, 103
　Douglas *132*
　Lockheed *149*, *150*
　McDonnell Douglas 166, 167
Tyrolean *118*
Tyumen Airlines 181

U-Land Airlines 167
Uni Air *55*, 71, *119*
United Airlines
　Airbus 25, *27*
　Boeing *72*, 73, 76, 78, 85, 100, *102*, *106*,
　　107,
　　109, *114*, 114, 115
　Douglas 126
　Lockheed 128–9, *153*
　McDonnell Douglas *154*, *157*
United Express *134*
United Parcel Service (UPS) *39*, *99*, 100,
　105, 127
US Air
　BAe *8*
　Boeing 80, *82*, 82, 85, *103*
　Douglas *128*
US Air Force
　Boeing 64, *65*, 100, *100*
　de Havilland Canada 124
　McDonnell Douglas 155, *159*
　Raytheon 169, *169*
US Airways 25, 33, 85, 100
US Army *124*, 125, 169
US Civil Reseerve *126*
US Navy 87, *133*
UTA 126, 155
Uzbekistan Airways *20*, *146*, 147

V-TA 46
Valmet 171
ValuJet 71
VARIG 67, *84*, *157*, 162, *163*
VASP *160*
Venezuelan Forces *124*, 125
VFW *22*
VFW-Fokker 16
VIASA 166
Vickers VC10 63
Vietnam Airlines *52*
Virgin Atlantic *36*, 37, *39*
Virgin Sun *84*
Vladivostock 187
VLCA (Very Large Commercial Aircraft) 38
Vnukovo Airlines 187
Volga-Dnepr 46–7
Voronezh Joint-stock Aircraft 145
Vyborg North-West 147

Wardair 67
West Air Sweden 61
West Airlines *135*
West Coast Airlines *132*, 139
Western Airlines *62*, 66, *157*
Westland Engineering 171
windshear 85
winglets 23
World Airways 63, 67, *162*
Worldways Canada *153*

Xerox Corporation 117